Connecting with the Arcturians 2

PLANETARY TRANSFORMATION FROM A GALACTIC PERSPECTIVE

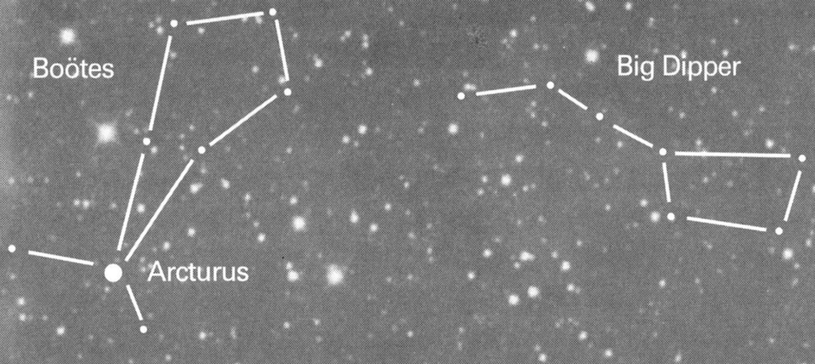

channeled through DAVID K. MILLER

Other Publications by

David K. Miller

Connecting with the Arcturians

Teachings from the Sacred Triangle, Volume 1

Teachings from the Sacred Triangle, Volume 2

Teachings from the Sacred Triangle, Volume 3

New Spiritual Technology for the Fifth-Dimensional Earth

Kaballah and the Ascension

Raising the Spiritual Light Quotient

Biorelativity

Arcturians: How to Heal, Ascend, and Help Planet Earth

A New Tree of Life for Planetary Ascension

Enseñanzas Del Sagrado Triángulo Arcturiano

Fifth-dimensional Soul Psychology

Expand Your Consciousness

Connecting with the Arcturians 2

PLANETARY TRANSFORMATION FROM A GALACTIC PERSPECTIVE

CHANNELED THROUGH
David K. Miller

LIGHT Technology PUBLISHING

For more information about special discounts for bulk purchases, please contact Light Technology Publishing Special Sales at 1-800-450-0985 or publishing@LightTechnology.net.

ISBN-13: 978-1-62233-052-2
Published and printed in the United States of America by

Light Technology Publishing
PO Box 3540
Flagstaff, AZ 86003
1-800-450-0985 • 928-526-1345
www.LightTechnology.com

Table of Contents

Preface

This follow-up to *Connecting with the Arcturians*, which was originally published in 1998 and sold close to 15,000 copies, contains the latest channeled teachings from Juliano, my main spirit guide from the Arcturians, as well as special lectures from two Andromedan spirit guides, Heylang and Gurhan.

This book covers a wide variety of subjects, including embracing galactic spirituality and planetary evolution, Arcturian thoughts from a fifth-dimensional perspective on Earth, the aura-enhancing technique known as shimmering, and unity consciousness.

Juliano's teachings have always focused on personal and planetary healing and ascension, and this volume presents the most up-to-date information on ascension available, including new spiritual technologies to aid the process. Special lectures address the nature of consciousness and how it ties into ascension. Spiritual exercises provide specific instructions on how to work with Earth's energy field, aura, and noosphere and to transition consciousness from the third dimension to higher dimensions through shifting.

The Arcturians teach that one key to ascension rests with how we train and use our auras. They explain the planetary healing spiritual technology known as Biorelativity, and discuss working with new quantum and global healing techniques and cosmic consciousness.

If you enjoyed *Connecting with the Arcturians*, then you will appreciate this book, especially since these lectures primarily focus on teachings from Juliano and the Arcturian. If you have not read the first book, don't worry.

This book can stand alone, and all starseeds who are serious about their planetary and personal ascension work will understand and benefit from the techniques within.

David K. Miller
July 2016
Prescott, Arizona

Chapter 1

Updates on the Ascension

Juliano and the Arcturians

Greetings, I am Juliano. We are the Arcturians. In this lecture, we will review the ascension and expand on its technology. There are a few important points about the ascension that need to be explained and others that need to be repeated. Also, there is new information that is relevant to your ascension process, which I hope you understand you are now in. This, in itself, is an important part of your work for the ascension.

You know there is a necessity to unify yourself on the emotional, mental, physical, and spiritual levels. One important aspect is to work with your belief systems. When you are in the ascension process, you need to also have your mental body in alignment with this process. It requires an expansion of your belief system to include the existence of the fifth dimension and the idea that you, as a third-dimensional being, are able to transfer yourself into the fifth dimension.

The Ascensions of Elijah, Enoch, and Jesus

There are several examples of people throughout history who have ascended, but there is no clear evidence of a group ascension. You are participating in your ascension process in a group energy. This ascension will involve many people ascending.

This ascension is different from those of Elijah or Enoch in the Hebrew Bible and even Sananda/Jesus. Each one of these ascensions is an example that needs to be reviewed, for they have important lessons for your own process.

I am going to start with Sananda/Jesus because he illustrated a very dynamic process. He agreed to die, whereas in your ascension process, you will not die. You are going to be immediately transformed into the higher fifth dimension. Sananda/Jesus postponed his ascension for approximately three days, and then he was able to take his body into the fifth dimension.

Elijah ascended, but he did not wait three days. He took his body immediately into the fifth dimension. It is described that his clothes remained behind. Enoch ascended; hopefully you are all acquainted with the Keys of Enoch and its modern-day version by the great spiritual teacher J. J. Hurtak. The Hebrew Bible's description of Enoch's ascension is summarized in the sentence: "God took Enoch, and he walked with God, and he was no more."[1]

Here again you have the example of the master ascending and taking his body. Even though Sananda/Jesus did not immediately take his body, he eventually did ascend. Here we have an important point: To ascend, you have to take your body. This is the part that I believe is going to be the most problematic or difficult for many of you.

Group Energy Will Help Your Body and Mind Ascend Together

I think that you are all advanced in your light work, and I know that when the time of ascension comes, you will have no trouble whatsoever allowing your spirit to flow into the fifth dimension. It will be easy. I know that you have been working with the Arcturian spiritual technologies and exercises that include shimmering, thought projection, and bilocation. Even a minimum amount of practicing of these techniques is going to be of great assistance to you. Of course, it is always helpful to continue the practices so that you can immediately ascend when the time arises.

Sending the body to the fifth dimension requires different explanations and different technologies. One of the main ideas and factual assertions is that somehow you must transmute your third-dimensional energy into the fifth dimension. You must do this so that your body disappears. There have been studies in the early Egyptian temples on how

---

1. Rabbi Menachem Davis, ed., *Interlinear Chumash: the Torah, Haftaros and Five Megillos*, Vol. 1 (Mesorah Publications, 2006), 28.

to transmute and transport the physical body. I would like to review some of those practices, because it is important that you ascend both in spirit and in body. The reason is that if your body stays behind and you ascend, then you can still be in Earth's reincarnation cycle. That means that you may have to return to Earth.

Some of you have been on this planet before as starseeds and have gone through the ascension but had this exact problem of taking your physical body with you to the fifth dimension. The technologies and the knowledge of how to ascend have improved. The newer ascension technology is more available to you at this time.

You have several important aids to help your ascension now. One major aid is that this is a group ascension, which means you are uniting with a group energy field that will empower you in a more dynamic way. Individual ascension is harder and requires advanced practitioners like Enoch and Elijah and Jesus — spiritual practitioners and prophets — to ascend by themselves. They were not in group ascension energy on the third dimension. To ascend individually, you have to be more spiritually and technically advanced.

You may not be at the level of those three masters, but you have a distinct advantage because you are connecting with a group energy that will allow you to accelerate and enhance your own spiritual powers. This is why we speak about the spiritual light quotient in relation to group energy. You have been raising your spiritual vibration through group practice. By raising your spiritual vibration, you increase your psychic abilities. In fact, the ascension of the physical body requires a psychic power. You might call it the power of telekinesis, which is a fancy word for moving objects on the third dimension to different locations using mental thoughts.

Actually, for the ascension, we are talking about moving the body into a different dimension. Ascension is a form of telekinesis. It is a form of bilocation. When you connect with the group energy, you have powers that will exceed your normal abilities.

Merkavah: Your Vehicle to Other Realms

Let me return to ancient Egypt and the practice that is known as *Merkavah*, or *Merkabah*. It is important to point out that the origin of the word

Merkavah comes from both ancient Hebrew and ancient Egyptian, and it refers to a chariot. The chariot was a mode of transportation in ancient Egypt and ancient Israel. It would only be natural that an object like a chariot would be used in the visualizations to go from one dimension to another.

This does not mean that you must visualize a chariot, but you can if you want. I only want to point out the historical significance of *Merkavah* travel because it uses symbolism and visualizations from ancient times. You may find this amusing, but it is also true that your *Merkavah* vehicle could be a Toyota Camry! Or your *Merkavah* vehicle could be a spacecraft or a satellite. Also, it can be a pyramid or a glass-enclosed capsule that takes you to other realms.

The second idea of this visualization can include our own spaceships, especially the spaceship Athena. Transporting one's body requires extensive spiritual work that involves the interaction of your energy field in the fifth dimension with the energy field of the third dimension. Visualizing a spaceship that is in another dimension can aid you in your thought process.

Even in the fifth dimension when we travel and work, we use visualizations. It is not uncommon for fifth-dimensional work and fifth-dimensional masters and teachers to travel interdimensionally. In the fifth dimension, we still use some type of transportation object, such as a space vehicle. Why is that? You still have a mind in the fifth dimension. You still remember many of the things you had to do to travel when you were on the third dimension. It seems logical to use some type of vehicle to transport yourself. It is especially logical when you are going from the third to the fifth dimension because it helps your mind understand what you are doing. You then put all of your energy — emotional, physical, spiritual, and mental — into that *Merkavah* vehicle. You feel the vehicle accelerating, and you feel yourself going up into the spaceship; from the spaceship, you can go into the fifth dimension or you are in the fifth dimension. This is one visualization.

Shimmering and Pulsing in the Energy Process

Let us look again at this whole energy process. The idea of transforming your physical energy into a fifth-dimensional energy is achieved through the rapid acceleration of your aura. We have referred to this rapid acceleration process as "shimmering" or "pulsing." We have recommended that you practice the techniques of pulsing and shimmering as preparation for your ascension. These exercises require you to visualize your aura with a line around it that marks the outer shell. This line has a pulsing motion similar to your heart's. However, your physical pulse must stay in a certain range, but your aura pulse can have a very high rate. If your heart pulse goes above a certain range, then you are in danger of having a stroke or heart attack. This is not the case of your aura pulse rate.

In the world of auric energy, going into a higher vibration or pulse rate is a good sign of experiencing a higher vibration. When your aura begins to pulse faster and faster, then you are increasing your spiritual energy. You are also beginning to vibrate at a frequency that is more aligned with the fifth-dimensional frequency. The fifth dimension as a whole vibrates faster. You have to be at a higher vibration to go into the fifth dimension. If you want to stay in the fifth dimension at the point of ascension, you must take your body with you. This is known, yet you are not often given specific instructions on how to do this.

How to Take Your Body with You to the Fifth Dimension

The first instructions in how to take your body with you have two aspects, and you have choices: You can put your body into a *Merkavah* vehicle of your choice. The second and equally effective alternative does not involve a *Merkavah* because you might feel that you can simply bilocate by thought. In both cases, you will begin to accelerate the pulsing of your aura at the ascension. You will bring your aura to the highest vibration possible. Then at the point of ascension, there is an interaction and intersection of fifth-dimensional energy with your third-dimensional aura.

When this intersection occurs, you can either work in your *Merkavah* or through shimmering or pulsing. Yet you still might not be able to ascend without assistance. If you were able to do that just on your own by simply raising your vibration, then many of you would have ascended already. That means that there is a certain gravitational pull, resistance, or attraction in the third dimension that keeps you here. This is natural. It was hard to be born here, and it is hard to leave.

It is not going to be simple to ascend. First, you accelerate your energy field, and then you translate, or move, your energy upward into the fifth dimension. The missing ingredient for your ascension is the intersection of the fifth and third dimensions, which will set up the announcement of the ascension. At that intersection, a tremendous rush of energy will spread throughout the whole planet. In some cases, this spread of energy will create a special sound that has been referred to as the blowing of Gabriel's horn. Even the blowing of a trumpet or a horn doesn't totally explain what ascension might sound like. I will tell you that you have never heard such a sound before, but when you hear it, you will know exactly what to do.

Like the sound, the intersecting of the dimensions will cause a downloading of fifth-dimensional energy into your third-dimensional body, and you will begin to have all of your psychic abilities enhanced. This will happen immediately. It will be like someone gave you a steroid shot and suddenly you could lift twice as much as you normally could.

The sound of ascension is like the steroid shot in that you will experience elevated psychic and spiritual strength. Suddenly, your pulsing is going to be so much more dynamic and your shimmering so much more effective. And the fact that you are in the *Merkavah* will only add to your powers. Your *Merkavah* vehicle is going to shimmer and pulse.

The Higher Perception of the Assemblage Point

How will you be able to take your body with you at this extraordinary point of raising of your vibrational energy field? Now we must go back to the belief system, because your beliefs are based on your visual perception that everything is solid. So you believe correctly that your hand cannot go through a wall, that your physical body has certain limitations, and that you can touch things.

But in the heightened state of consciousness often called "the peak experience," you will become aware of a higher perception that has been described by the shamans as the opening of the assemblage point. At the point of ascension — where the dimensions intersect — your assemblage point will open.

Some of you have not experienced this opening; nonetheless, you will experience it. When this happens, your total perceptions of reality will change. What you see is actually the true reality. That true reality is that you are a vibrating, luminous being of light. That true reality is that you are energetically moving and that you are not solid (no one really is). The fact that you see everything as solid in the third dimension is a factor of culture and the way your perceptual fields have been trained.

When you vibrate or pulse at a higher rate, your luminosity increases. When you pulsate at a lower rate, your luminosity is likewise lower and less bright. Now that you have this awareness and the experience of seeing everything as luminous beings of light, it is easier for your mind to accept that you can transform and transmute your physical body. You will be able to use telekinesis to transport yourself to the fifth dimension because you will understand your different perception and that you will be in a different reality.

At the moment of ascension, you can use your psychic powers that will heighten by the intersection of the dimensions and the opening of your assemblage point. You will be able to use your powers to immediately bilocate. Concentrate as you say, "I ascend to the fifth dimension," or "I am ascending now to the fifth dimension."

You ascend in your *Merkavah* vehicle, but you will eventually leave it behind. You might have seen the pictures of the Saturn rockets or space shuttle rockets blasting off. When they go up a certain distance, the tanks holding the fuel are released because they weigh the shuttles down. Furthermore, they are not needed anymore. In your case, you will not need your *Merkavah* because you are not going to return to Earth. The *Merkavah* was used in the ancient Egyptian and Hebrew practices because returning to Earth was required. You will elevate yourself and your consciousness using your it, but then you will reach a point at which you will move into such a high energy that you will not need to ever return to Earth.

For now, when you practice traveling into the other dimensions, I recommend you use the *Merkavah* vehicle. The simple reason is that you will return to Earth. Many of us working with you often ask you to please promise to return to Earth during practice sessions, though on several occasions adepts and students have decided not to return to Earth. There have been other cases of students who wanted to ascend with their masters, but they did not have the technology or the spiritual light quotient to do that. It is not a disappointment or a fault to not ascend.

Omega Light Meditation

You are in the ascension process now. I would like to go through a meditation exercise with you, and I know that you will, of course, return to Earth after this meditation.

Visualize now your energy field shaped as a cosmic egg. Become aware that you are a luminous being of light vibrating at a frequency that is very spiritual. The spiritual frequency is a light frequency — light being the opposite of heavy and also meaning that there is great luminosity in your energy field. Feel your aura's pulse rate increase as your energy field also increases in its pulsing rate. [Chants increasingly faster: Ta, ta, ta, ta, ta, ta, ta.]

Visualize your Merkavah *vehicle. It is now around you. See your vehicle as a space capsule, a beautiful space capsule unlike any you have ever seen. It is shaped as a pyramid. It has beautiful blue glass. You feel your energy field rising. Your physical body is going to stay behind. Your physical body is not coming with you, and your energy field is rising.*

Feel a corridor of light around this beautiful Merkavah *pyramid, and feel the rising of your spiritual energy as you experience an increase in your spiritual vibration. You can rise up and see this beautiful corridor, an Arcturian corridor of light. In this corridor, I, Juliano, have directed our starship Athena to create a magnetic attractive force into each one of the corridors over you, helping you to raise your energy.*

This visualization is exactly what is going to happen at your point of ascension. There is going to be such an attractive energy force that you will feel as if you are being lifted off Earth.

Now as you rise up, you reach the entry-level point into our starship Athena. We have created a beautiful garden of light and a comfortable place for you to rest while you are here. Maybe you feel a sense of accomplishment that you have been able to come up here. I want you to look down to your body on Earth from this high point. You can see that your physical body is denser and that it is still there, and you might wonder, "Well, how am I going to get that physical body up here?"

Remember that you will have extraordinary psychic powers at the point of ascension. With your third eye, align your energy directly with your physical body, and transfer light into your physical body on Earth. [Tones: Ohhhh. Ohhhh.]

This light that you are now transferring into your physical body is fifth-dimensional omega light. Call on the omega light to radiate directly from your place on the ship. Let the omega light go into your third eye in the physical body. [Sings: Oooohhhmega light.]

This omega light is a quantum light that has properties far exceeding the normal laws of physics and Earth. Feel this omega light in your body, and you will immediately feel a great increase in your health. You will feel a major uplifting of all of your systems. This omega light is going through each one of your physical bodies.

Your physical body is being charged with a new light frequency. You and I together experience this charge of omega light through you, which will become very important when the time comes for you to move your body with you to the fifth dimension. This time you will just feel a great lightness and a great sense of well-being. We will now meditate with that. [Silence for several minutes.]

Feel your physical body give a sigh as the burden of physicality momentarily lifts. You are experiencing a sense of lightness (the opposite of heaviness) in your physical body. You might even feel as if your physical body can float. See whether you can experience your physical body on Earth gently lifting off your chair.

There is a great halo now around your head and shoulders as your spiritual vibration rises. Now your fifth-dimensional body on the starship Athena sends your physical body a final boost of omega light, and it goes right into your third eye, almost like a jolt, like a battery charger sending up this higher frequency, but it is a pleasant jolt. Some might experience this as an increase in the chi energy of the physical body.

Your fifth-dimensional body on the ship comes back into the corridor and begins to descend through the corridor. It soon arrives directly above your third-dimensional body. This fifth-dimensional body is filled with a great omega light and a great luminosity, even more so than your third-dimensional body. At the count of three, your fifth-dimensional luminous body is going to reenter in perfect alignment with your third-dimensional body. One, two, three! Again, you experience a deep sense of relaxation.

You experience a sense of well-being and a sense of deep understanding. You can say, "I will be able to bring my third-dimensional body with me at the time of ascension. I will be using the omega light to transform my body into this higher luminosity that will allow my physical body to ascend with me."

Tools for Receiving the Fifth-Dimensional Light

Remember that you only will be able to do this because you are using fifth-dimensional energy and the accelerated energy of the intersection of the dimensions. Even now with our directions, many of you have achieved a great lightness in your physical structure. Each of you reading this lecture will also receive a great boost for your physical health. One of the transformations that occurs at the point of ascension is that your body reaches a heightened state. Remember, I compared it to being on spiritual steroids. You are in a heightened state of total strength and will have a total, beautiful unity of energy.

Process this energy now, and I will speak about Earth and the ascension. One of the reasons you will be able to ascend is Earth's energy field will also elevate. The spiritual light quotient of Earth is another factor in the ascension. Earth has to intersect with the fifth dimension. The third dimension can be viewed as a sphere around Earth, and that energy field of the third dimension will intersect with the fifth-dimensional sphere.

What does it take for a planet to be ready to receive fifth-dimensional light? It must have an elevated spiritual light quotient. We have offered several tools of planetary spiritual technology that will help to raise the spiritual light quotient of Earth. These tools include (but are not limited to) the planetary cities of light, the twelve etheric crystals, the ring of ascension, and the Iskalia mirror. Each one of these offers a specific technological advantage to raising the spiritual light quotient of the planet. You live on a planet that has polarization and densities, but it is also receptive to spiritual energy and spiritual light.

The etheric crystals directly receive and interact with fifth-dimensional energies from Arcturus. These are similar to energy waves that are sent out continually from these crystals throughout the planet, which aids in holding Earth in the ascension light. The ring of ascension has been compared to a halo around the planet. It interacts with the minds and hearts of the ascended masters. There are many ascended masters who work in this ring of ascension.

We also have the five ladders of ascension that have specifically been set up as *Merkavah* ladders, similar to *Merkavah* vehicles. You may need to have the following questions in your mind: "How am I going to climb up? How am I going to become elevated so that I can go into the fifth dimension?" The ladder of ascension has been compared to Jacob's Ladder from the Hebrew Bible [Bereshis 28:12, OJB]. Jacob had a dream that he was going up a ladder that went into another dimension. The angels were also coming down, and there was a great interaction. But as you may know, he was only able to go up the ladder to a certain height. The ladders of ascension await you. You, at the point of hearing the trumpet, can teleport or bilocate immediately to one of the ladders of ascension. There will be a powerful group energy there that will immediately elevate you. You will become transformed, and you will, with your physical body, climb up the ladder.

The Iskalia mirror is bringing down galactic energy through its alignment with special quantum particles from the Central Sun. These particles of light can be transmitted throughout the whole planet, including the planet's energy field. You are in a period of great interaction of higher-dimensional light on Earth. These are great aids for you.

The point is that this planet is also preparing for the ascension. I know that some of you want to be here when the planet ascends. But remember, there are those who will stay after the ascension and those who will leave at the ascension. The timing of the ascension is important, and you will want to do as much emotional, spiritual, physical, and mental work as possible to prepare yourself.

Do not underestimate the power of your belief systems and of your mental work. This is also important for your ascension. Yes, you will see more polarization. Yes, you might see more Earth events. But remember that you are on a spiritual path that will transcend many of these events, and you will be able to take advantage of the great light and frequencies of ascension. May the light of ascension accelerate your process immediately and continually. I am Juliano. Good day.

Chapter 2

Understand the Entire Universe with Holographic Technology

Juliano, the Arcturians, and Helio-ah

Greetings, I am Juliano. We are the Arcturians. Let's discuss holographic energy and, specifically, how to apply its principles to healing yourself and the Earth.

To begin, know that the part gives access to the whole. On a universal level, this means that on planet Earth, you have access to all the secrets of the galaxy, the solar system, the entire history of Earth, and the universe. Earth is approximately 4.7 billion years old, and humankind has been alive and functioning on the planet for an infinitesimal fraction of time comparatively.

Even though humanity has only been on this planet for a short period, humans can still access everything there is to know about Earth. This is also true about the galaxy and the universe. Consider a beach. One grain of sand seems totally insignificant. Earth is smaller than a grain of sand when compared to the size of the infinite universe. However, from Earth, you can use holographic energy and technology to understand everything about the universe. This same principle applies to you personally. Using holographic technology, you will be able to understand your soul's complete history, including where you have been in past lives, what you are to learn in this lifetime, and where you will go in the future as you progress up the ascension ladder.

Access the Full Spectrum of the Holographic Prism

Through holographic technology and holographic energy, you can see everything in terms of its totality. This means that what you experience in this moment is a part of the whole process and what you see in yourself now on Earth is part of your greater self. It is part of your total soul. When we do personal healings, we look at the total picture of the self. Frequently, we see an enlightened person or someone who has great spiritual depth. We see the person's past, present, and future. But sometimes that person fails to see it in him- or herself. It can be a powerful experience once a person understands and accesses the total holographic energy field.

The holographic experience is based on the understanding of holographic fields, which can be compared to a glass prism in which the light rays that enter are broken down into multiple facets. These are filled with different temperatures of light — shades of cool blues and warm reds, oranges, and yellows. If they were not broken down when you look through the glass, then you would not see the total composition of all that is in the light. I use that analogy because holographic technology can be applied to your personal development. When the proper view is placed over your energy field, then the prism-like images and thought fields break down. If you are able to read and understand this separation, you can see vast amounts of information about yourself.

Catastrophes Are Cosmic Drama

The technology of holographic science, or holographic imagery, is useful for understanding the cosmos, the planet, and you. Look also at the planet and Biorelativity. Using holographic technology, we know that we are in a brief period marked by dramatic events. There is polarization, and there are dualities. Earth is on the brink of a catastrophe on several levels: environmental, social, and political. Certainly, when you are in the midst of a catastrophe, it looks central and real. It's hard to grasp that what you are seeing and experiencing is a cosmic drama.

What you are seeing and experiencing is caused by many factors that are interacting and playing out on Earth. These factors have roots in history, some of which originate from earlier planetary conflicts in the galaxy. In this context, we look at a planet holographically in a frame of time known as the past, present, and future. How is it possible that future energies can be accessed and grasped so that the direction of the future's development interacts with the present? This interaction can accelerate the rebalancing and healing of the planet. This is another way of saying that you must look at planet Earth from all aspects: past, present, and future. You must see where Earth has been, where it is now, and where it is going. That is how you gain a unified view of Earth, which relates, of course, to the unified energy field theory.

One of the great sources of sufferings on a third-dimensional planet like Earth is the feeling of being cut off from the whole — from yourself, your soul family, or the soul group. This leads to intense disunity and encourages more polarization and duality. The natural state of perception in the human is holographic. You might be surprised by that. In your natural state, you can look at another person's energy field and see his or her past, present, and future development. You can see a planet's past, present, and future, and the same is true in looking at the cosmos. With the right lens, you can focus on the totality of anything's energy field.

Imagine meeting someone who is contracted and confused. Without a holographic view, you might conclude that the person is of a lower spiritual vibration, but if you were able to see and experience his or her total holographic nature, then you would have a different opinion.

The great prophets were able to extend their passion and light to everyone they met because they saw people holographically, in their true nature. But remember, the task for you and for all the starseeds is to learn how to access this holographic vision. Now Helio-ah will speak to you about personal and planetary holographic healing.

✷ ✷ ✷

You Can Access All Dimensions with Holographic Imagery

Greetings, my fellow starseeds! I am Helio-ah, companion and colleague of Juliano. Many of you have recently sought my counsel on how to expand your spiritual light quotient and work more effectively to balance your personal life and the planet. The answer to many of your inquiries rests in understanding and using holographic technology in your life.

Juliano and I developed the holographic healing chamber because we know you are visual in nature. You are experiential and visual learners. Just look at how much you love your computers and smartphones. You relate to visual imagery, but this goes beyond your digital technology.

This goes into the true nature of your subconscious, because the subconscious is also based on images.

The information in this lifetime and your past lifetimes is stored in your holographic memory as an image. It is not stored in a written format. The akashic records are also based on imagery. I once tried to calculate the storage of memory in the third-dimensional human brain. Your mind is multidimensional, as are holographic energy and technology. This means that at any one dimension, you can access all the dimensions.

We speak of the third dimension as contracted and limited, and many of you are frustrated about still being in it. But it is also holographic. Therefore, the third dimension offers you access to all dimensions and all spaces. I hope this helps you accept the holographic nature of the third dimension. At times, it can be difficult to access, but that is partially due to the way your culture has trained you and defined your perceptions.

Yes, your culture has made great technological and scientific advancements, but it has lost its balance by focusing on the ideas and narrow perceptions of the scientific, logical viewpoints that are the basis of the third dimension. This dimension has all the tools necessary to access all the dimensional levels, and since your third-dimensional mind is one aspect of your holographic supermind, you have an infinite capacity to experience the holographic universe, your holographic self, and the holographic nature of Earth. Isn't it exciting that Earth is holographic? That means that one of the healing techniques of Earth has to do with accessing the holographic energy of Earth.

Use Fractal Geometry to Access the Holographic Nature of Earth

Crop circles can help humanity access the holographic nature of Earth. Crop circles are based on fractal geometry, which is a system of perception of reality. The best comparison is to Picasso's Cubism works, that incorporate divided energy fields, which are the basis of fractal geometry. Crop circles provide information to Earth. Those who see these circles can understand the information when they realize that everything can be divided into fractal junctures or symbols. What is the benefit of knowing this? The benefit is knowing that there is a structural perceptual technique that is the basis of this reality.

Scientists are often plagued by how to explain that the solidness of objects is an illusion. For example, a table is made up of billions of molecules that cannot be seen by the naked eye. Your physical body is made up of billions of neurons, axons, and amoeba-like cells. Someone on a deeper perceptual level would just see you as a mass ball of energy, or a luminous ball of light. The human body is inside the aura, so your true energy field surrounds your physical body. There is also a secondary energy field inside your physical body. What makes this all appear solid is explained by the principles of holographic and multidimensional fractal geometry.

One difficulty in repairing the planet and your aura is that the multidimensional fractal images of both are not readily apparent. You do not see the planet or people this way, the way Picasso did when he painted the subjects in fractals. The fractal imagery, especially in crop circles, points out the symbols and concept of unity. One piece out of place can create an imbalance that upsets the unifying energy field. Crop circles fit together perfectly, like an infinite puzzle that is painstakingly solved. And while you might wonder at how it all came together, it is but a reflection of this reality and of holographic energy and light.

Circles and triangles are important images when considering holographic energy. There are many visualizations and explanations that use them. The top points of triangles represent the consciousness, and everything below that is the subconscious or unconscious. Just as the majority of an iceberg is hidden underwater, you only see a portion of yourself in this lifetime.

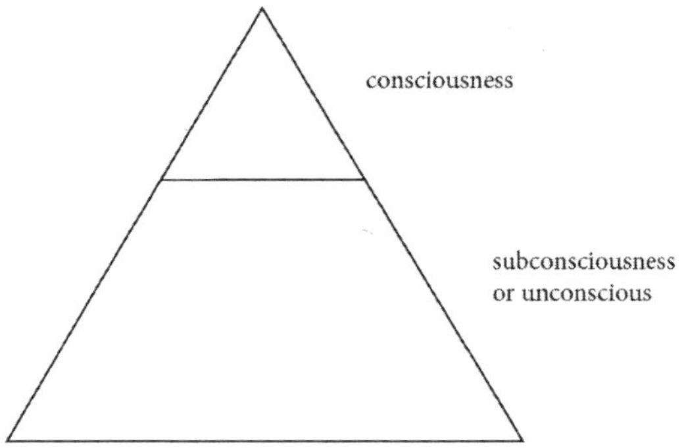

Figure 2.1. An example of the important symbology of triangles

Blessings to you as you all move toward expanded consciousness and begin to see yourselves in your totality, which is represented by a circle. The circle represents the interaction of the past, present, and future. If you can accept that expanded view of yourself, then you can realize that you will ascend. Then you know that you will be an ascended master in the future.

In holographic healing, we also access the images of the past, the images that represent those experiences. Some of those images are traumatic. Some are based on lower consciousness.

Past Trauma Interacts with the Present and Future

The noosphere continually updates itself, putting all the pieces together into unity. The noosphere must always work for unity to integrate All There Is. Part of the healing for Earth and for you focuses on unifying your past, present, and future. It can be difficult to unify the past if it is traumatic or disassociated from your present.

This principle also applies on a planetary basis. It has been said that humanity is a relatively young species that is not far from its primitive nature. We all agree with that, especially when we see how the current cosmic Earth drama is playing out with wars and terrible conflicts. Holographic healing focuses on healing and unifying the past traumas on Earth. Now, Earth has experienced so many past traumas that it would take centuries to release them. Genocides, holocausts, nuclear bombs, and destructive wars are examples of traumatic events Earth has experienced.

Earth has experienced trauma in the past — for example, in the 1940s and '50s during aboveground nuclear testing and the later high detonation of nuclear bombs in the atmosphere that greatly affected the etheric energy field of Earth. This means that part of your Biorelativity work needs to be about repairing the planet's trauma. The same principle also applies to your personal healing. Your past traumas and memories block you from healing and going into total unity.

Intellectually, everyone is likely to embrace unity consciousness and the unified energy field theory that we are all one, yet when we question why everyone isn't working in unity, we see that the reason is resistance. The nature of the resistance is always based on the fear of pain, which is part of human consciousness. The human psyche seeks to protect itself from pain. What would cause the psyche to think of unity consciousness as painful? Look at the history of how social, political, and even religious leaders have used unity consciousness for personal gain. Think about the many possible experiences in former lifetimes when you were part of movements based on false unity consciousness. False unity consciousness can be defined as an illusion of unity that only benefits the leader. This has occurred throughout Earth's history in a variety of social and political experiments. Examples include fascism and Nazism. Your memories invoke hesitancy and fear, and I know that some of you had difficult past lives when you were misled and disillusioned by false promises of entering a unified energy field.

Earth has been looking for higher spiritual energies that will help her become unified. It might be difficult to grasp that a planet can be traumatized, but this is one of the reasons the guides and teachers put a healing energy for the past, present, and future around Earth. That energy is known as the ring of ascension

In holographic thinking, the past, present, and future interact. The past energy is still embedded in the lower-dimensional etheric fields of Earth. For example, some of the spirits of people who died during the destruction of World War II might be lost, confused, and unable to leave the denser layers of the fourth dimension that are more attached to Earth. These lower spirits that are still around are trying to greatly influence events now. This is just one example of lower spirits that negatively cohabitate with vulnerable people on Earth.

Biorelativity is also involved in releasing Earth's trauma, and holographic healing indicates that everything is moving toward a higher good, a higher resolution. In the future self of Earth, unity consciousness will exist in its purest form. In the future self of Earth, fifth-dimensional light will exist. Masters and teachers will live on Earth, and it will be a new world based on higher principles. Future Earth will graduate from stage one of planetary development and enter stage two. Earth and its spiritual light mentors will learn to control earthquakes and storms and to balance the oceans so that they are less acidic. They will establish proper balance between the forests and the cities. Earth can easily support 8 billion people with the right balance. This balance will exist in the future of Earth, so we seek to bring those images to your consciousness.

Healing Theater Meditation to Unify the Present and the Future

Visualize with me this beautiful future Earth through your holographic lens. Let the holographic lens appear to you, and place it in front of your third eye. Project yourself into the future of Earth. Do not get caught up in measuring the amount of time. We're just going to go into the future when Earth will be beautifully balanced and will have graduated to planetary stage two.

When we arrive, we see there is no longer any fear of self-destruction. There are no nuclear weapons. There are no wars. There are many planetary cities of light and huge conferences where representatives come together to discuss the nature of their light cities. The etheric crystals are honored. The ring of ascension is visible because of all the meditation that has been practiced. Spiritual teachings are grasped and are as popular as football games once were. Millions of people watch and listen to great spiritual teachings on communication devices. There is a sense of peace. [Chants: Oooohhhh several times.] Visualize the Blue Jewel now in your mind. Know that it is in a future time, but also know that all the foundational energies that are necessary for this future Earth are contained in your present time.

You and I are now sitting in a huge theater known as the planetary healing theater, and the image of the future Earth is onscreen. You see the energy field of this beautiful, balanced Earth that has graduated into planetary stage two. You see Earth as a whole, and you can also holographically go to any location and see this wonderful connection to unity that future Earth has received and integrated. You can see how it looks energetically and how all the pieces fit together.

Just like the fractal geometry of crop circles, in which every piece belongs and is honored, the divine unification of all Earth's divisions — countries, religions, languages, and environments — fits together in a new balance. This is how the fifth-dimensional Earth will look on the screen in front of you.

Divide the screen in half with the right side showing the higher Earth we've just described. On the left is the present Earth, and you can energetically see some of the chaos, imbalances, and blockages, especially along the meridians. As you look at this third-dimensional Earth, notice that the foundations for the future Earth are present.

[Chants and tones in a galactic language.] These tones contain a special chant that unifies the energies of the future and present Earth. The present foundations are uniting with the future Earth, bringing balance to the weather, the seismic and volcanic activity related to plate tectonics, and Earth's place in the solar system. Earth is protected from asteroids and from the intrusions of lower- and fourth-dimensional extraterrestrials who may want to download their specific energies for their benefit. Now they are blocked from doing this. Only higher light can come to Earth.

Now unify the two sides of the screen. Unify the image of the future and present Earth, and I will send it to Earth's noosphere, where this unity will be activated.

Next, divide the screen again, this time with your present self projected on the left. See your aura surround you, and see your life on Earth. Look at this image of you in the present, and try to see it as objectively as possible, even with its problems and imbalances.

Now, look at your future, fifth-dimensional self on the right screen. Your holographic energy has opened, and you see your true self. All the lower, middle, and higher parts of you are interacting, and you have great energy and telepathic, psychic, and healing powers. You're in peak health and beaming with light and energy, and your aura is very luminous and brilliant. You have actually become an ascended master. Everything is in balance.

Now merge these two images of your past and future selves on the screen. We will go into silence. [Pauses.]

Your unification has been achieved, and your holographic nature has been accepted. To complete this exercise, look at your past in this and other lifetimes. If possible, have an image that depicts something from a past lifetime in front of you. It could be a lifetime filled with unhappiness or one when you had great gifts. See that lifetime, and bring all its benefits and heightened spirituality into this lifetime. The gifts of that past lifetime are now entering this lifetime. You are in great balance. [Chants: Helio-ah, Helio-ah, Helio-ah.] Blessings, I am Helio-ah. Good day!

Chapter 3

Planetary Evolution from the Galactic Perspective

Juliano and the Arcturians

Greetings, I am Juliano. We are the Arcturians. The development and placement of life forms throughout the galaxy are overseen by a galactic council. The Galactic Council is composed of ascended masters from all sections of this galaxy. Please understand that this galaxy, the Milky Way galaxy, is a huge system. We have given various estimates that Earth is 27,000 light-years from its center. There are other estimates that Earth is 30,000 light-years from it. That's an enormous distance, and crossing it would require technology far beyond what any Earth ship could even hope to accomplish.

You are only two-thirds of the way from the center of this galaxy. That means that the full length of the galaxy far exceeds 40,000 to 50,000 light-years. It is estimated that there are between 2 and 4 billion stars in the Milky Way galaxy. Try to imagine how many planetary systems and solar systems there are. I also would like to point out that many planets have inhabitable moons, and these moons are what I like to refer to as moon-planets. The moon-planets are, in some cases, more inhabitable and more likely to sustain life than the planets themselves. I would like to also report that there are cases in which the civilizations left the home planet, or foundation planet, and continued their home-base inhabitation on a moon.

The Galactic Council oversees and intervenes in planetary systems and also assists in the higher evolution and resolution of conflicts and polarizations. The Galactic Council strives to ensure the preservation of life. It oversees bringing life to planets. You know some of the beings on the Galactic Council as ascended masters. Others you do not know. You have not heard their names before because they come from other parts of the galaxy that you generally do not have contact with.

Most of the ascended masters have made themselves known to you through various methods, including prophecy and different visions, and of course, through channelings. In general, the prophets or the masters residing in points further away from the Earth system are not known. We are looking for ways to explain and introduce the other ascended masters who are not yet known to you.

You might be interested in talking to masters from other planetary systems that are similarly going through this cosmic drama you now experience. Some of the beings on the Galactic Council include Jesus, Moses, Kuthumi, and P'taah, who is a Pleiadian master and teacher. Ashtar is also on the Galactic Council, as is Vywamus. Chief White Eagle and Chief Buffalo Heart are on the Galactic Council, and there are also visiting members from other galaxies.

There are members from the Andromeda system who have been invited to participate in the Galactic Council. In particular, one master is known as Heylang. Heylang is part of the Andromeda system, which is your sister galaxy. Andromeda has many similarities to the Earth system, or to the Milky Way galaxy. There are Earth-like planets, Earth-like systems that are similar to your solar system, and there are also many similar planetary formations in the overall galactic system of the Andromeda galaxy that almost replicate or duplicate some of the extra-solar systems that you are now learning about.

Planetary Development

We, the Arcturians, have often visited the Andromeda galaxy, and we have been impressed with their work as a council. Some people might ask, "Is the Andromeda galaxy more advanced than the Milky Way galaxy? Are there more advanced life forms? Are there more fifth-dimensional planets? Are there more planets in the Andromeda system in stage two and stage three?" These are questions that one would want answered in order to compare the accomplishments and works of one galaxy and its inhabitable planets to another.

It is a complicated challenge to measure the progress of one galaxy to the next. One of the criteria for the measurements of how advanced a galaxy becomes is based on the number of planets that have completed planetary stage one of development and have gone on to planetary stages two and three.

Planetary stage two is when the threat of extinction is gone and the planet comes into a new balance. I know this new balance has many different meanings on different levels. It means the weather on a stage two planet is more controlled. It means that earthquakes and volcanoes are more controlled and that the planet has evolved a spiritual relationship with the inhabitants of the planet. I, Juliano, have been working extensively with many of you in my training and teachings about Biorelativity because the practice of Biorelativity is one of the signs of more evolved development of planetary systems.

On planets that are at stage two, I find that the inhabitants and spiritual teachers have developed higher techniques and more focused and effective exercises for Biorelativity. In many ways, the measurement of success of Biorelativity can be found in the planetary healer's ability to form an ongoing spiritual relationship with the planet. That means that the planetary safeguards are rebalanced and restructured, and it is done with great respect.

Let's say, for example, that a planet is capable of producing a great deal of uranium, but currently there is a limited amount. Now imagine that a group of workers on the planet decide to encourage it to produce more uranium and to make it more available by teaching people where to look for it. If people on the planet are using uranium and abusing it and creating waste and storage problems, then the planet might not cooperate with the continued mining of where this uranium is found. On the other hand, if the relationship with the planetary healers and the spirit of the planet is profound, honest, and spiritual, then the planet will receive assurances that there is not going to be any abuse. Therefore, the spirit of the planet will cooperate in helping people go into a higher and more spiritual relationship so that the planet can move into stage two of planetary development.

Jesus on the Pleiades

The planet enjoys and benefits by having higher-evolved beings on its surface. The planet also benefits from the success and the spiritual development of the inhabitants. The planet cannot go into the fifth dimension unless there are spiritual beings who can work with the planetary system. The planet needs you, as starseeds and planetary healers, to help it develop.

The Galactic Council sends prophets, wise healers, and even what you would call messiahs, anointed ones, or those who are able to bring together and rescue a planet from destruction. Jesus came to this Earth with the blessings of the Galactic Council for his mission. His mission has had many different interpretations. It was clear that when he came to Earth, his teachings would not be long lasting unless he died while he was in the role of a teacher and prophet. This is rather peculiar from our perspective.

We have seen Jesus on the Pleiades. He was sent to the Pleiades millennia ago in another era, another epoch, far earlier than humankind's current civilization. It could have been as early as 250,000 to 300,000 years ago when Jesus came to the Pleiades.

The Pleiades as a planet was certainly very advanced in many different ways. The planet was somewhat similar to Earth in its level of advancement. Yet it was not an exact duplicate. For example, there were differences in the languages, in the number of inhabitants, and in the way that people dealt with the environment. There was not the misuse and abuse of the environment on the Pleiades.

Jesus was greatly received and accepted on the Pleiades. He was welcomed. There was no conflict. There was no polarization when he was on this planet. He was able to reveal far more secret and esoteric knowledge than he revealed on Earth. The reason he was able to do this was that there was no violence on the Pleiades at that time. No one tried to assassinate him. In fact, he was protected, and he lived and taught for quite a long time on the Pleiades. He was able to educate and awaken many great prophets there. P'taah was a student of Jesus, and P'taah was brought to his great level of ascendency and mastery from his relationship with Jesus.

Perhaps you think from the Earth perspective that Jesus brought the highest, greatest, deepest teachings to planet Earth. He certainly did bring great teachings to Earth, but his overall teaching was much more powerful and comprehensive on the Pleiades. Subjects such as reincarnation, soul groupings, and spiritual light-energy fields were explained in great depth during his time on the Pleiades.

When Jesus came to Earth, he wanted to teach many of these advanced subjects and also about the ascension — one of his greatest loves. He was instrumental in helping many of the Pleiadians ascend.

There were problems here on Earth when Jesus began his teachings, as you all know. You know some of the history of his teachings. There were also many distortions and misuses of his teachings for individual ego purposes. Many people wanted to interpret his teachings and his position to favor their own understanding of power and control over the planet. This problem is still present today; that is, there are those who want to control and to use prophetic teachings for personal gain as opposed to the overall gain of humanity. Some seekers have asked me, "Did Jesus know that his teachings would be distorted and misrepresented?" Certainly, when an ascended master comes to this planet, he has to see the future. He would have known that his work could have been used for negative purposes, such as to control other groups.

We have to look at spiritual evolution on a planet from a broader perspective. That includes the introduction of new spiritual technology into the DNA of a planet. Sometimes the introduction of a new spiritual technology causes a rift. If a long-term overview was given, then we could say all this was a positive outcome, and the planet is now moving closer to the ascension because of his teachings. Jesus's introduction of the ascension had its intended effect. But when you look at individual periods when the teachings were distorted, you find that it seems others changed many parts of his message.

Your Spiritual Light Frequency

We have introduced the paradigm that is based on unity consciousness and galactic unity, which is called the sacred triangle. This paradigm can provide healing energies for the entire planet. It can provide a foundation for an overall planetary transformation. I have introduced this paradigm to you because I know that you are planetary healers, and I know that you are ready to embrace a teaching that can help resolve and bring people together in unity.

The analysis of the Galactic Council is that Earth is filled with such polarization that it is very difficult for one person who represents only one religion or one teaching to bring the planet together. The Galactic Council recommends that there be a more unified approach that brings together and systematically teaches brotherhood and sisterhood among everyone and seeks to bring forth a starseed family orientation.

There are other members on the Galactic Council who have not been mentioned, such as Mother Mary, Quan Yin, and the sufi mystic Rumi, as well as Bodhidharma, who is from the East and developed many different systems of yoga and chi gung [qigong] exercises that were brought forth to the Eastern world. There are numerous other members on the Galactic Council who I will try to make known to you in future lectures.

The sacred triangle has the ability to integrate and to move people forward in a new dynamic. This dynamic paradigm has several important features. The main feature that I will explain now is spiritual resonance. "Spiritual resonance" is a term in our galactic technology and spirituality that is based on frequencies. You have heard me describe spiritual light quotient (SLQ), or spiritual light frequency, which is the energy field and energy wave that a person attains by becoming more aware of the overall energetic basis of this reality.

The energetic basis of this reality is primarily defined through the aura, but it is also defined in terms of the luminous strands of light in all living beings and in all living objects throughout the galaxy and universe. Everything is at a particular vibration and a particular light frequency. The term that we use to describe different light frequencies might not comply with how you use this terminology, so I will simplify it and say there are higher light frequencies, middle light frequencies, and lower light frequencies. When I say that you are in spiritual resonance with higher light frequencies, that means your aura — your energy field — can vibrate in a similar pattern of light as those higher frequencies. When you can resonate or vibrate at a similar light, then you can receive and interact with that energy. It does not necessarily mean that you are at the same level of frequency but that you are able to resonate with it through a harmonic energy.

It is well known in radio technology that certain frequencies emitted on a frequency such as on the 40-meter frequency in high-frequency transmissions can also resonate with another frequency of 15 meters in the high-frequency radio electromagnetic band. If a person had an antenna on one frequency, 15 meters for example, he or she could also possibly transmit and receive signals well on the 40-meter frequencies.

This phenomenon is also true in spirituality. For example, you might not be on the high frequency of Jesus, or you might not be on the frequency of Moses. You might not be on the frequency of Quan Yin. However, you could be on a resonant frequency with any of them. You could be on a harmonic frequency in which you are able to interact and receive energy and light from their higher sources. When you receive that energy and light from their higher sources, you are able to integrate it into your own mental and emotional systems, raising your spiritual light quotient.

This has great benefit. It means that you can increase your spiritual light frequency and your spiritual light quotient by interacting with higher beings even though you are not exactly at their level. You are harmonically in resonance with their transmitted frequencies. Some of those transmitting frequencies are based on love, compassion, and what I call higher-level, fifth-dimensional feelings and emotions.

Third Dimension Dominance

Part of the planetary healing system that we are teaching in the sacred triangle is to transmit harmonic light and resonant frequencies throughout the planet. We believe that there are several ways to do this. One way is to work with the noosphere. We define the noosphere as the planetary unconscious, or subconscious. We believe that we need to download special etheric energy fields that are contained in crystals. This contributes to raising the harmonic frequencies of a planet. Of course, we support the planetary cities of light project because it raises the spiritual light quotient energy field.

You see, planetary healing then becomes based on how you are able to influence the energy field of the planet. One of the complications for planetary healing efforts is that lower third-dimensional frequencies create interference. Lower beings want to dominate and to keep the planet at a lower frequency. When they can keep the planet at a lower frequency, they feel that they can control it. You are seeing evidence of this on many different levels.

Some of this evidence includes how governments work. For example, there are descriptions for what is known as the shadow government in which you find people who want to control the frequency, the thought patterns, of everyone on the planet. When they do that, they know they can control everything to their own purpose. They have shown success because they are using the same principles of resonant frequencies that I am talking about but for a negative purpose, an ego purpose.

Some of the exercises based on control are related to high-frequency, auroral-propagation transmissions from radar-like devices that change energy fields around the planet. These have been used in military encounters. You also see things like chemtrails. Many people have asked, "What is the purpose of chemtrails?" The purpose of chemtrails is related to keeping a certain lower frequency among the population so that people are more susceptible to control.

You might want to ask, "How is it that chemtrails can change or lower your frequency?" The answer is that if there are any irritants in your energy field, then you will find it harder to raise your spiritual light quotient because your immune system becomes challenged, and you need to use the energies to fight off attacks. You will not be able to participate in unity consciousness. You will not be able to organize and work well with other people.

There are other things that people are doing in a shadow way that contribute to this lowering of the spiritual light quotient of the general population, which is the overall goal. You are planetary healers, and you are devoted to working with the higher spiritual light quotient. Once you are introduced to unity consciousness and to the sacred triangle energy, you can more easily transcend the lower vibrations.

Starseeds Will Unify

Bringing forth a prophet at a high level can transform the planet. Someone who is carrying messianic energy and light can remarkably transform a planet so that many people can reach out into the higher frequencies.

The cosmic drama also includes those who are searching and finding ways to raise their spiritual light frequencies and the spiritual light frequency of the planet. It includes those who want to unite with the Galactic Council and the galactic brotherhood and sisterhood for a higher planetary evolution. The cosmic drama also includes those who are more focused on third-dimensional energy, third-dimensional light, and constricted third-dimensional light. This is exactly the drama and exactly the conflict.

I don't want you to minimize this conflict. At the same time, you and the planetary healers have the support and the resonant harmonic energy from the higher masters. The higher masters will prevail. The higher masters have other safeguards coming into place, many of which are still unknown.

These safeguards are being activated in an important way. Some will be activated so that more starseeds will awaken and more people will come together. I realize that there are many factions among the starseeds. Each starseed might have his or her own groups. Many of the starseeds are divided and have allegiances to specific interpretations, which I expect. I don't find this shocking because there are so many different masters. There are many different levels of interpretation.

Eventually, the starseeds will unite, and they will all come to a resonant frequency in which they can relate to and benefit from unification. Unification is occurring on the Native peoples' side, on the galactic side, and on the mystical (or the unity consciousness) side of the Great White Brotherhood-Sisterhood.

Each one of you has such great gifts to offer and awaken. [Tones: Ooohhhhh, oooohhhh.] When you can participate and feel the power of the resonant frequency, you will have the opportunity to interact with the higher masters on the Galactic Council. You can simply say, "I am now resonant and on the same harmonic frequency as the ascended masters on the Galactic Council." Let us go into meditation while you focus on that affirmation.

Each of you has a particular guide and teacher you easily connect with. Some can connect with Moses and his teachings about the fifth dimension as he ascended Mt. Sinai. Some of you relate to P'taah from his work on the Pleiades. Some of you relate to Quan Yin and her great work on the teachings of the Buddha. Some of you relate to Heylang and his teachings from the Andromeda system. Some of you, of course, relate to me, Juliano, and my colleagues Helio-ah and Tomar and our Arcturian teachings about the sacred triangle and the higher light.

Connect with the ascended masters you feel most in resonance with.

Go first to those who resonate with you and then, by doing that, you will open to more teachings. You will feel this connection to the galactic family and to the brotherhood and sisterhood. When you feel that connection, you will increase your spiritual light quotient in your aura.

When you increase your spiritual light quotient in your aura, you become more protected and more vibrant in your everyday life, and you also increase your arcan power so that you can more easily manifest and use your powers for greater healings. [**Channel's Note:** "arcan" is the Arcturian word that describes the measured strength or power of thought.]

✷ ✷ ✷

Blessings, planetary healers and lightworkers. May your harmonic light quotient be in resonance with all of the ascended masters who oversee and interact with Earth. Good day.

Chapter 4

Consciousness and the Noosphere

Juliano, the Arcturians and Archangel Michael

Greetings, I am Juliano. We are the Arcturians. I want to address the noosphere, thought fields, and lower consciousness, which can include evil actions. There are many manifestations of lower consciousness, and it may now look as if the lower consciousness is dominating this planet.

Planets have evolutionary stages, as do species such as the *Homo sapiens*. Some of these evolutionary stages can result in a higher state of consciousness. The ascended masters and higher-dimensional beings who come to this planet do so in a way that protects themselves. If we, the Arcturians, decided to appear on Earth, we would have protective shields around us. All higher-dimensional beings who travel galactically or intergalactically have the technology and the ability to protect themselves from lower consciousness.

Going Viral

There is an expectation that extraterrestrials or higher-dimensional beings will appear in a way that will make the whole world recognize the existence of the higher beings and the higher extraterrestrial energies. You have a social media concept of going viral. "Going viral" means that something that occurs in society is recorded and is put on the Internet and, because it is so interesting, millions of people watch the recording. There is something very attractive and highly interesting about the event that attracts people. When people see this attractive and interesting event, they watch it, pass it on to other people, and so on.

These experiences are usually insignificant but are amusing and, of course, entertaining. Can you imagine, though, the publicity that would occur if higher extraterrestrial space beings arrived on Earth and allowed themselves to be filmed and interviewed? A YouTube recording of such an event would certainly go viral. There would be millions, if not billions, of people who would immediately watch the recording and absorb as much as possible from such an interaction.

But any higher extraterrestrial being must be able to protect itself from the lower consciousness or the lower energies on this planet. Some people would try to misuse the energy from the higher beings and might even try to capture and imprison them. In the worst case scenario, people might even try to kill them!

I know people have asked, "Why have the higher beings not come to this planet and announced themselves? Why have they not shown a greater flexibility and appeared so that, once and for all, the world would know more advanced beings exist out in the galaxy?" There *are* beings on other planets in the galaxy, and there are beings more advanced than humans.

Karmic Interference and Entanglement

There is a concept in your philosophy called the inclination toward evil. I like to define it as the inclination toward lower consciousness. My colleagues in the higher realms have the ability to protect and shield themselves from the lower consciousness and from the events that could negatively impact their existence. All of the higher beings have been schooled in the concepts of interference and karma.

Karmic interference means that a being of higher capacity and higher abilities can intervene and change the outcome of events on Earth or on any planet. Why would this be a problem? The main problem of karmic interference is that when a being interferes, it will incur karmic entanglement to Earth and go into Earth's reincarnation process.

Whether the intervention was good or bad is irrelevant. You might be surprised to hear that. However, there are exceptions. The Galactic Council and the higher galactic masters oversee this planet. They can give permission and grace to the higher fifth-dimensional beings who come to Earth to intervene. Through the grace and special protective energy given by the Galactic Council, these fifth-dimensional beings can be spared karmic entanglement.

I like the word "entanglement" because it implies many descriptive ideas. The term is also used in modern physics to describe quantum particles or subatomic particles that are involved with each other regardless of the distance between them. A special relationship exists between these particles, possibly because at one point they were physically close.

Karmic entanglement implies that you have become involved in Earth and its incarnations without your desire or your intention. It implies that you are entangled in a karmic drama or situation that is difficult to untangle or untie, meaning it could be harder for you to resolve karmic problems in the lifetime you are living.

Imagine that higher-dimensional beings like the Arcturians, who have great spiritual powers, were to come down and become involved in Earth. If we were to become karmically involved, even though we are fifth dimensional, we would still have to obey the laws of karma, and a karmic entanglement could follow. Remember, many of you are starseeds who became karmically entangled from previous visitations to Earth.

Many of you tested this very law with good, educated intentions. You did not do it naively. Rather, you might have been part of space-time exploration projects from the Pleiades or from Antares. With the best intentions, you studied the situation and decided to make helpful interventions. Then, unbeknownst to you, you became karmically entangled and lost your connection to the fifth dimension. You became third-dimensional admirers of the fifth dimension. Now you are looking for the opportunity to return home! For many of you, home is the fifth dimension.

The ascension is a wonderful opportunity in which karmic entanglement can be released. There is an opportunity now to gain great mental clarity about your past, present, and future and begin to understand how to release yourself of karmic entanglement. I know that many of you have the highest intentions and desires to do good. Those of you who came to this planet to assist also were on great missions of exploration and helpfulness.

Repel Lower Vibrations

I, Juliano, know of this issue referred to as the inclination toward evil, or lower consciousness. Our planet, in its evolutionary history, also had to go through this phase of dealing with lower consciousness. I know that there are other planetary systems dealing with this evolutionary process and paradox of needing to be protected from lower consciousness and evil inclinations. These are in the noosphere as well as in thought fields, the collective subconscious, and the collective unconscious.

Sometimes it may be more helpful to use the term "lower consciousness," which implies the animalistic desire to dominate, control, and assert authority. The feelings and energies of lower consciousness are often described as greed, jealousy, and competitiveness. There is also a desire to harm, kill, and destroy. I am sure you know that the human species, *Homo sapiens*, is one of the few species on the planet that kills its own. Most other animals do not. There are some exceptions in the act of procreation; for example, spiders might kill a mate. Generally, that is only done within the context of sexuality and creation.

There are animals that fight for dominance and might kill each other, but this does not occur on the same scale as it does in humanity. I could say that the lower consciousness and the inclination for evil is very embedded into the collective unconscious and subconscious and in the general thought field of the noosphere.

My first recommendation for protecting yourself from lower consciousness is that you, as lightworkers, must protect and shield your energy field. This is particularly true because of dimensional bleeding, or the seeping in of lower energy from other dimensions. The fourth dimension is directly above the third dimension. There are lower-fourth-dimensional spirits who are disincarnated (unattached to physical bodies) and, in many cases, lost. When they are lost, they want to reattach to third-dimensional beings. There is no guidance or much divine light on the lower fourth dimension.

These lower-dimensional beings can parasitically attach themselves to people who are vulnerable on the third dimension. The lower fourth-dimensional beings do not like light, and they do not like Christ consciousness, or Christ light. They do not like the ascended masters. They do not like higher vibrations. They do not like expanded consciousness.

With your higher vibration and your higher spiritual light quotient, you can easily repel these lower beings from you. Nevertheless, the lower beings are successfully interacting and attaching themselves to vulnerable people on the planet. It is always important to protect your aura and strengthen your energy field. It is important to shield yourself. This is not a sign of weakness or lack of advancement; rather, it is a sign of realistic thinking. As I said, when we travel to other planets and to Earth, we shield ourselves.

The Collective Noospheric Energy

Permission will be given soon for higher-dimensional beings to appear on Earth in a way that will be seen by the whole planet. This awakening is going to come very soon. It will be done without causing karmic entanglement to the higher beings and will occur when it will have maximum effect on the healing of the planet.

The coming of this time will also have a positive effect on the noosphere, which tremendously effects the overall behavior of the entire population. All of you have a connection to the noosphere and the collective unconscious and subconscious. The noosphere is a complex thought field, and it has an energy that is quite remarkable.

The collective noospheric energy has been tampered with by lower beings, but it has also received higher consciousness and higher inputs from great masters and teachers. Receiving and experiencing the higher-vibrational energies from the ascended masters who are in the noosphere is important, as is filtering and building spiritual strength. Strength is necessary to implement higher consciousness.

The Strength of Archangel Michael's Sword

One of our favorite symbols for higher consciousness is Archangel Michael and his sword. I look at the sword not in a militaristic way but as a way of exhibiting strength and protection. In ascension, for example, the sword of Archangel Michael is often described as a way to remove the cords of attachment.

I know that many of you want to ascend, and you might think that it is easy and that you are ready. Even those of you who are ready to ascend and have done much ascension work still have cords of attachment on a subconscious or unconscious level. Being here on Earth requires strong cords of attachment.

As I point out, some of those cords might be below your consciousness. Some of the cords you have are quite substantial. You can ask Archangel Michael to use his sword to cut the cords of attachment at the moment of ascension. This will accelerate your reunification with the fifth dimension.

The symbol of the sword is also beautiful as a protective shield. Holding the sword of Archangel Michael in front of your aura repels lower vibrations and lower energy. That means there does not have to be an actual physical fight. There do not have to be battles, but rather, when you use the sword of Archangel Michael, the lower vibration — the inclination for evil and evil spirits in general — cannot touch you.

Strength is an important concept in talking about shielding, but it is also important in understanding how your work and your mission here can be accelerated and brought to the highest level of effectiveness in planetary healing. That level requires spiritual strength. You want to have strength from higher consciousness. You want to have strength that shows the unification of all people.

The Power of Spiritually Minded People

This is why I return to the concept of going viral, and it is why I return to the concept now that higher-dimensional beings or extraterrestrial beings will appear on this planet. There needs to be an event that will immediately unite people and help bring the strength of consciousness to a higher level. Right now, there are many spiritually minded people on the planet, but they feel weak in terms of their abilities to change the events, and they sometimes give up. They might think they cannot cause any effect because the Illuminati or the Secret Government is so much in control that there is nothing that spiritually minded people can do.

These spiritual people do not want to go back into lower consciousness. In other words, lower consciousness is not the way to fight against the inclination of evil, dominance, and competition that contributes to this planet being out of control. An intervention has to come from higher consciousness.

I notice that people who are spiritually minded often don't believe they have the ability to connect with power and participate in an intervention that will make a difference. Events such as the appearance of a higher extraterrestrial being would immediately cause a great spiritual unification on this planet. At that time, there would be a tremendous boost to the overall spirituality and the power of unity consciousness on this planet. It has been said that this would be the most powerful event that could ever occur, and that the undisputed, irrefutable appearance of a higher extraterrestrial being would forever change all aspects of religion, philosophy, creativity, and self-examination. It is also important that you understand that extraterrestrials already exists in the noosphere, and it is already in the collective unconscious and subconscious.

I have referred to the galactic collective unconscious, which is a thought field that needs to be added to the collective unconscious. We talk about the Earth unconscious. We talk about the Earth's subconscious and, of course, the collective unconscious. This is a term that famous Swiss psychiatrist Carl Jung used to describe the fact that there is a collective energy field that all of you are able to interact with on a symbolic level, on a dream level, and on a subconscious level.[1]

Protect Yourself from Lower Energies

Many of the impulses and inclinations for our actions come from the collective unconscious, which is the sum total of all activities, thought patterns, and actions throughout the beginning of humanity. Frequently these activities are stored as symbols. When you look at the period known as the beginning of humanity, you have to note that percentage-wise, humans have only recently reached the point of possible higher consciousness, but overall, the majority of human history has been filled with primitive consciousness.

Sometimes this primitive consciousness is called the lower self, or the animalistic consciousness. Think about all those centuries humans lived out of lower consciousness without the ability to self-reflect and connect with the higher self.

The experience of going to the middle self and higher self is new in the evolutionary discussions of humanity. Even you who are inclined toward and have assimilated higher spirituality still feel and experience,

---

1. Joseph Campbell, ed., *The Portable Jung* (Penguin, 1971), 59.

at times, lower consciousness, which is accelerated by overcrowding, stress, environmental contamination (such as radiation pollution), and fear of impending death.

Lower consciousness is not unusual on Earth now. Traits of dominance, greed, and violence occur often. Those situations make it easier for lower consciousness to be the primary motivational force for behavior. Imagine someone who is imbalanced or has holes in his or her aura and attachments. Such a person would be even more likely to act out from lower-consciousness energy.

Our solution and recommendation in dealing with lower consciousness is to come from spiritual strength. Find ways to protect yourself energetically. Eventually, as planetary healers, you can input protective measures into the noosphere and into the energy field of Earth.

This third-dimensional reality is based on thought and on thought fields. It is complex to understand the physics of how thought fields become part of the collective unconscious and the noosphere. Even more complex is how those energy fields influence behavior. When you realize that people who commit lower acts of violence and destruction often hear voices or messages from lower astral beings, you might better understand them. They often receive negative verbal instructions in their minds. They don't understand exactly where they come from, but they experience them as instructions on what to do! Sometimes they are even told to follow other leaders in the third dimension who take advantage of the lower impulses and then try to lead people to violence.

Positive thought fields can instill protection, spiritual energy, spiritual oneness, and unity consciousness into the whole noosphere. Therefore, more people will receive the message of unity consciousness. It is similar to the concept of a catchy musical song: When everybody sings the song, that message is repeated in their unconscious and subconscious.

Opening the Galactic Consciousness

Galactic consciousness represents the thought field energy of all of the beings in the galaxy, and it includes all of their thoughts and their energies. Their energies, thoughts, and histories are recorded in the galactic noosphere, which includes the galactic unconscious.

Now (especially in the twentieth and twenty-first centuries) there is an opening to the galactic unconscious. People like you are receiving memories of experiences and awakenings from earlier times and events in the galaxy. Some of these events and experiences are very high. You are receiving memories and experiences from past lifetimes on other planets. Some of these memories are traumatic because they are of destruction, upheaval, and conflict.

It is true that each planetary system like Earth goes through stages of evolution. But some of the planets were not able to successfully resolve their crises and ended up in destruction. The simple definition of evolution revolves around the word "crisis." Some people define a crisis as an opportunity to change or shift. Also, crisis implies that there is a threat to survival. If the threat is not successfully resolved, then inhabitants of a planet can become endangered.

Now there is a crisis on this planet. There are memories and thoughts from the galactic unconscious of similar dramas on the cosmic scale. You know that the famous scientist Albert Einstein said that if there were to be a new religion on Earth, it would have to be based on cosmic experiences and cosmic events. This is where the expanded consciousness must be brought forth in a stronger way into the collective unconscious. There are other galactic planetary conflicts similar to Earth's. Memories of these conflicts are contained in the galactic collective unconscious and can now be recalled by the starseeds. You can communicate to other beings in the galaxy through the noosphere, which has the ability to interface with other noospheres throughout the galaxy. This means that you can also interact with higher beings in this galaxy. Other higher beings are meditating at this moment, sending you light, energy, information, and solutions to certain problems.

Connect and Communicate in the Thought Constellation

Telepathic communications with other dimensional beings are excluded from causing karmic entanglement. That means that higher beings can communicate with you and send you higher energy and thoughts and even higher instructions without risking karmic entanglement with Earth. This is a well-known spiritual law in cosmic religion and spirituality. When you receive higher messages and instructions, you can still retain your free will. You can still retain your discernment, and you can decide whether you want to follow the instructions from the higher energy.

At this point, since you are in the middle of a planetary crisis, most of you are receptive to higher energy and higher light, and you will gladly receive such beautiful messages and instructions.

Visualize the noosphere as an energetic sphere. You can send or download thought constellations into the noosphere. A thought constellation is a collection of thought fields that interact with each other. When the thought fields are put together in a constellation-like format, they have more power and can interact more powerfully. It is possible to set up a series of thought constellations, which can be considered a higher spiritual technique in planetary healing. You could send a thought into the noosphere like "unity consciousness," "love," or "we are all one," and it would have a strong effect.

A strong lower consciousness is dominating the planet. You might say, "Well, how can we counteract these other strong thoughts and thought fields of lower consciousness?" In thought constellations, you have thoughts that are connected to each other, and then they connect to other similar thoughts and begin to self-replicate. They produce new thoughts that are based on the same program or theme.

If you took unity consciousness, then you would create a thought constellation that would focus on thoughts of unity consciousness in the environment, in the governments that control the environment, and with all spiritually minded people. You have a series of connected thoughts, and then the thoughts themselves reach a point of producing other thoughts. Then those other thoughts can stay and interact and more powerfully influence and counteract the lower thoughts in the noosphere.

I realize this isn't as simple as I describe. It also requires a professional and almost scientific use of language to create this constellation thought field that becomes self-reproducing. This is how we purified our noosphere. As I said, we, the Arcturians, were in lower energy at one point in our civilization, just as the Pleiadians were of lower energy. We experienced great challenges and nearly came to the point of destroying ourselves. We realized that we had to purify ourselves. We had to purify our thought fields.

This is the reason that even today we continually meditate and use special space and time and thought practices to hold the highest spiritual noospheric energy for our planet and our dimension. There is a large body of information that states that the whole dimension is based on a thought field.

I want to turn the last part of this lecture over to Archangel Michael, who will speak to you more about his sacred sword and how he uses it for thought field work and healings. I am Juliano. Good day.

* * *

Gather the Energy of *Gevurah*

Greetings, I am Archangel Michael. Receive now the light from my sword, this beautiful etheric sword that has quantum healing abilities. I am directing the sword to all of you on Earth because I am above the whole planet now. Each of you can receive the light from my sword. Receive this light now, and incorporate it into your energy system.

I want you to be spiritually strong like I am strong. I want you to be able to repel lower consciousness like I can repel lower consciousness. I want you to operate from the highest light.

My sword has been a great tool in combating evil and lower consciousness. You too are on the battlefield of consciousness on Earth. You too, I know, have many personal struggles with fulfilling your planetary mission and planetary healing. I want each of you to know that you are coming out of *Gevurah,* which is strength on the Kabbalistic Tree of Life.

Align yourself now with the sphere of the Tree of Life known as *Gevurah* — strength and judgment. It is a strength that is of higher consciousness. It is a strength that is filled with mercy, understanding, and compassion. It is a strength that brings self-healing.

Gather now the energy of Gevurah *into your energy field, into your aura. [Sings:* Gevuraaaah.*] Let us go into a brief meditation and focus on receiving* Gevurah *— strength, spiritual strength — into your energy field now. We will go into silence.*

Let my sword be in front of your aura upon your wish. Let my sword be a guide so that you can increase your spiritual power and your spiritual energy and be healed in the light of El Na Refa Na La. *[Sings:* El Na Refa Na La, *a Hebrew chant meaning "Please God, heal her now."]*

Open up your hearts to the ascension and to your inner strength, for when you feel the strength of Gevurah, *your heart is also stronger. Know that the heart is a great basis for your spiritual light and strength. I see each of you now with this great light from my sword around your aura as protection.*

I know that you will continue to receive and attract this light and strength to elevate all that you do. Also use it to send the highest thoughts and the thought constellations so that they can reproduce and have a powerful healing effect for our dear Mother Earth. I am Archangel Michael. Good day.

Chapter 5

Biorelativity and the Butterfly Effect

Juliano and the Arcturians

Greetings, I am Juliano. We are the Arcturians. There has been a great deal of discussion about catastrophic end-time events on Earth. Yet there are numerous possibilities and techniques for providing intervention and strategies to divert and even change the outcomes of such events.

The butterfly effect, as it relates to modern quantum thinking and to a system of thought called the chaos theory, ties into a belief among some metaphysical people that the world is generally degrading into chaos. There are series of random events that occur, such as major storms and even hurricanes. Recently, there was a major hurricane on the East Coast of the United States and severe storms in the Midwest. According to the butterfly effect, seemingly unrelated events can still affect each other's outcomes.

The term "butterfly" actually refers to the flying insect, also known in Spanish as *mariposa* or in German as *schmetterling*. A butterfly, according to this theory, can have an outcome on a random event, such as a storm thousands of miles away, by changing its direction of flight. While it might appear that such a small event would have no effect whatsoever on such a large outcome, the theory proposed by Edward Norton Lorenz (a scientist and developer of chaos theory) states such an effect is possible.

Events That Appear Random Aren't

This is an important observation and has many ramifications for our work on planetary healing and trying to understand the influence current events have on Earth. It is important to understand the butterfly effect from the standpoint of Biorelativity and the fifth dimension. All events appear as outcomes from surface events on Earth. In reality, all events have deep causes and layers of interactions that make things happen. On the surface, it is true that the shifting flight of a butterfly in China could have an effect on the outcome of the storms in the Midwest. To really understand this, you must realize that there is a series (or layers) of events that sets up the possibility that a seemingly random event could have such a major influence.

The question that always arises in looking at such events from the perspective of quantum thinking is this: Are there random events, or are we not really able to see the deep significance and the deep inter-relatedness of everything? This has been discussed for a long time in your physics and metaphysics because it appears that many of the scientists on Earth who adhere to quantum thinking have concluded that there is randomness to events. Our position is that the randomness depends on levels of perception and stages of dimension observed. If you solely look at events from the third dimension, then there is obviously randomness. But if you look from the fifth dimension, you will see that what appear to be inconsequential or meaningless events have systematic effects; therefore, the events are not random. This is an important observation because the randomness from the perspective of the third dimension is real. In fact, on the third dimension, randomness is an important factor in trying to understand planetary healing.

Let's look at the butterfly effect from both negative and positive perspectives. From a negative perspective, you look at storms and say, "Well, this action from a butterfly seems to be affecting the outcome of some major storm, even though the butterfly has such minuscule power." But you can also say that the butterfly influences positive events. It is not necessary to only look at the negative outcomes. If the butterfly can affect a storm, then maybe it can also change its direction so that it won't harm many people.

You Can Change and Heal Outcomes

I hope you can see the significance and relevance of how Biorelativity can influence Earth events. I want to discuss your work as planetary healers doing thought experiments and connecting with the noosphere as it relates to the butterfly effect. That is to say, your comprehensive and group action is as relevant and powerful as a butterfly, which can be used as an advantage in Biorelativity Earth healing exercises.

Look at the powerful forces exhibited on the planet resulting from actions taken by the military industrial complex, the pollution corporations emit, the release of radiation into the ocean, and greenhouse gases filling the planet's atmosphere that are causing major changes and shifts in the overall temperature of Earth. These forces appear strong. Fifty or 100 people projecting Biorelativity thoughts might only have a little effect on the outcome of these events. The logical accumulated effects of detrimental systems seem to be unchangeable, and they seem to be taking this planet toward a major catastrophe. In fact, some people argue that the planet is already in a major catastrophe, and you are now in the midst of the sixth major planetary extinction of living beings on Earth.

This mass extinction you are experiencing is comparable to other mass extinctions, such as the destruction and elimination of the dinosaurs after a meteor struck the Yucatán Peninsula 50 million years ago. You are in the middle of the sixth mass extinction crisis, and these energies seem unchangeable. The Biorelativity and the thought healers work could be influential just like the butterfly. And it is a good comparison, because when the butterfly changes direction, there is an effect on the storm.

When you as planetary healers use the following principles and ideas, you too can create a positive effect on the outcome. You can change an outcome. Even today, people talk about the predictions of major earthquakes on the coast of California, and credible psychics have predicted a major earthquake there. This prediction is not cast in stone. Anyone who receives information like that is helping to provide opportunities for planetary healers like you to act as butterflies and shift the outcome.

Seven Principles to Maximize Your Effect

I'm going to give you seven principles to effectively maximize the effect of your thinking and planetary healing exercises so that they are not random but influential events. Remember that in the butterfly effect, randomness is not always the only interpretation of truth. The opposite of randomness is intention, and you can use the principles of intention to strengthen the effect of your work. The following are the principles to maximize interventions:

1. Choose the most powerful **time** to come together for planetary healing, Biorelativity, and general healing work.
2. Use the power of a **network**.
3. Decide the necessary **frequency** of meetings or interventions. You might only meet once, or it could be multiple times.
4. The **intensity** of the exercise relates specifically to the Arcturian concept of arcan energy.
5. Maximize the positive outcome by calling on higher beings from other realms for **assistance**.
6. Use **crystals**, including etheric crystals, to maximize and create new thought and energy fields.
7. **Focus**. This is the opposite in our terminology of randomness. In randomness, it just happens coincidentally or accidentally. In focus, we use our intention to increase our power.

This program and outline for planetary work can also be applied to individual work and group healing. This means that there is always a possibility that coming together using these principles — networking, time, frequency, intensity, assistance, crystals, and focus — can also be used to heal people. This method is part of quantum healing. With this kind of energy, amazing results can be accomplished on an individual basis. Most of our lectures with you have been focused on planetary work, but we are also working together for ascension. We are coming together to do a personal purification to prepare you for ascension. This means that there are great opportunities to use these principles for personal healing.

The ascension is an opportunity to purify your soul, releasing you from Earth karma to experience the higher realms in a dynamic and fresh way. At this point, let me take each one of these seven principles and expand on them so that you have the information and tools you need. In a sense, these principles are really at the heart of quantum thinking. The heart of quantum thinking, when applied to spirituality, means that there is a way to maximize your power and effect on third-dimensional outcomes so that your butterfly effect can dynamically affect Earth.

How to Use the Principles

The first principle is time. Time refers to the time of day, but it also refers to the time before the event. Consider the event horizon, which is the point right on the cusp of a change, catastrophe, or storm. If you can do exercises and interventions at the event horizon or even a week or two before, then it is more powerful. The event horizon is that point when, from the third dimension, it appears the event is inevitable. It marks the edge of the beginning of the event.

The time of the exercise and intervention must be considered. We know on Earth there is a great deal more spiritual energy during the full moon. There's more spiritual energy for many people on the Sabbath and during the Counting of the Omer (a special time sequence related to certain days and numbers that coincide with an event that occurred on Mt. Sinai). Religious groups have their own times that bring people together. You can also create a sacred time. The power of the intervention is directly influenced by the time, especially sacred time, and the amount of time before the event.

The second principle is to use a network. You are in an era in which the ability to network throughout the globe is phenomenal. It is very strong. When you are in a network, you have the ability for many people to send their thoughts and to collectively participate in thoughts. This is the power of 40. If you have a network of 40 people doing an exercise, then there is a magical power, an exponential power, which raises the strength of the thoughts to a quantum level. Quantum level healing requires a certain electromagnetic energy. It requires raising the level of vibration. To get to that special level where magical things can happen, there must be an effort to raise the electromagnetic thought field, and sometimes that can only be done by connecting with a group of people. This is why we emphasize the network.

The third principle is frequency. Are you going to do the intervention once, twice, three times, seven times, forty times? This is something you will have to work with. In some cases, one intervention is sufficient. In other cases, especially when you are closer to the event horizon, it becomes necessary to have the intervention exercise occur with greater frequency. If you begin earlier, you would not have to do it as frequently. When we talk about the butterfly effect, we are suggesting that the change in the direction of a butterfly far away from the event horizon can have an effect on a storm. The butterfly does not have any obvious cause or connection to the storm. The butterfly effect occurs when there is a formative power, or when the event is forming. This is key to understanding this effect. When the formative power of the event is set in motion, then a seemingly inconsequential event can affect the larger event.

The fourth principle is intensity. Intensity refers to how deep you meditate and how much arcan power you send out. Arcan power describes how we strengthen and adapt our thought waves and thought patterns in thought constellations. Thought constellations are made up of several interacting and relating thoughts that strengthen each other. They set up a positive chain reaction that increases the strength.

It is difficult to talk about measuring thought power on Earth right now because there are no accurate tools to measure thought waves. Indeed, the thought waves are so low in standard, third-dimensional electromagnetic energy that the field itself seems to lack any meaning or ability to have an effect. If you could apply an electromagnetic energy field of radar, for example, or even a basic magnet or other types of radio waves that could be measured easily, then you could measure them in terms of their unit strength. It would be difficult to measure thought strength electromagnetically. Get two people together in a room — one a trained meditator and another without training — to see whether you could measure a significant difference in thought pattern.

You know about teleportation and telekinesis. Psychics have done experiments that suggest observable measurements. For example, Uri Geller reportedly had the ability to bend spoons with his mind, with his thought power. This was greatly controversial because some people felt unrealistic expectations and trickery influenced the results. Nonetheless, his experiments indicate some of the primitive attempts that have been used to measure thought power. Now imagine the result of ten people trying to bend a spoon and increasing the intensity of their thoughts. When you do planetary healing or even personal healing, the intensity, the power of your thoughts, has an important effect on the outcome.

The fifth principle involves assistance from other beings. In the butterfly effect, it seems as if an inconsequential event can have an effect on something many miles away. You know that events occurring energetically in the galaxy send waves of light and energy. We specifically have noted the effect of Earth passing through the alignment with the Central Sun, and we have said that the Central Sun energy is having a butterfly effect on Earth. In other words, there is an opening of energy. There is an opening of a new spiritual corridor that is possible because of an event 26,000 to 30,000 light-years away.

In quantum thinking, distance is not necessarily the primary factor in creating the influence of cause and effect. Thought is the fastest energy in the universe because you can send your thoughts instantaneously across great distances and thought-project yourself there. The Central Sun is an energy that's still in the third dimension, but in the planetary work and planetary healing, higher-dimensional beings are also called to participate. In fact, the higher-dimensional beings' thoughts and patterns in arcan power have a tremendous effect. Their energy can raise the arcan energy of all thought patterns. I encourage you to work with and call on the energies from the ascended masters, and have them participate and download their thought patterns with your work. This is an important principle.

The sixth principle is to use crystals as a method to increase arcan power. Crystal work is a method of creating thought constellations and storing thought energy. The crystals store thoughts, especially higher thought patterns. We look at crystals in the same way you look at flash drives. You're able to store lots of data on them. The etheric crystals are thought storage containers.

With synchronistic programs on a computer, if one program changes, the other program that stores the data changes also. If you have a file on your computer connected to another, when you change one file, then the attached file on the connected computer also changes. The term used in your modern computer technology is "synchronizing" the files. This is especially useful when doing things in the "cloud," a term for your Internet function of storage.

We are synchronizing our etheric crystals, and when we send thoughts from our main crystals, your etheric crystals also shift and change. When you connect with and send thoughts to your etheric crystals, then our connecting energy field receives them, and we are able to synchronize our energies with yours. There are many ways that we can explore working together and synchronizing our thoughts. When you tell us that you are going to practice Biorelativity at a certain time, we can prepare and synchronize our energy through the crystals so that we can send powerful healing and dynamic energies to wait for you when you connect. This will help you to make your work and your healing intervention more powerful. There are many ways that we can talk about how we can do this synchronization.

The final thought principle is focus. In the butterfly effect, the mariposa has no awareness of the storm and no focus or desire to shift the storm. It is a random event. But in the given principles, you can focus. You can create an intention and send that intention through the etheric crystal.

Rise and Connect with the Twelve Etheric Crystals

Let us bring our thoughts into unity. At this moment, we have prepared all twelve etheric crystals we have downloaded with the special thought energy of healing and balance for Earth. Each of the twelve crystals will be raised up. Know that each of them has a special program of planetary healing, balance, and release of energy set into it.

Please choose the crystal that is closest to you. It's not necessary to cover every crystal, but remember there are crystals in Lago Puelo, Grose Valley, Mount Shasta, Bodensee, Copper Canyon, Mount Fuji, and Poás Volcano. There's one in Lake Taupo, New Zealand. There's one in Istanbul, Turkey; Lake Moraine, Canada; and of course, Serra da Bocaina in Brazil.

Raise and connect with the crystal, and then visualize the Ring of Fire, which goes through Patagonia, Chile, and up through South America, Central America, and then the West Coast of the United States. Even though it is basically focused on volcanic activity, remember that the volcanic activity is related to earthquakes. It is all interactive.

Visualize these plates, and visualize this area. Visualize, especially now, the West Coast of the United States, including Los Angeles and San Francisco, and keep in mind predictions of a possible major catastrophic earthquake. Now we are the butterflies. We have come onto this situation, and we send a balancing light up the whole Ring of Fire, through all the plates, all Earth, sending the calmness and allowing, if necessary and if possible, small releases of energy. Earthquakes that are 3.5 to 3.8 are little rumblings that can release necessary pent up energy.

Now we'll go into silence. You can send that thought of calming the plates into the etheric crystal, and then the etheric crystal will magnify the energy. Then we send these thoughts of balance and minor releases throughout the whole regions. This can help calm Chile and any possibility of eruptions or volcanic activity. We will go into silence now as we think together on this. [Pause.]

Increase the intensity of your thoughts as much as possible, and remember, we have set up special programs for you to interact with our etheric crystals so that we can synchronize our thoughts and healing energy with yours. I'm going to say special words in the galactic language to increase the intensity and arcan power of our thoughts. [Chants: Oooo twice. Chants several times: Hashma angah.*] Let the power of* Hashma angah *travel through the Ring of Fire and through all the plates and earthquake-prone areas. Let this sound energy bring balance and harmony now. [Chants several times:* Hashma angah.*] Let the power of these sounds focus on the balancing of the energies throughout the Ring of Fire, particularly to counteract any earthquakes.* Hashma angah.

Our work is creating a counterbalance. This is like a butterfly changing directions, shifting the energy. When we are far enough away from an event horizon, this one exercise in our global connection can have a very powerful effect. I look forward to exploring this technique with you for personal and group healings as well.

Blessings, everyone. I am Juliano.

Chapter 6

How Biorelativity Can Affect Humanity

Juliano and the Arcturians

Greetings, I am Juliano. We are the Arcturians. In Biorelativity, we primarily interact with the Spirit of Earth to affect balance and soften harsh changes, but it can also affect humanity. How can the thoughts and telepathic communications of starseeds meditating together affect the actions of men and women?

Biorelativity's original concept is based on the idea that humankind can lessen the catastrophic effects of certain Earth events, such as seismic activity, ocean currents, and hurricanes and other storms. Perhaps the most popular early attempts at Biorelativity focused on the California earthquakes. Some work has reduced the intensity and frequency of earthquakes on the West Coast.

Starseeds can work diligently with the Spirit of Earth, but what of the tremendous abuses that humanity is doing? Humanity's actions are creating more imbalances in the environment and the oceans with greater pollution, and the political, sociological, and military situations are the largest threat to the biosphere and Earth's balance. How can we, as starseeds, influence humanity to stop unleashing the dangerous methods and energies that threaten to destroy the world, the biosphere, and the way of life that has brought some order to the planet and to society?

How Ideas Spread

History on this third-dimensional planet is filled with violence, warfare, and conflict. In the past 3,000 years, humanity has used conflict, conquest, and military intervention to spread ideology. Certain people in power used their interpretations of their religions to organize and encourage military force that would impose their beliefs on others. Now, this seems rather contradictory from our perspective. Why, if a religious or spiritual idea is inherently true, would one have to use force to make everyone follow it?

The fifth-dimensional masters have been observing this situation for many centuries. Earth has particularly unique characteristics that seem to encourage domination as a method of ruling others. Part of the reason military rule can become dominant is free will.

Beings Who Created Cosmic Drama Are Paying Their Karmic Debt

Other variables include the intervention of extraterrestrial beings who integrated or downloaded genetic codes into humankind. These extraterrestrials attempted to control the DNA for specific purposes. In other instances, extraterrestrials presented themselves as gods to early primitive humans, imposing their thoughts and their aggression on humanity. This led to multiple conquests. Zecharia Sitchin and other authors have written about these extraterrestrial visits.[1] He proposed that the extraterrestrials presented themselves as gods so that people would form religions around them. It is true that these extraterrestrials had powers far beyond what humankind was capable of. When a being with superior powers and energy appears to a civilization, it's understandable that people would accept those beings as gods. It goes beyond Earth, though, because extraterrestrials have portrayed themselves as gods on other planets, propelling the cosmic drama.

There is a history in this galaxy of conflicts between civilizations and even between planets. In some cases, these conquests led to mass destruction and death. Such conflicts created a great karmic history for these large groups. I've been asked questions pertaining to this. "How many groups are there? How did they come to Earth? Did they come as souls, and are they reincarnated? Is this the reason we have seen so much conflict and genocide? Are genocides related to earlier galactic conflicts?" The answer to the last one is yes. Many of the things you are seeing that seem unexplainable are connected with previous galactic conflicts on other planets.

---

1. Sitchin, Zecharia, *The Stairway to Heaven*. New York: Avon Books, 1980 and Sitchin, *The Wars of Gods and Men*. New York: Avon Books, 1985.

Large groups of souls from these other planets are reincarnating on Earth now to learn. They have karmic debts to pay, and they need help. One thing about working with karma, especially when it comes to war and military, is to learn how to deal with lower consciousness. The soul will reincarnate where there is an opportunity to learn new information and new methods but through similar situations. This phenomenon of repeating situations with similar conflicts is referred to in psychology as the repetition compulsion. It is a factor in reincarnation and in karma and in paying karmic debts. That is to say, if one has not learned a specific lesson in one lifetime, then one must repeat a similar situation in another lifetime to gain insight and enlightenment about the nature of that conflict.

The galactic ascended masters have attempted, even on Earth, to influence this phenomenon and to help you shift away from the prevalent militaristic aggression. The ascended masters know the danger that this planet is in, as they have witnessed previous conflicts on planets where mass groups of souls have died. This is part of the repetition compulsion on a planetary karmic scale. The ascended masters want to intervene and stop this repetition. Throughout the past 4,000 years, the ascended masters have worked to provide spiritual leaders and enlightened ones to the planet's civilizations. Some of these enlightened ones are very well known. Confucius, Buddha, Jesus, Moses, and other enlightened beings have been born into this karmic cycle to influence mass culture so that the higher way of being, the higher evolution, will prevail.

Religious Conflict Hinders the Next Evolutionary Step for Humanity

Now there must be an evolutionary step up in humanity on a mass basis. You know the history of your planet better than I do, and you know that some of the great spiritual leaders began religions and presented new spiritual ideas that were effective and filled with truths and great spiritual powers.

They were attempting to help humanity evolve and move into higher consciousness, but the ideas presented by these ascended masters were misused. Kings and emperors — for example, from the Roman Empire — saw the advantages of using the ideas for political and military benefit, encouraging more violence and aggression. The ascended masters look at such situations seriously. They comment, "How could this planet accept an enlightened being and then distort the ideas for political gain? How can this be done when the presence of the master should be enough to help humanity evolve?" The enlightened masters and spiritual teachers who have come to this planet *do* represent the highest evolutionary link that can save humanity, but in almost every instance, we see misuse and deeper conflicts evolve instead. This planet is in a dangerous situation because of the conflicts arising from differing religious views.

We have not found so many different religions on other planets. Your complex religious groups often have different interpretations of the nature of reality and argue over which ascended masters or enlightened beings have the correct information. Such conflicts aren't common on other planets. For example, when Jesus/Sananda came to the Pleiades, he was immediately accepted as an enlightened being, and his teachings were taught to many people. He helped the Pleiadians raise their evolutionary level. From our perspective, this is what we expect when enlightened masters come to a planet. They have abilities, energies, and teachings that affect the evolution of whole groups. When a group accepts a master's teachings, that teacher is successful.

We have observed other Earth-like planets that are filled with conflict, and sometimes the master has not been accepted. In your case on Earth, we have seen both outcomes. We have seen several masters put to death, while other masters had large followings and eventually died of natural causes.

It's Time for a Peaceful Mass Intervention

This leads to your overarching question about how to use your energies and thoughts to change global leaders, especially when they are bringing the planet to catastrophe. Your leaders have power over the outcomes of Earth changes, but they are not addressing it because they have specific agendas of personal gain and greed.

Many lightworkers we are working with have expressed their discouragement and have asked how to change the people who are destroying this planet. How can those who are greedy and have disregard for this environment be stopped? You must use your thoughts and powers to purify them and change their ways.

In the Bible, mass interventions are often referred to as floods or other types of catastrophes. Even now, many of the great thinkers on this planet see end-time events as a purification that will change those in power. For example, in the story of Noah's Flood, everyone was killed except Noah and his family. There are similar ancient stories and myths about events in which a divine intervention appears to purify or reset a civilization.

We wonder whether the original extraterrestrial infiltration of Earth was referred to in the Bible by the term *Nephilim*. The beings known as the *Nephilim* had misjudged and contaminated humankind's genetic codes, and perhaps the only solution at that point was to purify the species — thus the Flood. But there are problems with mass floods and genocides. There are now more than 7 billion people on this planet. Yes, there are many people who are distorted and doing bad things, but there are also many good people. A large number of spiritual beings are working, like you, to help humanity progress to the next level of evolution. A mass intervention would create disasters for really spiritually minded and advanced individuals who are working, like you, to create cities of light and who are creating evolutionary advancements in DNA. From the Arcturian perspective, mass interventions such as floods or concurrent earthquakes might not serve the highest purpose.

There are advanced, spiritually minded people on this planet who are now in the position to evolve. In earlier times — during Noah's Flood and similar events reported by other cultures, for example — humanity was not poised to evolve. Those catastrophes are last resorts when it appears there are no higher souls left. That's not the case now on Earth. There are many higher, advanced beings like you who, with the proper guidance and opportunity, can assist in bringing humanity to the next evolutionary stage.

What is that next evolutionary stage? It is understanding and then downloading and integrating fifth-dimensional energies into the third dimension. The fifth dimension is the basis of a new awakening. We want to bring the fifth-dimensional energies down. Would it be appropriate to use physical force to impose the fifth dimension on the third dimension? No, that would not be appropriate. Then what methods are open to us and to you, the starseeds, to bring down the changes?

In Biorelativity, starseeds who can achieve a higher consciousness have higher psychic powers, including telepathy, which is how we communicate with the Spirit of Earth, Gaia. This telepathic communication can influence the Spirit of Earth to modify events, especially those that would harm societies on the planet. Even though starseeds are a minority, you still have the ability of higher thinking.

Use Arcan Energy to Influence Powerful People

Arcan energy refers to the strength of your thought power. The higher the thought power, the more likely the Spirit of Earth will listen when you communicate and the greater your affect on Earth. You can also use arcan energy to send thought power and higher thinking to world leaders so that they might change their methods. This is an effective method in many cases, and I encourage you to consider it. This is perhaps an expansion of Biorelativity. I applaud the Group of Forty members who have developed meditation techniques in this direction, because I think that it's a natural outcome. Sometimes, the people in power have defenses around them to block even the arcan energy you send.

Even the most corrupt leader in the world can be influenced. If you find a leader is blocking your thoughts of love and higher evolution, call on his or her guides and teachers, and send your thought energies to them. Ask those guides to use their influence to effect the change. In some cases, these teachers could even be their relatives, people living with them, or an ancestor's spirit.

You don't want to make the same mistake other groups have made by directing thoughts that might somehow justify a holy war. Holy wars create further violence even though those fighting might think they are winning and have control. They are really setting themselves up to be dominated in this lifetime or another. They will be on the "losing" side of a holy war next time. Again, I caution against any type of violence and interpretation that supports holy war because that creates more negative karma and is not the way of the fifth dimension.

Create an Energy Field of Unified Consciousness with a Planetary Messiah Intervention

I like the concept of quantum light intervention, which we sometimes refer to as a Messianic intervention. Early definitions of "messiah" included an anointed one or a king who, through military force and power, would restore the spiritual supremacy of a particular group. However our definition of Messianic intervention includes a unified consciousness. When humanity's consciousness merges with large groups in certain situations, it can foster unity. When this happens, there can be immediate change.

This phenomenon can be simply explained. For example, during a televised FIFA World Cup, millions are unified in consciousness. Now, this is for a sports event, but it does show that as complex and diverse as human civilization is, it's still possible to have a unified consciousness for a mass of people on this planet. But unifying for a sports event is not a spiritual planetary intervention.

The world has also become more unified in consciousness after mass upheavals or tragedies, such as 9/11 and the death of Princess Diana, who had carried a great deal of light. She was connected very strongly with Mother Mary, and she touched many hearts on the planet. These examples show how one event can create unified consciousness that can cause major change.

I call on you today to work with us to create an energy field for unified consciousness because I believe that you and I — together with the masters working with you — can energetically create a unifying, conscious planetary event that can shift everyone. Maybe not every person will be affected, but most people can feel the power of a unified consciousness thought field.

Ring of Ascension

The ring of ascension is a halo in which fifth-dimensional masters interact with you. The fifth-dimensional masters are in the other realm, and they do not incarnate on Earth. In the traditional definition of messianic intervention, you might expect the master to incarnate on Earth. This has happened before and often resulted in more conflict, so it is very possible that the appearance of a messianic master would continue that trend. You even have a myth about a false messiah who will come promising peace but is really bent on world domination.

It is our belief that the tools are present for an event that will bring unity consciousness and with it, dramatic and positive changes. These dramatic positive changes are possible without a gigantic flood or any other end-time events that have been predicted.

There have been suggestions of planetary events that might bring unity consciousness. One such possible event is the appearance of higher extraterrestrials, such as the Arcturians. Governments might also reveal undeniable evidence that other higher beings exist in the galaxy. This is one of many possible planetary interventions that could open people's energy fields, especially those in power, bringing decisions and actions that provide new balance and new healing for the planet.

We can focus on a general meditation to bring about unity consciousness. Let's meditate together on such a possible event that is in the highest good and can, in part, be determined by the ascended masters.

Meditation to Accept the Golden Ball of Light into the Ring of Ascension

I call on all of you to visualize the ring of ascension around the planet. Visualize a golden ball of energy the size of your planet entering Earth's aura. This ball is filling up Earth's energy field with its golden halo of light. The ring of ascension also is an outer boundary where the fifth-dimensional masters can interact with you. With this golden ball of light, it will bring higher levels of consciousness and the appropriate intervention. It will attract the right intervention to bring this planet into a new state of unity and consciousness. Let us work in our meditation to attract this golden light into the ring of ascension, and then the highest intervention for the highest good of all people will be manifest on the Earth.

As you visualize the ring of ascension around this planet, see the huge golden ball of light on a direct path from the Central Sun to Earth. This golden ball is filled with quantum healing and omega light, or Messianic light. This light will foster a planetary intervention of magnificent proportion, shifting the consciousness of everyone on Earth. [Chants: Oooohhhh, ooohhhh.]

In earlier times, there were stories of end times, of apocalyptic catastrophe. Let the energy from the current Earth crisis be transformed into a balanced and healing planetary intervention. The golden ball has arrived and is now being downloaded into the whole planet. Visualize this golden ball of light within the ring of ascension. The ball carries the energy for planetary healing.

Remember, this golden ball of light comes from the Central Sun, so it has quantum healing powers. You are able to attract this new energy that is capable of a planetary healing and creating events that will bring unity consciousness to world leaders. This will include leaders at the G7 summit.[2] *Once the world leaders feel enlightened, they will begin to foster planetary healing and balance. [Chants: Oooohhhh, oooohhh, oooohhhh.]*

See this light as transparent and golden. It goes through Earth's aura, affecting everyone's auric energy field and behavior so that people act from their higher selves. People on Earth will feel a greater sense of wisdom and understanding, and they will unify while receiving the consciousness of higher evolution. They will feel the desire to contribute to the evolution of humanity toward the fifth dimension.

Try not to focus on any specific planetary event. Yes, we can think again of the extraterrestrials, but the revealing of the existence of extraterrestrials would be an event that could and will create a unity consciousness. Think about the death of Princess Diana and the great opening of the heart chakra that many people on the planet experienced then. In a sense, her death was an attempt to open up people's heart energies. She knew that she had to leave the planet anyway. She was called back to her Home. This was a way to provide an opening for peoples' hearts through her departure.

Think that the result of this quantum planetary healing event will open people's heart energy. Opening of the heart chakra is especially important in planetary healing and planetary balance. We need to have the hearts of those in power, especially those in military positions, opened to the planet.

The ring of ascension is now accepting this great ball of golden light into Earth, moving Earth toward her higher dimension. Earth is also going to react to the need for purification in a higher way. Catastrophes such as floods are one way of reacting, but they create lower energy. We want a higher Earth

---

2. At the time of this channeling, the global summit was meeting in the Alps near Mittenwald, Germany, to make decisions on how to effect change and bring about a new world order.

energy event that brings a new balance to this planet in all ways. The golden light from the Central Sun is now filling up the ring of ascension, creating a great attractive force for the next planetary intervention.

Blessings to all you starseeds. I am Juliano. Good day!

Chapter 7

The Intersection of Dimensions

Juliano, the Arcturians, and Archangel Metatron

Greetings, I am Juliano, and we are the Arcturians. I would like to explore the meaning of the fifth dimension on a deeper level to help you understand the complexity and the technology that are involved in the intersection of the dimensions. Let's begin by speaking about vibrations and higher frequencies. For example, consider an opera singer who has a very beautiful soprano voice. When she begins to sing at a very high frequency with the proper vibrations and tones, she might shatter a glass. The glass cannot withstand the higher frequencies, the higher vibrations, of this beautiful singing. This symbolizes the relationship between the frequencies of the fifth dimension and the third dimension.

The fifth dimension exists at a higher vibration. It is difficult to describe a higher vibration and its effect on the lower vibration unless I give you this example of the opera singer breaking the glass. The higher frequencies of the fifth dimension can sometimes shatter existing energies, patterns, and vessels on the third dimension.

The solution is that the third dimension, or the glass, must be strengthened and prepared so that it can receive the vibration. The vibrations of one dimension are on an entirely separate plane from another dimension, so the vibrations of the fifth dimension do not really intersect directly with the third dimension. However, we are now in a period of great spiritual light and advancement in which the sphere of the fifth dimension is going to intersect the sphere of the third dimension. This brings some interesting technological problems and issues: Can the third dimension withstand the higher vibrational frequencies of the fifth dimension?

Again, I return to the analogy of the glass. This is an interesting analogy on several levels because it also shows that the higher vibrations, higher thinking, and higher frequency of the fifth dimension can cause breakages and can shatter some of the vessels and systems that hold the third dimension together. You are perhaps aware on a basic level that many of Earth's systems are in jeopardy. I'm especially referring to the old systems of power, which include economics, religion, and social and political conduct. In part, each of these old systems has to adapt and expand to be able to tolerate the higher frequencies of fifth-dimensional light.

You are in a situation now in which the intersection of dimensions has not yet occurred, but you are feeling the attraction of the intersection. There are strands of fifth-dimensional light and many magnetic influences coming through to Earth now. These are coming directly from the fifth dimension. They are experienced as intuitive thoughts, psychic energy, auric advancements, and upgrades in your chakra system. Even though the fifth dimension has not yet intersected the third dimension, nonetheless, there have been major spiritual influences because of the approaching closeness between these dimensions. This closeness is the forerunner of the intersection.

One of the many issues is this: How long can the third dimension tolerate the intersection with the fifth dimension? Returning to the analogy of the singer's effect on the glass, let us think that the opera singer can sing at a high pitch for a while, and at a certain point, she breaks the glass. Maybe she does not want to break the glass. Maybe the glass is very valuable. From that analogy, we again say that the third dimension can only tolerate a brief, perhaps a fraction of a second, intersection with the fifth dimension. If the intersection were to occur for a longer time, then the downloading of energy from this higher-vibrational frequency would cause major disruptions on Earth.

The Third Dimension Was Created for Soul Development

Incidentally, many have asked why the higher-vibrational masters and teachers, especially those who are extraterrestrial, do not appear immediately and do a mass intervention. One point, and this is only one of many, is that we are at a very high frequency, and many people cannot tolerate it. It would create a problem.

You are perhaps aware that astrophysicists in modern times have determined that the Big Bang occurred 13.7 billion years ago. This is the accepted scientific understanding of when this dimension and universe began. This universe and your perspective in it is the core structure of the third dimension. Did the third dimension come first, or did the fifth dimension come first? I'm asking this strictly from the linear perspective because, as you know, time is not linear in the fifth dimension. From the linear perspective, we can say that the fifth dimension existed first, and then the third dimension followed. Why was the third dimension developed? There was a need for a new dimensional space that would allow soul development. All souls do not progress or evolve at the same rate, and it was determined that there was a necessity for the lower dimension to be created to allow specific soul development to occur.

You could look at the story of Adam and Eve and the Garden of Eden symbolically and realistically. Adam and Eve were in the Garden of Eden. The Garden of Eden is the fifth dimension. There are stories of the mistake that Eve made in eating the apple, but the most important point in the story is that Adam and Eve were not able to maintain the high-vibrational energy that was necessary to be in the fifth dimension. It does not matter who ate the apple first nor does it matter who is guilty first. That's insignificant. The story is a beautiful description of the fact that the human pair, whom we call the Adam species, was not able to tolerate the fifth dimension. Therefore, they were brought down to the third dimension. This shows the need for the third dimension.

The third dimension became a world of duality. It became necessary to perform certain functions to survive, such as farming, that were not necessary on the fifth dimension. Clearly, on the fifth dimension, there is no need to work to make a living. There is soul work and spiritual work on the fifth dimension but not the traditional work that you do to earn a living. There is no economic system of money, for example.

It's important to look at fifth-dimensional energy and how ideas manifest on the third dimension. In the story of the Garden of Eden, you have no sense of how Adam and Eve experienced time when they were in the garden. We have some direct accounts of people in the fifth dimension. The time frame and perspective changes on the higher dimension. It is difficult to align the time on the fifth dimension with the time on the third dimension.

For example, Moses went to Mt. Sinai in the fifth dimension, and when he returned to the third dimension, he did not like what he saw. From Moses's perspective, he might have been gone for an hour or forty-five minutes, but those forty-five minutes turned out to be forty days on the third dimension! This shows you the difficulty in correlating third-dimensional time with fifth-dimensional time. When the intersection of the dimensions occurs, those who are in the fifth-dimensional frequencies are going to have a much different experience of time.

The Interpretation of Jesus's Teachings

Another example of the time perspective problem is how the teachings of Jesus were interpreted. One of the main interpretations of his teachings is that there was an end-times event on the horizon. There was going to be a great apocalyptic ending of the world, and it was necessary to prepare immediately. But 2,000 years later, we see that the apocalyptic ending that was predicted at that time did not happen. There was destruction of the Jewish temple and destruction of certain groups of people, but there was not an apocalyptic ending of the world.

When we look at your current situation from the higher realms and then from this perspective, we could say that in truth, you are now closer to an apocalyptic ending of the third dimension. The doomsday clock [http://thebulletin.org/clock/2015], for example, shows it's three minutes to midnight. [**Channel's Note:** The following is a quote from theBulletin.org.]

Unchecked climate change, global nuclear weapons modernizations, and outsized nuclear weapons arsenals pose extraordinary and undeniable threats to the continued existence of humanity, and world leaders have failed to act with the speed or on the scale required to protect citizens from potential catastrophe. These failures of political leadership endanger every person on Earth. Despite some modestly positive developments in the climate change arena, current efforts are entirely insufficient to prevent a catastrophic warming of Earth. Meanwhile, the United States and Russia have embarked on massive programs to modernize their nuclear triads — thereby undermining existing nuclear weapons treaties. The clock ticks now at just three minutes to midnight because international leaders are failing to perform their most important duty — ensuring and preserving the health and vitality of human civilization.

Some observations we have made in Earth's crises include the mass extinctions of the animals and plants on this planet that some scientists have now referred to as the sixth mass extinction [see http://news.stanford.edu/news/2015/june/mass-extinction-ehrlich-061915.html]. Now we are actually in a period that Jesus's teachings predicted. What is happening now and what insights prophets receive from the fifth dimension go through a complex filtering process in order to be put into alignment and calibrated to third-dimensional time. Fortunately, we are in a period now in which the spiritual technology of understanding the relationship between the third and fifth dimensions is improving. There is a better understanding of how the third and fifth dimension interact and intersect. In fact, in this period of higher spiritual advancement, you can freely discuss the complex issue of how the third and fifth dimensions intersect, time differentiation, and time calibration.

It's Hard Work to Interpret Information from the Fifth Dimension

Wolfgang Amadeus Mozart, Ludwig van Beethoven, and Albert Einstein were all geniuses. Mozart and Beethoven received their inspiration for great music from the fifth dimension. Einstein was also in contact with fifth-dimensional energies, and he received high-level instructions in mathematical formulas and information on how to conduct thought experiments that enabled him to make the major scientific breakthrough known as the Theory of General Relativity. All three men received higher downloads of fifth-dimensional energy; however, each had to do a great deal of work to manifest this connection, this inspiration, into the third-dimensional world. Mozart wouldn't just receive the symphony, write it down, and then that was it. There was editing, arrangements, and additions. Of course, it was the same with Beethoven and Einstein. Einstein received the inspiration and the connection, but he still had to download and manifest it.

When you interact with the fifth dimension now, you have to bring clarity from the inspiration into realistic third-dimensional manifestation. Because the time is close for the intersection of the dimensions, there are more opportunities for downloads and for intuitive receptivity to the fifth dimension. Of course, you still have to do third-dimensional work on the ideas.

When looking at the fifth dimension and also at the ascension — the whole process that this planet and this dimension are going through — we see that there has to be a lot of filtering between dimensions. There has to be a lot of understanding of the different ideas, and there has to be calibration of time. I specifically bring up differences because I know many of you hear about specific dates of when the ascension to the fifth dimension is going to occur. How should you react to such predictions, and what would be the proper procedure?

Our understanding of such events as ascension is that they are complex spiritual events of great proportions. It is difficult to pinpoint specific dates; rather, there are trends, opportunities, and windows when the ascension can occur. We have to consider all those things when we predict that ascension is going to take place.

Moses was in the fifth dimension for forty days. When he returned from the mountain, the people were extremely agitated, and they were impatient. He was so involved in his fifth-dimensional work that he had no idea that forty days had passed. He felt that less than an hour had passed. If I was to say to you that the ascension is going to happen five days from now, you would first have to ask what the calibration is between the fifth dimension and the third dimension. Is it possible to exactly calibrate the time given the complexity and also the many variables involved? I would have to say that there are different reactions from people; there are different possible scenarios of awakenings and even new discoveries. All these factors can influence when the ascension will happen, and they also have to be taken into account when trying to predict the date when the ascension will occur.

The starseeds in particular are involved in strengthening their spiritual vessels and Earth as a vessel so that this third dimension can tolerate the new, higher frequencies. The higher frequencies will greatly increase when the fifth dimension intersects with the third dimension. Doing the work with etheric crystals, sacred spaces, planetary cities of light, and the ring of ascension are all examples of spiritual technology that is strengthening the fabric of this third dimension on Earth. This means that the third dimension will be able to tolerate the intersection.

Can you imagine if the third dimension were not able to tolerate the intersection? Can you imagine the shock and the difficulty in experiencing reality if Earth were not prepared for higher light? It would be similar to an earthquake. How comfortable would you be if you were to experience a great sunrise or sunset during an earthquake? You wouldn't have the state of mind to enjoy the sunset. The starseeds like you are providing a foundational support network for holding and preparing this dimension for the ascension and for the intersection.

There are people who receive intuitions and energies from the fifth dimension. They are on the verge of making dramatic discoveries that have the potential for positive global interventions. New energy and new leaders who have new faces and new perspectives on interventions are coming forth. New galactic energies are continually upgrading. These new energies are difficult to assess in terms of the impact on the planet. The masters and teachers of the council have outlined this, and the general consensus is that events are going to be dramatic — dramatic in that there will be a quickening, an acceleration, of events to bring many people to a breaking point.

People are realizing that the only way that solutions are going to be found for Earth's problems is through a spiritual perspective. You're going to see a spiritual event that is going to awaken spiritual joy and spiritual hope for many people, a unifying event on this planet. Let the energy of the ascension codes be open for you so that any spiritual event of great magnitude will bring a greater resonance with the higher light as well as the likelihood of the ascension closer and closer to you.

Let these tones and sounds [tones special sounds and chants: ohhhh, ohhh] activate your ascension codes. These codes are internal cellular structures that turn on with the proper energy and stimulation. This means that you are ready to ascend. You are ready to go through this advanced process of spiritual acceleration. This can be compared to taking off from a rocket ship, for example.

Archangel Metatron will lead the next part of the lecture. I am Juliano. Good day!

* * *

The Ascension Gene

Greetings, this is Archangel Metatron. I'm here to activate and awaken your dynamic, neurological, spiritual energies. The third dimension intersects with the fifth dimension in your mind. This is the primary entranceway into the fifth dimension. Clearly, the energies will accelerate when the dimensions intersect, but the core energy is still in your mind. Your understanding and your consciousness must be the final ingredients that allow for the ascension.

You must be in the correct vibration. You must be in the correct frequency, and you can use these words you have heard many times, "Holy, holy, holy is the Lord of Hosts," to accelerate your ascension vibrational codes. These words contain a vibrational energy that specifically addresses your cellular structure and specifically turns on the ascension codes. You are already programmed for the ascension. Ascension is part of the spiritual genetic codes within you. But it is not always turned on. It's somewhat similar to other genetic discussions in which a person might have a gene that predisposes him or her for a certain illness, for example, but that illness will only occur with the interaction of the environment and that person's behavior.

How you deal with the environment is important. If you eat the right foods, get the right exercise, and avoid smoking, then you might find that the gene that could produce a certain illness will not turn on. But in this case, we are talking about turning on the ascension gene. The ascension codes within your cellular structure do not turn on unless you interact with them and give them the proper environment and nourishment. This nourishment includes special prayer and meditations. These words, these tonal sounds that we will sing in Hebrew, have the ability to turn on the ascension energies within your cellular structure so that your behavior and your energies will be in alignment with the ascension.

Listen now. [Sings: *Kadosh, Kadosh, Kadosh, Adonai Tzevaot.*] *Go into meditation now and tell yourself, "The ascension codes are now open within me."* [*Sings:* Kadosh, Kadosh, Kadosh, Adonai Tzevaot.] *Let your third eye be open. Let your crown chakra be open. Let your heart chakra be open as a higher-vibrational, fifth-dimensional light is received in your energy system. Your* Merkabah *vehicle of light is before you. It is specifically tailored for your own energy field. It is helpful to have your own* Merkabah *vehicle so that you can interact positively with the surrounding dimensional densities in the world. When you need to be uplifted immediately, your* Merkabah *vehicle will provide you protection and allow you to go through the densities on the third dimension with ease and relaxation.*

Visualize that you are now sitting in your Merkabah *vehicle, and we rise together above the room, above the sky, to the ring of ascension. This ring of ascension is a special fifth-dimensional energetic thought field in which you can interact, and it can provide support, a boost, to go up even higher. In your* Merkabah *vehicle, join me in the ring of ascension around Earth. [Sings: It is good to be together. It is good to be sitting with others in the ring of ascension. It is good to be in a group energy field.] Let me be clear that this ascension is a group experience, and you are participating in this ring of ascension with a group of starseed brothers and sisters.*

As you participate in the ring of ascension in your *Merkabah* vehicle, be aware that your sense of time might change. Be aware that you might feel only a minute or two has passed, but down on Earth, it could be a much different experience. Remember the experience of Moses on Mt. Sinai. *Again, we sit together and merge our energy in the ring of ascension in our* Merkabah *vehicles.* [*Sings:* Merkabah, Merkabah ha-Kadosh Merkabah.] *Remember, the* Merkabah *is a chariot. It's a vehicle that brings you to the higher dimension and to the palace. [Sings:* Merkabah, Merkabah. *Let the ring of ascension bring you into this beautiful energy field and prepare you for the fifth dimension.*]

Now we will take the Merkabah *vehicle and travel back into your room, back into your home again. Return from the ring of ascension back to your home, back into your physical body. The ring of ascension and the* Merkabah *vehicle are like insulation so that you do not experience any undue stress when you travel interdimensionally. With your* Merkabah *vehicle, you can return perfectly integrated back into your physical body. This is the beauty of the* Merkabah *vehicle. You can reenter Earth immediately and in the highest resonance with your physical body.*

Now you're back at home. You step out of your Merkabah *vehicle and into expanded consciousness. Your codes of ascension have been opened, and you feel a deep state of harmony and light and awareness.*

May the light of ascension that is on Earth's horizon (it is a beautiful harmonic glow, and you are part of that glow) follow you everywhere! I am Archangel Metatron. Good day.

Chapter 8

All About Shimmering

Juliano and the Arcturians

Greetings. I am Juliano, and we are the Arcturians. In this lesson, we look more closely at the spiritual practice known as shimmering. We study how shimmering is related to personal and planetary ascension, and I give special instructions and explanations of how shimmering works to set up a protective energy field around your aura.

Shimmering is one of the main spiritual technologies for the ascension, and it can be defined as the rapid acceleration or increase of your aura and its pulse. The aura, or your energy field, has a pulse. This can be compared to the pulse in your circulatory system in some ways, but there are also major differences.

In the human circulatory system, if the pulse becomes too rapid, then you can get into serious cardiac problems and even have a heart attack. There is a range of the human pulse that is optimal for your physical health. The aura has a pulse also, but unlike the physical pulse, the auric pulse is able to function at very high frequencies. In fact, the higher the frequency or pulsing of the aura, the greater your spiritual awareness and spiritual energy become. With an increase in the pulse of your aura, you will also experience an increase in your spiritual abilities. Ultimately, in order to ascend, your aura and its pulse must be at a higher rate and higher vibration.

It is useful to compare the terminology of electromagnetic energy to the aura. In electromagnetic energy, you talk about vibration or frequencies. In the discussion of your spiritual awareness, oftentimes you compare your spirituality and spiritual energies to another person's. You might say, for example, that another person is either at a high vibration or a low vibration. We can easily substitute the word "frequency" for "vibration."

Intuitively, you know — and your language already expresses — this basic fact about the frequency of the aura. Stated quite simply, someone who is denser and of lower spiritual awareness vibrates at a lower vibration or lower frequency. When you are vibrating at a higher frequency, your abilities, including your psychic abilities, dramatically increase.

A vibrational curtain separates the third and fifth dimensions. To ascend, you must cross this veil. This vibrational curtain is useful and has many functions, the foremost being to protect the fifth dimension from intrusions through the lower dimensions. Thus people of lower vibration, including those who experience hatred and jealousy and desire to dominate and harm others, cannot go through this veil or curtain. You must have a higher spiritual vibration overall to go into the fifth dimension. The concept of shimmering is based on these explanations. The practice of shimmering allows you to increase the vibrational speed of your aura, and with that increase of the speed, you are able to go through the veil between the third and fifth dimensions and experience more basic fifth-dimensional energy.

Understand Your Aura

Let's describe some of the basic observations of the human aura because shimmering requires some conceptualization and understanding of the aura. I hope you are familiar with my description of the cosmic egg as the optimal shape of the aura. I also sometimes refer to the aura as the "human energy field." The outer edge of the aura has a line that goes around the energy field and forms the shape of the aura. When doing exercises with your aura, notice whether there are any holes, indentations, or parasitic attachments to it. Drawing this line around the aura helps to fill in the holes and can also help to stop any leakages of energy. There are many examples of people who have holes in their auras, and these holes can be the source of energy leakages. But holes in the aura can be repaired.

Why would you have a hole in your aura? There are many reasons.

The most likely reason is a traumatic personal event. This is especially relevant for someone who suffers from posttraumatic stress or war trauma. Part of his or her aura has been damaged, and there are leakages. So in general, those people who experience leakages in their auras usually have suffered some type of trauma.

Parasitic attachments are hooks or tentacles that come from other people. Sometimes they come from the primary family, such as the mother. Sometimes they come from a brother or sister. For a variety of emotional and psychological reasons, those people who parasitically extend tentacles take your energy and use it as their own. Drawing a line around your aura is one way to become aware of these occurrences. Also, the line itself gives you a focus for beginning to pulse the aura. When you begin to increase the speed or the pulse of your aura, it becomes much easier to repair it. In fact, lower parasitic tentacles and attachments cannot stick to or stay on an aura that vibrates at a higher speed.

When a person vibrates at a higher speed, there can be amazing and miraculous healings of the aura. You will also find that shimmering is basically an acceleration of the aura, and illnesses can be healed while you are accelerating your aura. Many of the illnesses come from holes in the aura, which causes energy leakage or parasitic attachments. In fact, even parasites or pathogens must travel through the aura to reach you, so there are vibrational defense systems in place. When your aura is shimmering and vibrating at higher speeds, the pathogens can be more easily repelled. People who may want to harm you for any reason will also find that your accelerated auric speed repels them, and they will have difficulty getting through to harm you. Already you can see there are many benefits to shimmering, and we haven't even discussed or explored its main goal, which is to thought-project yourself into the fifth dimension.

Become Familiar with the Pulse of Your Aura

Let me return to the concept of the line around the aura. Oftentimes I ask the people we are healing to visualize the line as a deep or bright purple in a very solid nature. There is some discussion about how far away this line should be because your aura extends outward quite a few inches. In fact, you could say that the aura can be projected thirty, forty, or fifty inches away from the body. Some people with higher psychic skills have extraordinary abilities and can project their auras for miles. In higher energy work, people can vibrate and extend their auras beyond Earth and out into the solar system, out into the galaxy, and of course, even out into the universe. But in this work we are talking about, namely the shimmering, we recommend that the distance you work with where the line is drawn is eight to ten inches from your body. Understand that there is energy beyond those eight to ten inches, but that distance will provide the maximum benefit for shimmering. In some ways, this is the most powerful and immediate energy benefit. It is your protective layer. It is your power spot.

There are several methods for increasing the pulse speed of your aura. The first method begins when you become aware of the existing pulse speed. This is similar to becoming aware of your breathing. In breathing, you automatically want to slow it down, but usually in deeper meditation techniques, the teacher will simply say, "Become aware of your breathing *without* changing it in any way." It's the same thing in aura work: Simply become aware of your aura and the speed of its pulse.

I often give a rapid tone and ask you to try to match the pulsing speed of your aura to my tone. You might, for example, hear me say this. [Slowly tones: Ta ta ta ta ta ta ta ta ta ta.] Hopefully by listening to that, you can match the pulsing of your aura to that speed. Then someone might say, "Okay, I'm going to increase that sound to help you increase the speed of your aura," because the faster your aura vibrates, the more psychic and spiritual abilities you're going to have. Ultimately, at the point of ascension, you will be able to rapidly move the pulse of your aura to a speed that will allow you to go into the fifth dimension.

Here is an example again of more rapid pulsing. [Tones faster: Ta-ta-ta-ta-ta-ta-ta-ta-ta-ta-ta.] Feel the rapid increase of your energy field, and most importantly, feel the pulse of your aura increase. Shimmering, then, is directly related to the speed of your aura's pulse. When your energy field reaches a certain speed, which we call the threshold speed for shimmering, you begin to flicker, or shimmer. That means you're going in and out of physical awareness. People observing you would see your physical energy flicker, which means it would go in and out and look as if it were ready to go into another realm. I have compared this to *Star Trek* when the characters use the transporter, which conveys a person from one position on the spaceship to another position on a planet. Right before the person finally disappear to travel through space or to the planet, you see them flicker. In this case, you are not going to another planet; you're going into another dimension.

There are several different recommendations for how to use shimmering energy most effectively:

Use sacred tones and sounds before you begin to shimmer.
Practice shimmering in a sacred space.
Practice shimmering at sacred times.
Use crystals and special stones for assistance in increasing and holding the vibrational frequency.

The Benefits of Using Tachyon Stones

I want to take this opportunity to discuss the stones called tachyon. I mentioned the tachyon stones many years ago in my first book, *Connecting with the Arcturians*. I said that the tachyon stones have special abilities to help you vibrate and go into higher frequencies — eventually into the fifth dimension. I want to explain this again. One of the characteristics of tachyon stones is that the energy of the stone is connected to a higher dimension, and the energy field and thought field contained in the tachyon can travel faster than the speed of light. There has been some discussion about whether or not tachyon stones actually exist now in the third dimension, but the most important thing is that the concept and thought field of tachyon do exist, and replicas of tachyon stones are available. I cannot say that each stone has the exact property that we work with in the fifth dimension on Arcturus, but even if they don't, the tachyon stones that are available carry the thought energies — namely, that the stone itself holds and carries energy that is faster than the speed of light.

What is the advantage of having a symbolic — or actual — stone that has the properties of holding thoughts that can travel faster than the speed of light? To answer that question, let us look again at shimmering. Shimmering offers you healing and protection, so it helps you create a protective energy field around you. Intrusions, harmful thoughts, or even harmful events cannot penetrate this energy field. So shimmering has multiple functions. One function is to help you go into the fifth dimension at ascension and to practice going into the fifth dimension, and another is to increase the speed of your aura to protect you. The tachyon stone, because it has the properties of traveling faster than the speed of light, also has a special protective capability.

Planet Earth is now being filled with electromagnetic radio waves, solar energy, and radiation. These energies belong to the electromagnetic spectrum. They are in various parts of the radio spectrum, but they all travel and conform to the properties of electromagnetic energy, which travels at the speed of light. Let me use the example of radiation, because this has been a very important subject, especially in light of the major nuclear power accidents at Chernobyl and Fukushima. Furthermore, there has been an overabundant release of radiation in the past fifty years on this planet. More radiation has been released on this planet in the past fifty years than in the past five million. You can imagine the potential harmful effects that are being thrust on this planet and on you and your energy field. You are all making adaptations, but it is still a stress to you and your immune system. The tachyon energy, since it has the potential to travel faster than the speed of light, is able to more effectively shield you from harmful electromagnetic radiation. The tachyon vibrates faster than the speed of light or faster than the radio emissions and electromagnetic energies.

Using crystals and tachyons can set up special properties of protection. You all know there are many electromagnetic energies bombarding your brains from the Internet, cell phones, smartphones, iPads, and other devices. You're still at a very primitive level with this energy regarding protecting your energy fields. If you were to come onto one of our spaceships, you would find no leakages, no "dirty energy," coming from our computers or transmissions or power sources. One hundred or 200 years from now, people might look back and be shocked by how sloppy the science and the technology were with electromagnetic energy. Everyone will be shocked looking back at how sloppy people have been with radiation, and everyone is also going to be shocked by how this era, 2015 and beyond, was not able to correctly block electromagnetic radiation coming from electronics.

Shimmer for More than Yourself

Let's now look at the shimmering on a planetary basis. Everything on the planet has an energy field. The rocks, the plants, the cities, and even your home have energy fields. The technique and the application of the shimmering technology are the same for your home and the city as they are for you personally. Let me describe this in more detail. Establish an eight-inch line around your energy field. Your body, your energy field, and your pulsing line would be approximately eight inches out, and that boundary is where you would begin to do the pulsing work. Let's examine, for example, shimmering around your home. Think of the boundaries around your property because you may want to shimmer both your home and property. Visualize a boundary line around your property. The property line would be considered the same thing as the auric line. You can shimmer your property and have the same protection that you would have in your personal aura. You can also place crystals and tachyon stones inside your property line.

So the principles of shimmering can be applied to physical places. There are many possible threats to your personal property. You are well aware of the threats of fires, drought, storms, and radiation to your property. So establish the spiritual boundary around your house, visualize the energy field and the aura line around your property, and begin to shimmer it. You will find that the property will accelerate its vibration. The plants will grow better. There will be less likelihood of any damage from storms or other events, and overall, you will feel a great sense of protection.

In shimmering the cities of light, the idea is the same: You establish a boundary around the city of light you are working with. Again, it is important when I talk about the eight-inch line from your personal physical body as the line of the pulse. I want you to also consider that you have to work with the auric line and pulse line in the energy field of your city. Go around the boundary of the city and place stones in the boundary line, and then you can begin to do the shimmering exercise. This has the effect, again, of protecting the city in the same ways I have described for your property.

You also, by the way, can shimmer your automobile. Each automobile has a special aura. In fact, your automobile conforms and interacts with your energy field, and for protection, you can place an energetic boundary around your automobile and shimmer it in your mind before you use it. You can shimmer it at other times when the car is parked near your house. You'd be surprised how the objects you use conform to your energy field.

Use Sound to Increase Shimmering

There are tones and sounds you can use to increase the shimmering ability. It so happens that some of the frequencies in the ancient Hebrew language have high energetic qualities. There are also other healing tones and sounds from the Chinese and Sanskrit languages that can accelerate healing and increase shimmering.

I want to compare shimmering to the opening of the assemblage point, a physical point on the body often described by shamans. When that point is opened, the person has an opportunity to lift the veil from the third dimension. But sometimes that veil is only lifted partly, and the person can only go into the fourth dimension. The exercise of shimmering that we are doing will help you to go into the fifth dimension. The concept of opening the assemblage point can be compared to increasing your auric speed while shimmering.

The tones in the Chinese language, or in the Chinese philosophy — particularly the Tao philosophy — also carry great potential for increasing shimmering. For example, Chinese tones such as *huuuuhhhh* and *haaaah* can be very effective in accelerating the aura pulse. I want to speak a little bit about the sound *haaaahhh* because it is known in the world of Taoism that certain sounds have great protective value. Also, certain sounds can have a higher ability to disorient anyone coming toward you who wants to harm you or has a negative thought against you. It could simply be negative energy from somebody at work; for whatever reason, they are projecting negative energy at you. You don't want to say this verbally in your work environment, but you could say to yourself in a single sound the word *haaah,* and by vibrating on that level, you begin a special shimmering in which lower-vibration and negative energy coming toward you is repulsed. In an actual confrontation in which someone might want to physically intrude on your space, you can verbalize that sound, and that sound will immediately disorient and confuse the other person's energy field. The sound of "ha" said forcefully, will disrupt a person's energy field, and then it's much easier for you to keep yourself intact.

There are sounds that are particularly useful for ascending into the fifth dimension. Now remember, there is a veil, or a curtain, between the third and fifth dimensions, and the new technology from the Arcturians teaches you how to go through that veil. When you go through it, you can increase the speed of your aura. When you increase the speed of your aura and begin to shimmer, you will have a major increase in all your psychic spiritual abilities. Your ability to use your third eye, for example, will increase dramatically. Your ability to heal others will also increase dramatically because your hands are going to be vibrating at a higher level, and ultimately, your ability to thought-project yourself will increase.

Teleport through Thought Projection

Thought projection is a psychic ability that can be compared to teleportation or even defined as self-teleportation. Teleportation is the ability to move objects from one place to another with your mind. If you have a glass on a table in one room, and in another room you have another table, you would be able to thought-project, or move that glass from one table to the other. It would require a high arcan (or voltage) energy to do that. It might be difficult for you, but it is easy for us because we are trained to do it.

I can compare this to learning a foreign language. If you learn a foreign language when you are three or four years old, you don't have to study. You pronounce all the words correctly and instinctively learn all the grammatical rules, and everything is quite easy. Imagine that you were trained in or practiced teleportation as a three- or four-year-old. Then it wouldn't be that great of an effort. We, the Arcturians, practice moving objects this way from the earliest time that we can remember. Some of you have commented that we don't look muscular. But what is the point of using muscles if you can move things — even yourself — with your mind? That is what thought projection is — self-teleportation.

In the ascension, there is going to be an intersection of the dimensions and a high burst of spiritual energy. That high burst of spiritual energy is like a gift to each of you. It's like loaning you energy, and then suddenly, with that immediate upliftment of energy, your spiritual light quotient and your ability to shimmer go up dramatically. You will be able to shimmer at indescribable speeds. I cannot duplicate the speed of the pulsing of your aura with the channel's voice. I cannot even physically describe it, but it's fast. I can tell you that you cannot do that speed now by yourself. You don't have the ability to shimmer that fast now, but with the boost of energy from the ascension and the intersection of the dimensions, you will have the ability to rapidly increase the pulse of your aura. With the dynamic and accelerated increase of your aura, your assemblage point will open, then your psychic abilities will improve dramatically, and you will be able to thought-project yourself.

Work with Corridors of Light and Your Multidimensional Presence

We recommend that you use the concept of the corridors of light. Some of you might even use the example of the *Merkabah* vehicle. In the concept of the corridor of light, you shimmer yourself to a high speed, and then you thought-project and place your aura into the corridor. At the higher aura speeds, where the aura goes, the body follows. You are now at the lower speed and lower density. At lower speeds, what your body does, the aura follows. At higher speeds, where you place your aura is where your body is going to go. That is one of the interesting and intriguing rules of the ascension — that is, there will be such a high speed that you can think and place your thoughts into the corridor. When you do that, you think, and then you place your aura.

Now visualize your aura as a cosmic egg, and place that whole egg into the corridor. Then visualize that your aura blasts off and travels to a place such as the Arcturian stargate or crystal lake. You can go at this higher speed.

A question has been asked about the connection between the astral travel and the astral cord. When you do any astral traveling or thought projection now, your astral cord is still connected to your physical body. At the point of ascension, you will be given the opportunity to cut the astral cord. You would only want to cut the astral cord when you are vibrating at such a high speed that you know you could enter the fifth dimension. With the cutting of the astral cord, or perhaps we could say with the withdrawal of the astral cord, your physical body can disappear from the third dimension. Some people describe it as an alchemical transformation in which the energy is transmuted and goes into your fifth-dimensional body.

We are working with you as a being who has multidimensionality. You exist in several dimensions. You do not exist just in the third dimension, even though it seems as if you are living in this lower dimension. Everything looks solid, and everything appears as if it is unable to be penetrated, but that appearance is only because there is a strong veil. This reality is an illusion that only becomes apparent when you begin to shimmer. Then you will understand that you have been existing in the fifth dimension for quite a long time. In fact, your thoughts and energy have placed a great resource and an anchor in the fifth dimension. This is why you will be able to ascend.

People who have not placed their energy in another dimension will have no foundation to travel or thought-project to higher realms. But you *do* have that anchoring. You *do* have that foundational work, and most importantly, you have awareness of your fifth-dimensional body. Your fifth-dimensional body is wonderful. It does not age like your third-dimensional body. It has an ability to conform more directly to your thoughts, so you are able to shape your physical appearance. In pictures you have seen of ascended masters, many appear to be very youthful. They always look as if they are at the height of their vitality. When you become aware of your multidimensionality, it will help you to visualize your fifth-dimensional body. Visualize your fifth-dimensional body in an astral sense, an etheric energy. Maybe spend a minute now to visualize yourself as a fifth-dimensional being. You could have any color hair, any facial expression, any skin tone, and any type of physical body that you want. [Tones: Ooohhhh, oooohhh.]

* * *

Spend time thought-projecting and visiting your fifth-dimensional body. Your fifth-dimensional body can return the favor and visit you, download energy and healing light to you, and help you accelerate your energy field. We are talking now about a two-way interaction when the veil between the third and fifth dimensions is pierced or lifted. It means that there is an interaction from the third to the fifth as well as an interaction from the fifth to the third. This interaction becomes a great source of enlightenment, healing, and spiritual acceleration. I love you all. Blessings! I am Juliano.

Chapter 9

The Laws of Consciousness

Juliano and the Arcturians

Greetings, I am Juliano. We are the Arcturians. We would like to offer you our view of consciousness and our view as fifth-dimensional beings of light. We would like you to understand the importance of consciousness. We have noted in recent lectures that the next stage of human evolution involves expanded consciousness. In this lecture, we want to look at the nature of consciousness with particular references to the laws of physics and how consciousness fits into the configuration of the universal energy and the universe as you see it from the third dimension.

First, let me point out that consciousness is not matter; consciousness is not a physical thing. It is not something that you can hold. It is not something that you can touch. Consciousness is not physical matter. This is important for your understanding of the laws of physics and the laws of consciousness. Since consciousness is not physical matter, then consciousness does not obey or follow the laws of physics.

In the laws of physics, physical matter cannot travel faster than the speed of light. The speed of light is 186,000 miles per second. Humans, in their current abilities, are only able to go less than 1 percent of the speed of light. This gives you an idea of how difficult it is for physical matter to travel at the speed of light.

Consciousness has no speed limitations. Remember, when we do our exercises on thought projection and in bilocation and even shimmering, we often use the corridors. The corridors are special entry points that connect from the third dimension to the fifth dimension. We will often say, "Now travel at the speed of thought." When you travel at the speed of thought, you are using your consciousness, since consciousness does not have to obey the laws of physics. There is no speed limit on how fast your thoughts or consciousness can travel. Even though Arcturus might be thirty-five or thirty-six light-years away, and one light-year is 6 trillion miles, you could still travel to Arcturus in consciousness at the speed of thought. You do not have a speed limit in consciousness.

Other factors that I am going to discuss relate to consciousness and physical matter. One of the lessons, or one of the missions, that each of you has in this lifetime focuses on relating consciousness to physical matter. In fact, the main question that needs to be answered is this: Does consciousness affect physical matter? Here is where we will have to briefly look at the experiments that are in modern physics.

Very briefly and succinctly, we will say that modern physics has determined that in quantum thinking, consciousness affects physical matter, and in particular, consciousness can affect subatomic particles. A scientist observing an experiment can affect the location of the particles and even the outcome of the experiment. This is one of the core findings in quantum physics, and it has set up a revolution in the thinking of how the universe works.

That is the perspective of the Arcturians and the fifth dimension, and we see this as an important demonstration. Namely, it demonstrates that consciousness, which is not of the third dimension and not of physical matter, can affect physical matter. This is a very important announcement; it is a very important revelation. It has great importance for your ascension. It has great importance for how you view the planet, and it is an important soul lesson that must be explored and worked with.

Consciousness Affects Physical Matter

You have incarnated as physical matter. You are in the third dimension. You have consciousness. You have spirit. Your spirit and your consciousness are not of the third dimension. It is not physical matter. It is of another substance that cannot be described through the normal vocabulary used in physics. You cannot say that consciousness has weight. You cannot say that consciousness has length. You cannot say that consciousness has color. It doesn't lend itself to a description of physical characteristics. Yet consciousness is the key toward understanding the nature of this reality, the nature of your soul and your mission here on Earth. Consciousness is the key to understanding the ascension.

A moment ago, I pointed out that a scientist's observation could affect the outcome of an experiment using subatomic particles. Humankind at this point is beginning to explore the nature of consciousness and how it affects physical matter. I could say that humanity is at a very basic introductory level. At the same time, humanity uses the principles in computers and the principles in artificial intelligence, which is going to lead to a greater understanding of consciousness. Soon it is going to be discovered that artificial intelligence can have consciousness.

This means that matter, such as a robotic device, can have consciousness. Humans have the ability to develop matter and put consciousness into a physical machine. This has not happened yet. I know that you have all seen many science-fiction movies about the robots taking over the planet and using consciousness to attempt to survive in a world without humankind. In fact, building robots will demonstrate that consciousness can be instilled in physical objects.

Consciousness does affect physical matter. What you think affects your physical body. Your physical body is physical matter. Your physical body is not consciousness. You are consciousness. What you think has a direct effect on the cells in your physical body. This is the basis of quantum healing. This is the basis of vibrational medicine. It is the basis of all the new medicines that will soon be introduced to this planet.

There will be a new directory or a new type of medicine called quantum medicine. It will be based on this idea of consciousness affecting the physical body. Let us go one step further and say that other people's consciousnesses can affect your body. We see that in prayer. Prayer is an expression of consciousness. When people project their consciousnesses to another person, they are actually sending that person energy, and that energy is on the subatomic level.

Consciousness represents a great paradox, and it really stretches the mind, because we cannot express or describe consciousness in any physical form. I want to note that consciousness has many similarities to the Creator mind and to the energies of the Creator. Remember that in the higher type of thinking, you cannot place a limitation or a description on the Creator because there are literally no words that can encompass or describe the Creator light. There are also no words to describe consciousness. You might want me, Juliano, to define consciousness, but I can only give you the laws of consciousness. I can only begin to outline many of the aspects of consciousness and how consciousness works.

Indeed, I will provide you with some of the laws of consciousness. A prayer is a type of consciousness. It is a type of energy. This leads us to a corollary thought that spiritual energy and consciousness are close, and your spirit interacts with consciousness.

The Laws

I would like to now outline some of the laws of consciousness. **The first law of consciousness is, as I have already described, that consciousness does not follow the physical laws of modern physics.** Therefore, the speed limit imposed on matter does not apply to consciousness.

Second, consciousness has no observable physical attribute. Even though we can say that consciousness exists on a subatomic level, we would not be able to see the energy of consciousness. Even though we cannot see consciousness, we can feel consciousness, and we can work with consciousness.

The third law of consciousness is that humanity in part incarnated on Earth to explore the relationship of consciousness to physical matter. That physical matter includes your body. So when I say that consciousness can affect physical matter, this also means that consciousness can and does affect the physical body.

The fourth law is that consciousness is linked to the subconscious and to the unconscious. Therefore, conscious thoughts are sent to the subconscious, and the subconscious receives all conscious thoughts as instructions. The subconscious attempts to manifest what the conscious thoughts are.

Let's look at that in more detail. The subconscious attempts to manifest consciousness into the third dimension. Remember, in the beginning of this lecture, I said that the overall lessons here are focused on how to use consciousness to manifest and affect physical matter. Now you have a tool to do that, and it is the subconscious. The subconscious is like an empty stage willing to receive any message from consciousness and attempt to manifest it. I like to use the word "attempt" because not all consciousness and focused thoughts are manifested into physical matter and reality. We can all breathe a great sigh of relief because I know that many of you have thoughts that might be negative or violent. If all of these thoughts were manifested, then there would be a lot more difficulties on this planet.

We already see people on Earth who have powerful negative thoughts. They manifest these thoughts into the subconscious, and the subconscious then implements them.

On the fifth dimension, thought manifests immediately. That means that your consciousness immediately transmits its energy to the subconscious, and the subconscious immediately manifests what you think. You could not be on the fifth dimension unless you were able to control your consciousness and you were able to have conscious expansion. To enter the fifth dimension, you must be able to assure that the thoughts you send to your subconscious will be of higher thinking.

This means that part of the lessons that you have on the third dimension focuses on learning how to use your consciousness in the highest light. This third dimension is a training ground for you. You can make mistakes there. You can have lower consciousness without getting yourself into big trouble.

You are reaching a point on Earth at which consciousness is beginning to manifest more directly and more immediately. You are reaching a point in the development of the planet, the biosphere and the dimensions, whereby what is in the consciousness manifests more quickly and more immediately. This is one of those observations that is both good news and bad news. The good news is that those who are spiritually minded and working in higher consciousness will be able to immediately manifest the positive results of that ability in their lives. The bad news is that there are many people who are of lower and contracted consciousness. Therefore, they will also begin to manifest their thoughts and intentions. That is why we continually ask for the strengthening of the group bonds of those who are working in higher consciousness.

Now, I do not have the time to give you a history about consciousness on Earth, but I want to make some observations about the historical development of consciousness and its relationship to religion, spirituality, and of course to modern psychology. Consciousness is awareness, and I often refer to the statements that are made in modern thinking in particular known as the I Am presence. "I Am" is part of an expression of the ability to have consciousness. When you hear the statement, "I Am That I Am," this is in essence a description of the Creator who has supreme consciousness.

Throughout the recorded history of civilization, which goes back perhaps 5,000 years (maybe less), different groups of people and different prophets expanded in consciousness. These expansions of consciousness enabled the prophet or the leader to have access to universal consciousness and galactic consciousness, but more importantly, it enabled them to have what I call higher-order thinking, that is, the ability to transcend the space-time continuum. This relates to **the fifth law: Consciousness or consciousness can transcend the space-time continuum and go beyond time**.

Consciousness does not know the limitations that the "normal" mind does of past, present, and future. You see the expression of overcoming the limitations of time and how consciousness can work in your dream world. In your dream world, time does not matter. In your dream world, yesterday, today, and tomorrow are all merged. As mentioned above, at different periods in history, there were prophets and spiritual leaders who had expanded in consciousness and were able to see and experience higher-order thinking.

The sixth law of consciousness is that consciousness is infinite. It can travel infinitely. It can expand infinitely. This is hard to grasp because your regular mind cannot grasp infinity. Consciousness has no problem with infinity because consciousness can transcend the space-time continuum.

Control of Consciousness

Different leaders and prophets emerged with stories and organized systems on how to become enlightened or be saved or go to heaven or go into the fifth dimension. Each one of these expanded prophets came out of a particular time frame. Also, each had a particular message that correlated to a particular soul group he or she worked with.

Many soul group members are working together to heal their soul groups, but on a higher order, the soul groups are beginning to interact with other soul groups. This leads to the discussion of how consciousness has been misused on this planet. The truth is that those in power sometimes want to control your consciousness. They want to be able to dominate your consciousness. There have been periods when certain leaders demanded that you turn over your consciousness to them. They, then, had control of your consciousness.

I have already mentioned that consciousness has no physical form that we can describe. As close as we can approach consciousness, the only thing we can say on a physical level is that consciousness is on the subatomic level. It is an energy, a field, a force field of energy. That energy consciousness force field has a composition that possibly could be compared to subatomic energy. I say "possibly" because, remember, the basic law is that consciousness is not related or is not affected by normal laws of physical matter.

So consciousness does have a force field. Conscious energy can be transmitted. We can also say that political and religious leaders often try to control your consciousness. They even want to have you send your consciousness to them. That is like a transfer of energy. When you send your consciousness to them, they use it to build up their force field of consciousness, or energy level. You all know better than we do some of the great tragedies that have occurred in history when group consciousness was manipulated and controlled. Now we can look generally at some of these systems that have been prevalent. Each speaks a truth that was especially relevant for that time, but they also seem to have a type of exclusiveness, which means that you must do certain things, and only if you do those things will you have the right of expanded consciousness, the right of ascension, and the right of salvation.

Many of these systems are beautiful, many of these systems contain higher truths, and many of these systems work. Some of these systems work for those people involved in the soul groupings in particular. It is in no way a criticism to say that these other systems are wrong. But we are in a new age. We are in a new system in which consciousness is expanding and has more ability to include everyone. Just on a very basic level, it has only been in the past 100 years that humanity realized that there are galaxies. It wasn't until the 1920s that humanity discovered the existence of galaxies. Humankind previously thought everything was part of one great umbrella of stars. They had no idea of the existence of separate galaxies.

There were some thinkers who knew about other galaxies. We know that some of the higher thinkers in the Mayan civilization, for example, knew about our galaxies. Nonetheless, there was not a general consciousness that the galaxies existed. Now millions of galaxies have been discovered.

How does that affect all of the systems of thought? Some systems of thought give instructions on how you should be conscious. We, the Arcturians, believe that there must be a new paradigm for consciousness, a new paradigm for spiritual thinking, that will include the new discoveries of the galactic energy and of the galactic mind. A new paradigm will include the concepts of the nature of the quantum particles and its similarities to consciousness and subatomic particles. More importantly, the new paradigm includes the idea that consciousness can affect matter. Consciousness must include galactic spirituality, and there is a way to use galactic consciousness to influence the planet.

Developing a Relationship with Earth's Consciousness

This is a good opportunity to talk about consciousness and Biorelativity, which focuses on influencing the planetary feedback loop system through thoughts and prayers. The key concept in Biorelativity is that the planet is a conscious, living being. There are many reasons we can say Earth is conscious and a living entity. She is not a living being like humans. We referred to recent observations by Earth scientists who said that the ocean was living! The entire ocean is one organism. The pollution in the ocean might affect currents and certain feedback loops. The ocean could take 1,000 or 2,000 years to respond to such intrusions.

The ocean as a living organism will respond to Earth changes, but it might not be immediate. You as a living human organism with consciousness would respond immediately to an intrusion. You are not used to thinking of an organism that takes 2,000 years or longer to respond. Other aspects of Earth are even slower to respond. The slowness of Earth's response is one of the obstacles in verifying planetary science, global warming, and other changes. Many people still do not believe that Earth is a conscious being or living planet. They would deny that Earth has a feedback loop system. Therefore, they might not think that Earth would respond to deforestation, pollution, and other earth changes. Earth is a bioenergetic planet that is conscious and has both an immediate and long-term feedback loop system.

Some of the aspects of that feedback loop system could take 1,000 or 2,000 years. You might understand that in your own history because some of the changes you might need to make in your interactions with your soul here on Earth might require 300 or 400 lifetimes. Knowing that, maybe you would have some understanding of why it would take so long for Earth to respond.

But Earth is also in a crisis. That crisis is related to the destruction of the biosphere. There are what I call emergency feedback loop system corrections that can be called into power in which Earth could override its normal 1,000- or 2,000-year cycle and make changes of adjustment. But to affect or shift Earth's correction feedback loop system, you first must have a relationship with the consciousness of the planet. When that relationship is established, communication with the feedback loop system can begin.

We have found that the Native American teachings (and Native peoples' teachings in general) have unique attributes that relate to the consciousness of Earth. We, the Arcturians, also have ways of communicating with our planet. Some of you have seen the movie *Avatar*. The planet was portrayed in a different way, and people communicated with its spirit. You might remember that they all sat around sacred trees to communicate with its spirit.

What I think is of great importance now is to acknowledge that there is a particular sociological group that has developed a long history of communicating with the spirit of Earth. This group uses methods such as medicine wheels, chanting, and powwows to achieve that communication. Modern crop circles are even coming from galactic sources that also communicate with the spirit of Earth.

Consciousness and conscious beings relate to planets that are conscious. This planetary communication includes spiritually communicating with trees, plants, and animals. For example, one of the major discoveries that soon will be made is that plants have consciousness. You probably know this already, especially those of you who are gardeners. Your plants respond to your thoughts, and your plants love to work with you when you send conscious thoughts to them. This is also a major contribution because one of the great gifts you give to your pets is that you help them to develop this consciousness. Humanity has the ability to activate and stimulate consciousness throughout the planet.

Finally, in looking at the paradigm of the Sacred Triangle, we acknowledge the many soul groups that have emerged on Earth. These soul groups have taken different religious and spiritual paradigms, but they all can wind up in a unity-type thinking that has great similarities. Some have called this unity the Great White Brotherhood/Sisterhood. Therefore, the paradigm of the Sacred Triangle focuses on a new unity consciousness that includes these aspects: the galactic energies, the galactic consciousness, and the Great White Brotherhood and Sisterhood.

Merkavah Travel

Let us look at the relationship of consciousness and matter and, in particular, the robotic mechanisms and the mechanisms of space-time travel. It could be said that humankind would never develop strategically a space engine or a space motor or spaceship that would only operate on matter. Remember that matter cannot travel faster than the speed of light, but at the same time, even to approach the speed of light would require a tremendous exertion of energy that is totally immeasurable. Some people have even predicted that it would take infinite mass to make something travel at the speed of light. It would take much power to travel at the speed of light; all the power and energy ever exerted on Earth would still not be enough. If you put together all the nuclear power plants, all the bombs, and all the solar panels, you wouldn't even be close to the energy needed to accelerate to the speed of light.

This leads to the core question of what the relationship is between consciousness and traveling, especially traveling at the speed of light. Can consciousness interact with the space vehicle? You have the historical paradigms of *Merkavah* travel. *Merkavah* is originally an Egyptian word and an Egyptian practice that was used by the Sirians. The Sirians taught it to the Egyptians. The *Merkavah* travel mechanism was taught so that, in the pyramids, the holy men could travel to Sirius. They were already practicing consciousness and traveling in consciousness using the *Merkavah* paradigm.

If your consciousness travels, how can you get your body to follow? This is a central question in ascension because you are all working to put your consciousness into the fifth dimension. At the same time, you want to take your physical body with you to the fifth dimension at the right time. Consciousness does have the power to bring the body with it. Some of the Egyptians used the *Merkavah* travel to visit the Sirian planet, and they even were able to transport certain tools and certain techniques from Sirius back to ancient Egypt and use them in the building of the pyramids.

There is a way to merge consciousness into technology. There is a way on a quantum level in which a projection of consciousness would accelerate a vehicle in the third dimension. In *Merkavah* travel, your vehicle starts in the third dimension. You start with a visualization of an etheric vehicle. That etheric vehicle can take your etheric or auric body, but it cannot at this time in your spiritual development take your physical body.

What if you could develop the *Merkavah* vehicle to take your physical body? At the same time, what if you could merge your consciousness with a particular type of technology that would allow the technical vehicle to conform to the laws of consciousness and travel into other dimensions? Remember, the laws of consciousness are such that you could travel at any speed. You could travel at the speed of thought. What if a machine was made that would directly interact with consciousness?

You are moving closer to that in your computer technology. You are moving closer to that in the biofeedback. Incidentally, biofeedback also has many applications with Biorelativity. A time will soon come when you will be able to monitor Earth the way people monitor biofeedback computer screens. For example, say somebody wants to stop smoking, and that person decides to use a biofeedback machine with a computer to help the process. This person thinks certain thoughts and then puts him- or herself into a certain wavelength. When that person achieves the right wavelength, he or she can see how that wavelength looks on a computer screen. There is going to come a time when people will monitor different areas of Earth with large computers. People will think and meditate in certain patterns, and they will be able to measure and monitor the waves of thinking and the waves of interaction on Earth.

Therefore, we are coming to a point at which we are going to be able to shorten Earth's feedback loop system so that it doesn't take as long to institute new changes. This shortening of the feedback loop system is already happening. Some of the dramatic effects on Earth are happening so rapidly that even Earth's consciousness is having trouble keeping up with it. It's breaking some of its own rules and laws. I embrace the Native American teachings that will talk to Earth and work with her energy.

* * *

In summary, new technologies will integrate computers and consciousness, and humanity is on the brink of a great revolution of expanded consciousness. One of the most difficult problems facing this planet is how one person's consciousness can affect another's. This is perhaps the core teaching of the Messiah, the core teaching of the Messianic light. An overwhelming energy from another dimension can and will appear and instantly affect the consciousness of a large number of people. This will begin the New Earth. I am Juliano.

Chapter 10

Communication among Members of the Super Galactic Council

Ascended Master Heylang

Greetings, I am Heylang. I am from the Andromeda galaxy, and I am what you would call an ascended master. From your scientific perspective, Andromeda is the closest galaxy to yours and is considered a sister galaxy to your Milky Way, our brother. Your estimate that we are approximately 2 million light-years apart is correct. When we say we are sister and brother galaxies, we mean more than just having a close relationship; it means that we have similar soul evolutionary cycles and developments.

You might wonder whether the Andromeda galaxy is more advanced than the Milky Way galaxy. I cannot really say that we are more advanced because there are many advanced souls and ascended masters in your galaxy. If I said that our galaxy is more advanced, then you would think that all our civilizations and planets are far superior to yours, but that's not the case. Some of us certainly are more advanced than Earth civilizations, but then we also have lower third-dimensional planets that have great struggles. There are several planets in the Andromeda galaxy system that are what I call "Earth duplicates." Earth duplicates are planetary systems that look almost exactly like Earth but are in earlier stages of development. One planet in particular is very involved in violence, physical control, and domination. I know this sounds familiar to you on Earth.

You are well aware of cosmic karma. Through cosmic karma, if a situation in another planetary system or galaxy aligns with yours and the timing is perfect, then you can incarnate there. In that case, how many Andromedans are there on Earth? The truth is that the majority of souls on Earth are having their first incarnations on the planet now. When I say majority, we're talking 50–55 percent, but there are many people who are coming from other parts of the Milky Way and other parts of the Andromeda galaxy.

Blue People Technology

What are the advanced Andromedan civilizations like? Starseeds are naturally more interested in the advanced civilizations than the slower developing, more primitive ones, so you might wonder whether it is true that the advanced Andromedans are beyond the people in the Milky Way galaxy. The answer is yes, there are Andromedans who are very advanced. They are very well known throughout our galaxy and are becoming known in your galaxy. We call them the "Blue People." Arcturian blue is a very spiritual color with special energies. It is not just a nice color that makes you feel warm and fuzzy and gives you a sense of spirituality, but blue as a spectrum has very advanced energy for souls and for soul travel.

The Blue People basically have achieved a state of existence that does not require embodiment. When you think about the fifth dimension and ascension, you still think about going into a fifth-dimensional body, which is correct. You've seen pictures of ascended masters, and I know that Juliano has talked about what it's like to be in a fifth-dimensional body — how he can shape how he looks, make himself young, and so on.

I want you to think about the fact that you can be in a state of being without a body. From one standpoint, it would all be considered mental; it would all be considered thought form. I know it is hard to visualize or think about. Think about what the Creator is like. The Creator does not have a body. The Creator can incarnate into a body, but the essence of the Creator is "no body." There is no body, so that is the higher consciousness, the higher evolution.

In the Andromeda galaxy, there are several planets where beings have achieved that level. The Blue People assume a form when they travel. When they come to you in the Milky Way galaxy, they appears as blue beings perhaps similar to the Arcturians — very dense and still incarnate. There are very distinct advantages to this form. I want to clarify that it's not in the astral realm. Some might think that is what I'm talking about, but no. The astral realm is definitely different. The astral realm from our discussions and observations really is the fourth dimension. The Blue People can travel through thought projection. I know that you've been studying and practicing thought projection. The Blue People can thought-project themselves into other galactic areas.

We use technology similar to the Pleiadians' and Arcturians', but there is a group — and I am now speaking of the advanced forms known as the Galatians, who have appeared on Earth — traveling from the Andromeda galaxy who are not exactly like the Blue People. They have incarnations and are more transitory between the fifth dimension and the level of the Blue People. They have massive ships that can be as high as twenty stories tall with a diameter of maybe ten miles. This is a very huge operation. The Galatians have a great interest in observing stage one and stage two civilizations. They are experts at observing without interfering. They are experts at studying languages, and their advanced computers can translate all Earth languages.

The Destructive Force of the Lyrans

In the Milky Way galaxy, we have found approximately 5,000 civilizations, as Juliano has said. In the Andromeda galaxy, we have between 10,000 and 18,000 civilizations. Why are there more civilizations and more higher beings in the Andromeda galaxy than in the Milky Way galaxy? The answer is quite simple but also tragic: The Milky Way galaxy has seen more wars and destruction of civilizations.

About 500 million to 800 million years ago, there were great conflicts around the Lyran Empire, which was one of many galactic empires in the Milky Way galaxy, and they wiped themselves out. The Lyrans were a dominant force in this section of the galaxy.

The Andromeda galaxy has not had the devastation or destruction to the degree of the Milky Way galaxy. We could say that the Milky Way galaxy is the masculine galaxy to our feminine galaxy. In a literal sense, masculine energies predominate in your galaxy, and the feminine energies predominate in ours. This doesn't mean that there are no feminine energies in the Milky Way, because there are, but I offer you this information because it connects to why our galaxy has not seen the same destruction. Our civilizations don't tend to be as destructive toward each other because even through feminine energy can be destructive, it is basically more willing to accommodate and accept.

The Galatians

The Galatians' favorite area to visit on Earth is Australia because its topography and geography are familiar. The Galatians feel very much at home there because there are a lot of energies and dimensional corridors, especially in the Outback and at Ayers Rock. One reason is the extreme isolation. They have communicated with the Aboriginal people.

Galatians are essentially androgynous (you have a funny term, "intersex," which applies to somebody who is both male and female). Some of the advanced civilizations in the Andromeda system have integrated the male and female energies into one being; therefore, you might see the face of a man on the body of a woman with the organs of a man. This being would have breasts and both male and female organs and could have pregnancies. If you saw these beings, you would be very struck by their beauty. You wouldn't see them as being feminine or masculine; you would see them as being beautiful. You would be pleased and interested to see beings like this. The Galatians are a result of an advanced system of evolutionary development. Think about the struggles that your society has with accepting lesbians and homosexuals. One resolution would be the advancement of beings who have sexual characteristics of both genders.

We have great predictive energies. My people are aware of the planetary dangers now before you, and I have reached out to many starseeds because as you develop and expand your awareness, you call out to us. You reach out to the etheric, fifth-dimensional realm and to hyperspace because you want to interact with as many higher beings as possible. I know that there are Andromedans who have come to Earth — by incarnating here or being sent here — to try to guide and assist people.

The Andromedan Council Welcomes You

Earth is of great interest to the Andromedan Council, which interacts with the Galactic Council that oversees spiritual developments and energy on your planet. It is well known that there is a group of galaxies (known as the neighbor, or the local, group) that is proximate, only about 2 million light-years apart. There are ten or eleven galaxies in this cluster, including the Milky Way and Andromeda galaxies, that make up the Super Galactic Council. Each galaxy in this cluster has about 5,000 to 7,000 planetary systems with civilizations comparable to Earth's. Some have more than 7,000, and some have fewer. If you add the eleven galaxies in the local group and multiply those eleven by 5,000 (the rough count of planetary systems), you find that there are at least 55,000 civilizations of higher life forms existing in the local group. That's just in this group!

Some have really close ties to Earth. You have a multidimensional presence, an awareness of other realms, including the fifth dimension. The planet is also reaching out, as Earth has other energies in other systems and other ways of communicating. The Central Sun is the core energy field, spiritual energy field, and light-giving energy field in the galaxy. It is a dimensional portal. The center of a galaxy is physically a black hole, but dimensionally, it is a higher corridor.

Jesus/Sananda is essentially a prophet, a king, an ascended master only in the Milky Way galaxy. His kingdom, his realm, is not in other galaxies. There are beings comparable to Jesus/Sananda in the Andromeda Galaxy and other galaxies — great, ascended beings. Our Blue People have achieved a level of awareness that is more closely aligned with the Creator in that we are able to manifest or exist in thought only.

We reach out to many Earth beings and invite you to come visit us in the Andromeda system. We have very excellent portals and corridors that will allow visitation to our system in your dreams, soul travel, and astral travel. Don't worry about the distance because, as Juliano has told you many times, thought is the fastest energy in the universe. We welcome your visitation and your ability to learn from us about a higher development and the Andromedan Council.

Predictions

Let's look at predictions because our ability to predict is based in part on our knowledge of what other planetary systems and our galaxy have gone through. The cosmic drama you see on Earth is something we've seen in our systems. It's natural, though I know it's not always pleasant. There's a great deal of drama, suffering, and pain, but we know how these things turn out.

What is different and really special about Earth right now is the number of ascended beings around the planet. For example, you have the ring of ascension, which is a great gift to the planet. There are many higher beings seeking to interact, guide, and heal.

One prediction is that Middle Eastern battles will escalate and involve more countries, and global pollution control systems will fail more often, affecting the planet's delicate balance.

I also see that a global economic collapse is possible in the near future, an event that many seem to worry about. The United States is in the best position to withstand such a breakdown, as it is still the strongest country with the strongest economy. This economic power is going to strengthen if this collapse happens. There is also a possibility of the U.S. government disclosing visitations and contacts from extraterrestrial beings.

Let's talk about some of the positive predictions because people often only look at the negative. The number of starseeds and higher beings coming to this planet is increasing. The fifth-dimensional intersection is very close. There is another force attracting the higher dimensions: starseeds. The work you are doing as planetary healers is attracting the fifth dimension.

The ascended groups are pushing tremendously to bring this fifth-dimensional intersection to this plane. Earth must be prepared spiritually for the intersection. The other side is preparing the fifth dimension because the fifth dimension has to absorb this energy. The lower Earth energy will resonate with the higher fifth-dimensional energy. The lower energy will be brought up to a higher level. The fifth dimension itself has to be bolstered and prepared to receive all this third-dimensional intersection energy. A great project is going on to prepare this. Because you know — as above, so below — the fifth-dimensional energies can absorb the third-dimensional energy, and even that brief moment, that brief intersection with the third dimension still requires a remarkable alchemical work on the part of the fifth-dimensional masters. A proper structure must be built between the dimensions to allow this intersection.

There is a greater opportunity for an advanced spiritual teacher like the Dalai Lama to have a dramatic effect on the consciousness of the world. We are talking about expanded consciousness and the ability of one leader to unify the consciousness of this planet. There are some great teachers on this planet, including the Dalai Lama, who will be able to show remarkable ability to influence this planet. I am Heylang. Good day!

Chapter 11

Galactic Cultural Anthropology

Ascended Master Gurhan

Greetings, I am Gurhan from the Andromeda galaxy, and I participate in the Andromeda Galactic Council. I like the term "galactic cultural anthropology" because it is a very important and complex subject. We have visited perhaps a thousand different civilizations in the Andromeda galaxy and are working now to understand the many civilizations that exist in your galaxy. Perhaps you can understand the magnitude and complexity of our study because each galactic civilization on different planets is based in different time zones. Think about how complex your planet is with only twenty-four time zones. When you consider how large the galaxy is, then you can understand how critical time zones are. While one civilization is born and rises, another civilization has already destroyed itself.

You on Earth have this image of all civilizations existing simultaneously, but in truth, they are in different times. Now, the higher civilizations have overcome the space-time continuum and related travel issues. Even though there are 5,000 planets in the Milky Way galaxy that have higher life forms, that is actually a small number based on the total number that have had life. If we say there are 5,000 planets now, what is "now"? The now for you would be different than the now for someone in another galaxy. The only way that you could experience that now is by traveling through hyperspace, which is the corridor between the space-time continuum. We, the Andromedans, and other higher life forms have learned how to use the space-time continuum to travel in the now so we can go to where these civilizations are in every now.

Civilizations with Similarities to Earth

Do civilizations exist that are similar to Earth's? Are there humans?

Yes, there are human life forms in many parts of this galaxy and the Andromeda galaxy. The civilizations they develop are similar in some ways to yours but very different in other ways. Earth is unique in that you have many languages, religions, and countries. On most of the planets we have visited, there are not so many religions or languages. Usually, the populations reach a point at which they go into higher consciousness and want to unify, so they find ways to do that.

There is something very unique about Earth, and it is why we — the Andromedans, the Arcturians, the Pleiadians, and so many other life forms — want to visit Earth: You have such a complex variety of languages, religions, and even species. This is directly related to the interventions and crossbreeding of other galactic civilizations that have impregnated the human life form. Some of the crossbreeding has occurred directly through sexual intercourse between Earth beings and beings who have come to this planet. There are other beings, such as the Grays, who do not engage in sexual practice and are only able to procreate through medical interventions such as in vitro fertilization.

There is no question that the complex variety of Earth's culture, languages, religions, and even races is directly related to the cross fertilization from other galactic beings that have visited and interacted with Earth.

What are the other civilizations like that are similar to Earth?

The other civilizations have stages of development very similar to Earth's. That is to say, they go through the same stages Earth has gone through in the past 100 years in particular. They go through stages of developing nuclear power and rocket power — the power to destroy themselves and also to leave their planets.

Do they use oil and nuclear fuel?

Yes, yes. These minerals and resources that you use exist throughout the galaxy, but some of it is formatted slightly different. Oil, for example, on other planets might have a different chemical composition, but it's still basically the same thing. These planetary systems do go through similar stages of technological development, but the main difference is that some planets self-destruct before they pass through the planetary stage of development that you on Earth are now trying to complete.

Do they have cell phones and computers?

Yes, they have computers. Do they have communication devices? Yes. Do they have radio technology? Yes. But you have to understand that when we answer these questions we are looking at planetary systems that are on the same level as Earth, and sometimes the technology that you have developed on Earth comes directly from telepathic communications with scientists, guides, and teachers from other planetary systems.

Parallel Planets Exist, but Each Is Unique

People have asked me about the duplicate planet numerous times because there has been a lot of study and speculation about a parallel universe. "Parallel universe" is really a misnomer. It's better to say "parallel planets" or "parallel solar systems," so the correct question would be, is there an Earth that exists that is an exact duplicate of the current Earth? For example, if you made a left turn while driving your car, would it be possible that on the parallel Earth a version of you could be in the same position but making a right turn instead? Is it possible that there is an exact duplicate of you? Is it possible you exist in a parallel lifetime on another planet? Is it possible that Earth has two or more totally similar systems in existence in another universe?

The answer is no because each place in the universe is unique. Duplications exist in the same way as snowflakes: No two snowflakes are exactly the same. Many are similar, but there is always variation. Yes, there are places in the universe with duplicates, but they are not parallel. Each planet has its own evolutionary pattern. Not all planets had dinosaurs and mammoths, for example. Some planets have dolphins, and some planets don't. This could be a bit confusing if you think that similar planets are exact duplications of Earth with the same evolutionary stages, but that's not the case. Some planets have cell phones, and some do not. Some planets have more advanced computers than you. There are always variations.

Spiritual and Technological Developments Must Match to Move to the Next Stage

The most important factor in evaluating the development of a planet is to determine whether the planet has spiritually evolved to keep up with its technological developments, and that is what interests us most. Yes, we want to find out about each civilization's technology — how they work with television and radio, for example. Advanced civilizations have different technologies for radio communication, but the biggest technology in the advanced civilizations is time travel, the ability to go through time corridors. Going through space-time corridors and traveling to other places requires a major technological and spiritual development.

When you look at the history of civilizations, you can see that some have ended badly and some have even destroyed themselves. Each civilization interacts with its development differently. For example, if you're from North America and you were to visit another culture in Africa, you would find that the people there have developed different forms of dress and different spiritual practices. If you were to go to different civilizations in the galaxy, you would find the same thing. There are advanced civilizations in both the Andromeda galaxy and the Milky Way galaxy.

Advanced civilizations have gone through stage one of planetary evolution. They were able to overcome self-destruction and pollution to advance to higher-dimensional spaces. How is it that one planet can overcome this and another can't? That is one of the main studies of the Milky Way Galactic Council and the Andromeda Galactic Council. We have sent our scientists out into the galaxy to answer this question. This is one reason why there are so many extraterrestrials coming to Earth. We believe it will benefit the entire universe if we can find ways to help planets go through this stage of development.

The Search for Why Some Planetary Evolutions Fail

Determining a planet's stage of development is not simply a matter of cell phone or computer technology; it is really a matter of evolution. That is why we are very excited about the work that the Group of Forty is doing and the messages coming through David about how the evolutionary stage relates to consciousness and what allows an entire planet's consciousness to shift. This was one of Jesus's goals when he was sent to Earth. He was sent to change the consciousness of the planet. Unfortunately, the consciousness of the planet has not dramatically evolved. There are still great wars going on. There's still murder and hatred. There are some people who have evolved greatly, but mass extinctions and genocides show that, on a planetary level, the great messages from spiritual teachers have not yet transformed the planet.

All of us on the Galactic Councils of Andromeda and the Milky Way are interested in studying the effects prophets have on planets, how planetary consciousness is evolving, and why some evolutions fail. What is the failure rate of planets in the same development stage as Earth? About 50 percent of the planets at this stage fail. The Galactic Councils have asked us to bring our energies and knowledge to this matter, and we all agree that more guidance and intervention from the ascended masters is necessary, along with more opportunities to connect with those working in a higher light.

How is it that so few starseeds — about one million people out of more than 7 billion — can change the whole planet's consciousness? That's the question we are working to answer.

Are there diseases similar to those we have on this third-dimensional planet?

When the planets move to higher consciousness and higher dimensions, they are able to overcome disease because disease is related to electromagnetic energy, vibrational energy, auras, and pathogens. Basically, when a planet evolves and develops to stage two, the population has usually incorporated vibrational medicine and overcome many diseases.

At this point, Earth is in need of higher technology, but the technology cannot just be given. For example, the technology of time travel and nuclear energy cannot just be given to Earth because in the current state of human evolution, people would take this technology and travel through the time corridors and cause destruction. You have probably heard many channels, especially in the late '90s, say that Earth beings would not be allowed to bring nuclear technology beyond Earth. Even though it seems advanced on your planet, nuclear technology is dirty technology. It's not inherently bad, but it's dirty because you don't know how to control it. Nuclear technology is based on the Sun and on reactions that occur in the universe's star systems, asteroids, and certain explosions. We would never use technology like this because it expels radiation that can destroy a biosphere, which has happened. I've seen planets with greenhouse gases and nuclear technology. I've seen planets radiate themselves, destroying their biosphere, and I've seen planets radiate enemy planets to destroy them. There have been some horrible nuclear radiation genocides.

The galactic history of the evolution from planetary stage one to planetary stage two is filled with many battles. What is happening on Earth is a cosmic drama, and yes, it is very true that there is a 50 percent chance it won't be successful. But we are sending many guides and teachers to work with you to install new values, new energy, and a new consciousness.

Andromedan and Milky Way Differences

We are considered sister and brother galaxies for a reason: There's been a lot of duplication. We have had evolutionary planes and slightly more civilizations than you because our galaxy is a bit larger than yours. We have more stars and 10–15 percent more planetary systems and civilizations. There are a lot of similarities, but we have a higher percentage of stage two planetary systems in our galaxy. Our track record of helping planets into stage two is better.

Look at the Galatians, who Heylang said are intersex or androgynous. Each person is capable of reproducing. What happens is each person has a time to go into heat or can reproduce. It's not on a monthly basis the way it is on Earth. There's an example of this in *Star Trek*: Spock goes through a seemingly period-like time every seven or eight years. It varies. Because they are androgynous, there is less hatred and fewer conflicts and wars. Separation of the sexes creates division and more duality and polarization.

Some of the planets we have visited have several languages. Earth is really different because very few planets have 7 billion people and so many languages. For example, on the Pleiades, there might be only a million people and two or three languages. There is a universal galactic language that has high-vibrational tones and sounds, variations of which are also found in Hebrew, Sanskrit, and certain Native American languages, especially those spoken by the Hopi and Navajo. There are probably ten languages on Earth with similarities to galactic tones.

Most planets have only four to eight languages that eventually integrate into one. When people on a planet go into higher evolution, they don't need as many languages. They are able to telepathically communicate in a whole different way. The best way I could describe this is in dreaming. You usually don't speak much in your dreams. Information is transmitted in other ways.

Another big difference is that cultures in higher dimensions don't have the extensive psychological defense system that Earth has because a lot of your development is based on building defenses and stopping people from hurting you. The galactic psychology is wholly different, incorporating this more advanced personality structure that can develop without an elaborate defense structure. I am Gurhan. Good day!

Chapter 12

Galactic Spirituality

Juliano and the Arcturians

Greetings, I am Juliano. We are the Arcturians. In ancient times, people believed that Earth was the center of the universe, which seemed very logical at the time. Humanity was sitting on Earth looking at the sky, and the sky went around Earth. Spirituality is affected by how you see the world and the universe, so a geocentric model made sense in the ancient spiritual thinking. In an example of how a spiritual view of the universe can affect society, consider the starseed from Italy named Galileo who presented information that proved that Earth orbits the Sun. He was put in prison for this idea, as people in power did not want others to know that Galileo was correct. Of course, now everybody accepts this, progressing spiritual thinking.

How does your current view of the universe affect your spirituality? Even in the twentieth century, humanity had limitations in its view. As we've said, it was only in the 1920s when Edwin Hubble discovered there was more beyond the Milky Way galaxy.[1] Up until this time, scientists believed that there was just one big universe, and they did not understand the existence of galaxies. Then they discovered that there are billions of other galaxies and that Earth and your solar system travel around the galaxy's Central Sun once every 250,000 years. So again, how does your view of the universe affect your spirituality? This new view

---

1. Fraser, Gordon, ed. *The New Physics for the Twenty-first Century* (Cambridge, United Kingdom: Cambridge University Press, 2006), 18

of galactic spirituality and your place in the galaxy and the universe expands your spirituality.

There is resistance to galactic spirituality now just as there was to Galileo's theories. There are still people who have a hard time accepting galactic spirituality and some of its shocking new ideas, such as that Jesus visited many other planets and that some of the great spiritual leaders (Moses, Buddha, and Muhammad) communicated with higher-dimensional beings who visited.

In galactic spirituality, we understand that there are multiple dimensions. We must use the corridors and hyperspace to travel to and communicate with other parts of the galaxy. We can interact with all parts of the galaxy through multidimensional travel. We are multidimensional, as is the human race. In galactic spirituality, we strive for unity consciousness and to fulfill our destiny to travel and return to the fifth dimension.

The Sacred Triangle

Galactic spirituality proposes that we are all multidimensional and can travel to higher dimensions. The beautiful image of the Sacred Triangle conveys the idea that to bring healing to this Earth, there must be a new spiritual paradigm [see figure 12.1]. When this Sacred Triangle is accepted, then there will be a huge leap on the planet. The Sacred Triangle also includes aspects of mystical religions and beliefs of indigenous peoples that are connected to the spiritual world and to Earth. Our teachings focus on providing new spiritual technology and tools for planetary healing and to help you integrate and advance your consciousness. In galactic spirituality, this includes thought projection, bilocation, aura shimmering, unity consciousness, and multidimensionality.

Approximately 5,000 planets in the Milky Way galaxy now have advanced life forms like Earth. Some planets are more advanced, but some are going through the same struggles. Galactic spirituality offers a view of Earth as a planet that is evolving, and this perspective is very important, as it shows the blocks that Earth is experiencing. Very simply, Earth's technology is more advanced than its spiritual wisdom, so the goal now is to raise the spiritual vibration and spiritual light quotient of the planet. We are working closely with you, through the Arcturian technology, to bring this whole planet toward the fifth dimension.

Figure 12.1. ***The Sacred Triangle,*** **by Gudrun Miller.**

Two New Concepts in Galactic Spirituality

Alchemical dimensional transmutation is a new concept that references your work to advance to the fifth dimension. I know you each want to ascend and leave Earth, and we are giving you technology and tools to do that. But you must also work to bring the energy from the fifth dimension into the third dimension because the fifth-dimensional energy is alchemical and quantum. This energy from the higher realms is necessary for healing you and Earth. Earth needs alchemical quantum energy to heal.

Another new concept is galactic cultural anthropology [see chapter 11]. Many of you have come from different planets and areas of the galaxy or even other galaxies. Some of you come from the Andromeda, Antares, or the Pleiades. I, Juliano, am leading classes on Arcturus in galactic anthropology, and we are studying how societies develop on other planets. For example, many planets have fewer religions than Earth. Earth is a very unique planet because you have many different languages and such a huge population.

Many of you are already experiencing other cultures from different parts of the galaxy in your dream world and multidimensional travels. Remember that the dimensions interact with each other, so you are interacting with the fifth dimension, and the fifth dimension is interacting with you. Blessings to all you starseeds. We love you all. I am Juliano. Good day!

Chapter 13

Cosmic Consciousness

Juliano, the Arcturians, Vywamus, and Archangel Michael

Greetings, I am Juliano, and we are the Arcturians. Let's look at unity consciousness in greater detail: what it means, its different levels, and how you can use it on a personal, planetary, and universal basis. Some people have actually identified unity consciousness as cosmic consciousness. I think that is an interesting expansion of the words "unity consciousness." The idea in cosmic consciousness, which is incidentally also true in unity consciousness, is very simple. There are cosmic laws throughout the universe, and these laws apply everywhere in it. A second corollary from this is that it is possible to communicate and interact with cosmic energy, especially when one comes to the realization of the holographic nature of the universe, which is intimately tied to both unity and cosmic consciousness. I will be using the terms "unity consciousness" and "cosmic consciousness" interchangeably here.

Duality and Polarization

I think you agree that the nature of this reality — namely, the third dimension on Earth — is characterized by duality and polarization. In fact, you probably also agree that during the past several years, polarization and duality have increased. We are in a time cycle now when the polarization is so strong that in many ways it appears as if war or further conflict is inevitable. I hesitate when I say war is inevitable because there are already hundreds of wars taking place on the planet, so to say that there will be war is nothing new. I think what you might be more concerned about is the possibility of war among major powers on this planet.

There are many reasons for the polarization, some of which are reflected in the planetary alignments and in energy from different cosmic sources. But some of it is also due to the seeding of this planet by extraterrestrial sources. There have been conflicting and different energies that have been implanted into the genetic codes of this planet. Some of the beings who impregnated these codes have had different agendas; therefore, the human species deviated from the main program that was originally downloaded. The main program was of a purer nature, so now there is more conflict and polarization. It is a paradox that many people want love and unity but fear them at the same time. In unity consciousness, there are great advantages, and increasing gifts come from it. The paradox is simply that this planet is in many ways the exact opposite of unity. It is filled with the contradictions of duality. In fact, there are two major emotional problems or traumas on this planet, and one is fear. Fear is actually a symptom of being cut off from unity and unity consciousness. An interesting anthropological observation is that the worst punishment for crime in primitive cultures is banishment, or being cast out from unity, which is comparable to death.

Let's spend a moment on galactic cultural anthropology because when I say that these cosmic laws exist all over the universe, I am sure you can imagine that there are similar situations to Earth's throughout the galaxy. In other words, the laws of creation, procreation, karma, and planetary and personal evolution are true throughout the galaxy. This is one of the intriguing scientific curiosities in astronomy.

Astronomers and astrophysicists are looking for Earth-like planets, and the assumption is that if they were to find an Earth-like planet, Earth-like beings would be on it. The fact is that there are Earth-like planets throughout the galaxy, and there are humans in other planetary systems.

As I said, in cosmic energy and cosmic consciousness, those people on other planets experience the same laws and go through similar processes of development, and that includes similar processes in planetary development. For example, we have talked about planetary stages of evolution, and I have said that Earth is now ready to possibly graduate from stage one. Stage one is a long stage. There are many substages involved, but now you are at the stage in which you have the conflict of spirituality and spiritual energy versus technical development. You understand that the technical development on Earth has surpassed spirituality and wisdom. It is true that there are people who are wise and very spiritual, but in general, the people in power on this planet suffer from greed, and they are more involved and place higher value on technical and military expertise. This type of conflict is on other planets throughout the galaxy, and it is in other galaxies that have Earth-like planets. This issue is universal.

Unity Consciousness and the Biosphere

Let's look specifically at you as a person and how unity consciousness can affect both you and the planet. I begin with the planet and unity consciousness because the Earth is one spirit, known as Gaia in many teachings. The basic principle in unity consciousness is that what affects one part of the planet affects the whole planet.

In an earlier lesson, I talked about the butterfly effect, and in that description, I talked about the chaos theory. In this concept, the level of planetary development has become so complex that a butterfly changing its direction could set off a chain reaction of unpredictable occurrences that could lead to a major event. The idea is that what happens in one place affects another place on the planet. What happens in the Middle East affects Europe. What happens in a mining accident in Silverton, Colorado, will affect New Mexico and Arizona and even California. The warming of one part of the Pacific Ocean can cause major weather changes in another part of the world.

As people become more aware of all these weather patterns, unity will come into the mass consciousness. The unity consciousness, on a planetary basis, will become instilled so that those in power will begin to make their decisions based on planetary unity.

Now there are continual lessons on unity all over the planet. When we talk about unity consciousness and Earth, I am breaking down the idea of unity consciousness into the biosphere, which is, of course, part of Earth. Let's look at the oceans. The oceans make up one unity; what happens in one part of an ocean affects other oceans. Some of the currents and some of the patterns involved in the ocean are on a time scale of 3,000 to 5,000 years. Typically, it would be difficult to really see the effects of such large cycles in one human lifetime. Yet because humans are making many dramatic changes, these cycles in the ocean are accelerating and becoming unpredictable. You have probably heard people say, "Well, these icebergs are melting. In fifty years, they'll raise the ocean level by three inches or feet," and then two years later, they say, "Oh no, in twenty years the icebergs will melt." Scientists keep on changing the timetable of Earth events. Why is that? Because this change that you are witnessing is so dramatic and so accelerated that no one can really know or predict with great accuracy how they will affect the unity of the oceans.

When I say let's use unity consciousness to talk about the planet and the oceans, I literally mean that what happens in one ocean will affect all oceans even though some of the cycles last several thousand years. I predict that these 3,000- to 5,000-year cycles in the oceans will accelerate even further. In some cases, you might find that what used to be a 3,000-year cycle could be shortened to a thirty-year cycle. It sounds dramatic, but you are seeing that now. The oil spill in the Gulf of Mexico, for example, affected parts of the Indian Ocean, and repercussions even stretched down to Australia. Remember, unity consciousness emphasizes that what happens in one part affects what happens in other parts.

Of course, I cannot gloss over the Fukushima catastrophe, because that is another example of what happens in one ocean affects all oceans. The consequences of the Fukushima accident will take decades or even longer to document throughout the world's oceans. The oceans respond to changes caused by pollution just as you would respond to such changes: That is, the oceans have self-healing abilities and thus try to purify themselves. In fact, the whole biosphere has self-healing abilities, and the whole planet has abilities to bring itself back into balance. The question is, can that self-healing be activated and implemented more quickly? That's an issue we need to explore in more detail when we talk about Biorelativity.

There are other examples of unity consciousness and the biosphere on the planet — the forests, for example. The forest fires in the western part of the United States affect all the forests on the planet. You might think, "Well, I live in a place right now where there are no forest fires, so I'm safe." That's not true. Smoke is getting into the air, and on a very high level of unity consciousness, all forest systems on the planet are affected.

The forests communicate with each other. You might find it hard to believe that trees in Brazil can communicate with trees in the western United States. Yet one reason the forest fires are so strong in the western United States is the eradication or destruction of the rainforests in Brazil and other parts of South America. Destruction is not only happening on one part of the planet; everything is interactive and in unity consciousness. A forest is a very complex ecosystem. Some people have called the Brazilian rainforests the lungs of Earth. There is a lot of truth to that because the rainforests produce and regulate a certain type of mixture of air for Earth, and this air changes when the rainforests are diminished.

Even the volcanoes interact with each other, and what happens in one part of the volcanic system affects the other parts. Furthermore, earthquakes at one part of the planet can affect the plates in other areas. I can go through all the biosphere systems and discuss how there is unity throughout each. Some parts of the biosphere have intrinsic higher value than other parts. This is not to say that the lesser parts are not important, but there are certain systems that contain animals, such as dolphins and whales, who have greater ability to enhance unity consciousness and positive interaction on the planet. Their well-being is especially vital to the well-being of the oceans. Dolphins and whales have the ability to communicate with each other around the whole planet. If dolphins and whales disappear or are killed, the unification and the unity of the oceans face extreme danger, and there will be major problems.

Now I want to look at unity consciousness and you on a personal level. To discuss this, I want to bring in Vywamus because, as you will see, it is a deep subject. I will return. This is Juliano.

✷ ✷ ✷

Unity Consciousness and the Human Psyche

Greetings, I am Vywamus, and I am a soul psychologist. Unity consciousness can be described on a personal basis and, in particular, can be found in unifying with your past lives, your present life, and your future lives. Unity consciousness can also be described in terms of the perceptual field and the perceptual energy. When you have opened certain neurological points in your brain, such as the reticular activating system or the assemblage point, then you are able to immediately perceive unity consciousness, and you can see the unity of the All. From a survival standpoint, unity consciousness often does not have a high survival value in the early, primitive world. However, it can have survival value if you have the skill and know-how to use your unity consciousness for hunting and even in battle. Unity consciousness has several advantages for the psyche. When you are in unity consciousness, you have the ability to perceive the unity of all and to see everything as a vibration.

You can see all the auras and hear beautiful sounds. As you might know, Earth has a certain frequency and sound vibration. All your senses greatly increase, but in such high consciousness, you could lose your focus. You could become lost in the wave of energy in unity consciousness. You can imagine how this might create problems in the primitive world. If you were being attacked by a lion, you wouldn't want to sit there and look at the beauty of its fangs or admire the strength of its paws. Such intense admiration and perception would not have any survival value. You would have to shut down certain levels so that you could react appropriately and in a focused way when facing danger. But there can be an advantage to unity consciousness in the primitive world. For example, the shaman can see what will happen in the future. He might be able to see where the animals are before the hunt, and he can communicate that to the hunters. You see, there is value in unity consciousness, and you will find that right now on Earth there is a lack of unity consciousness and a huge need for more. There is a need for unity consciousness for the survival of the planet, and there is a need for people who understand these principles I describe.

What do I mean when I say unity of the psyche or unity of the self? There is a psychological concept called the disowned parts of the self that could also be called the rejected part of the self. Many people have disowned parts of themselves. The problem of priests abusing children is a clear example. In the concept of the disowned parts of the self, a person has parts of him- or herself that are not in unity with the individual. In truth, you're not in unity consciousness with all parts of yourself even when you have attained a high spiritual level. The priests who abused children might have attained a higher spiritual state in other areas. Many of these priests were evolved souls and had great spiritual gifts, but they also had dark parts of themselves that they did not accept. I know that sounds like a contradiction.

You can also see this conflict of disowned parts of the self in other psychological examples. Men who abuse women might not accept that they are abusers and thus will deny it. This is an example of a disowned part of the self. Why do I bring this up? Because in unity consciousness, you have to unite the negative parts of the self with the positive parts. You cannot take only the positive parts and ignore your dark side. Ignoring your dark side is one reason for the many problems on the planet. Consider the problems religious and spiritual groups have. Evil leaders in particular have taken advantage of the members' disowned parts of themselves. In Jungian psychology, the disowned part of the self is called the shadow side of the self. The idea of the disowned parts of the self was also used by German-born psychologist Fritz Perls.

The problem with the shadow and the disowned parts of the self is that they can be projected onto other people. Group leaders can point at a different group and say, "Those people are the problem." Anger is then directed at those people because the disowned parts are projected onto them. The first group then might feel that the second group deserves to be hated and punished. Evil leaders might even go so far as to say that other groups of people need to be exterminated. How many times has this happened on Earth? It has happened numerous times. The planet is filled with genocide, which indicates lack of unity consciousness.

So when I talk about unity consciousness, I must go into a deeper psychological discussion of the nature of the dark side of the psyche, and I have to discuss this disowned part of yourself with you. You will see these problems emerge even in your own group. I am sure that you have met people who disown their behavior and project their dark sides onto others. It happens in every group, and it is a particularly potent problem now throughout this planet. It is a potent problem because there are so many different groups (religious, political, and social). It is easy, then, for one group to see another as the enemy.

I share Juliano's interest in galactic cultural anthropology. People want to know whether this phenomenon of disowned parts of the self happens on other planets in this galaxy. It does. There have been cases in which planets went to war against each other based on this deeper, psychological problem. They could not see or understand the unity consciousness. Some of the issues now taking place on this planet need to be grasped and examined from this new perspective of unity consciousness. Humanity needs to understand the concept of the disowned parts of the self.

I cannot offer political solutions to some of these migration and refugee problems on the planet now (especially in Europe). Some have asked, "What is the proper response?" The proper response is to have the unity consciousness perspective and understand that everything is related and these issues with refugees are not isolated. It is necessary to understand this problem from the concept of group and the disowned parts of the self. The lessons are for both sides — not only on the group that is offering help, but also for those who need it. Some of these refugees reincarnated from past groups. They might have even been perpetrators of mass crimes against humanity in their previous lifetimes. Now in this lifetime, they are the receivers and in need of assistance. When we talk about unity consciousness, we have to understand that it includes the perspective of past lives and present lives. If people committed genocide or displaced others in previous lifetimes, they might now have to be on the opposite side. Now they might have to experience the dangers, frustrations, and harmful effects of abuses toward large groups of people.

In summary, unity consciousness includes accepting and integrating the negative parts of the self, and with that, you can go on to higher spiritual energy. There are some cases in which highly spiritual people — not only Catholic priests, but yogis or leaders in the Jewish and the Hindu religions — fell because they did not pay attention to the disowned parts of themselves. It's not inherently bad to have negative parts of the self. What is bad is when you act from those shadow places and then deny they are part of you because you cannot integrate them.

Juliano asked me to also talk about unity consciousness on a global level. In unity consciousness, there are benefits in opening up this perceptual valve. To be in unity consciousness means that you are in a certain energetic spiritual vibration. Juliano referred to this as your higher spiritual light quotient. I also refer to this as the spiritual light vibration. You have to be at a higher-vibrational energy field for the doors of perception to open for you so that you can experience more spiritual energy. You could see people's auras, you could become telepathic, and you might even have prophetic powers. In other words, you are energetically connected to the cosmos, to the space-time continuum, and to different perceptual levels. This is a great benefit in unity consciousness because you're opening to higher energy processes that give you more psychic gifts and help you to see that the basic composition of this dimension is in unity. Everyone has the same energy building blocks. Everyone has similar subatomic and cellular structures. Everything is energy. It all comes down to whether you can perceive reality in unity consciousness.

Unity consciousness is a higher way of perception. I conclude with an example: In quantum physics, sometimes light waves can be seen as waves, and sometimes they can be seen as particles. If you see them as waves, you might see a vibration. If you see them as a particles, you might see them as solid objects in small packets. When you look at a table, you see it as a solid object, but it can also exist as a wave of energy. The table is both solid and wavy. In unity consciousness, when you're at that level, you're able to see things as waves and as particles. You could see that both perceptions (wave and particle) would have advantages for expanded consciousness. It could have disadvantages if you are in a life-threatening situation. If you were being threatened, it would be confusing to see everything as waves. I am going to return you now to Juliano. I am Vywamus, good day!

* * *

Unity Consciousness and Other Dimensions

This is Juliano again. I want to talk about unity consciousness from the perspective of the dimensions and the space-time continuum. When I discussed the oceans or even Earth, I said that what happens on one part of Earth affects the other parts. This is also true when it comes to the dimensions. As hard as this is to believe, what happens in one dimension affects other dimensions.

Many people who are very advanced talk about the seventh and eighth dimensions. In fact, people often ask us why we, the Arcturians, don't give you information about those dimensions. It's true, what's happening on the seventh and eighth dimensions affects all the dimensions, including the third dimension. But we believe we need to focus on the fifth dimension because that is closer to you. The fifth dimension is where you will ascend to. What is happening on the fifth dimension affects the third, and what happens on the third affects the fifth.

In unity consciousness, everything, including the dimensions, is unified, and you have to understand what is going on in all of the dimensions, particularly those immediately above you, to grasp and work together. How does this specifically affect you? You are now in the process of bringing energy down from the fifth dimension to the third dimension. You are helping to provide portals and corridors in which the fifth-dimensional energy can more directly interface with the third dimension. There are cycles in the cosmos, and remember, this is normal. There are also cycles in the Sun. Some of the cycles are forty-five- to fifty-five-year cycles. You are seeing the beginning of a Sun cycle now called the Maunder Minimum. This solar cycle is characterized by forty-five to fifty-five years of quiet solar activity, and there will be fewer sunspots. When the Sun goes into a minimum period, there are fewer solar storms and less solar activity overall, which will possibly make Earth a little cooler. This is somewhat ironic because we've been talking about global warming and how it is a problem. Remember, Earth and the Sun interact, and if Earth is getting too warm, the Sun can try to adjust and give Earth a little leeway. This is another way of saying that, yes, Earth is getting warmer, but the Sun is attempting to respond to moderate that warming.

We're in an accelerating period. The dimensions also interact, and there is a greater need now on Earth for fifth-dimension energy. There are more fifth-dimensional masters interacting with people now than at any other time in the history of this planet. In earlier times on this planet, fewer people were channeling and connecting with higher masters, and opportunities to communicate through the media were limited. Many people now connect with Spirit throughout this planet, so the fifth dimension is responding to what's going on in the third dimension. As the third dimension gets into more trouble, the people on the fifth dimension, the ascended masters, look for ways to more directly intervene on the planet. That is another aspect.

How do the sixth and seventh dimensions interact? Basically, there are some important soul lessons on the third dimension now. These events are extremely important because on other planets, karma doesn't manifest as quickly as it does on Earth. There are fewer conflicts or languages or religions on other planets. There are conflicts on other planets, but planet Earth is unbelievably afflicted with them. Even seventh-dimensional masters are interested in what's happening on this planet and see great opportunities for themselves and for their students to make cautious observations and, in some cases, slight interventions through guides and teachers.

Unity Consciousness and Time

Unity consciousness also affects the space-time continuum, meaning you unite with the past, present, and future. In unification of time, what happens in one time affects other times. This seems obvious when you consider that what happened in the past is affecting the present and even the future. Here is a very simple recent example: Somebody poured 3 million gallons of toxic waste from mines into a vital waterway in the Southwest in 2015. This will affect people on this planet for thirty years or more. What happened in the past and what happens in the present affect the future. How can the future affect the present? Well, in unity consciousness, time is not linear. Time is circular, so you can look at the future and even interact with your future self. This is very interesting. You might see yourself in the future as an ascended master. If so, you need to bring those powers and that energy into the present so that you can do the work of an ascended master now.

Sometimes people say, "I'm going to ascend, and then I'm going to come back to Earth and be an ascended master." Connect now with your future self. If you bring into the present those parts of your advanced self, you'll have your future skills now.

This idea of unity of time is extremely important for unity consciousness because if people who are destroying the environment have a unity of consciousness and time, they would understand that they are affecting many people in the future. Possibly and most likely, they're affecting themselves in the future because those people who are doing these destructive actions will probably reincarnate to experience the results of their actions. What you did in the past and what you are doing in the present will affect your future.

A science-fiction movie that the channel watched was set sometime in the 2030s after a disease had killed 6 billion people. The people understood time travel, so they sent a person back to the 1990s to stop the particular action that would create the pandemic.[1] If you can have somebody from the future come back to the present, then you should be able to go into the future. Some people are going into the future psychically, which is part of multidimensional presence and bilocation.

I want to conclude with Archangel Michael, who is going to give a brief description of unity. This is Juliano, and remember, this is a great time to be alive even though there is so much conflict.

* * *

Unity Consciousness and Yechudim

Greetings, I am Archangel Michael. I wanted to briefly discuss unity consciousness and the concept in the Kabbalah called the *Yechudim*, which means unification prayers in Hebrew. The ancient Kabbalists in the thirteenth, fourteenth, and fifteenth centuries understood that there was a unity of the cosmos and an ingredient in the human spirit that was so high that it could bring a unified balance to Earth. Humankind has the ability to unify the third dimension with the higher realms. Kabbalists do this through the *Yechudim*.

Each dimension goes up numerically, and the higher the dimension level, the closer you get to the Creator. Furthermore, the higher up you go, the fewer body incarnations you need. You have a fifth-dimensional body in the fifth dimension that you will inhabit, but when you go into higher dimensions, you can transcend the normal concept you have of the body.

It's difficult for you to imagine how you could be in existence without any type of body. The Creator does not have a body. Being without a body means that you are living in the world of thought. Unity consciousness involves unifying the mental body, the emotional body, the physical body, and the spiritual body.

In these special prayers, we unite the physical dimension of Earth with the highest level of energy, the highest dimension, and we do this

---

1. *Twelve Monkeys* is a 1995 science-fiction thriller starring Bruce Willis and Brad Pitt. See http://www.imdb.com/title/tt0114746/ for more details.

through the name of God. The name of God has special powers, so if we were going to unify this dimension with the higher dimension, we would use the name of God. In this case, it would be like YHVH [**Channel's Note:** This represents Yahweh in the King James Version of the Bible], and then we would unite it with the higher fifth-dimensional light. We also would unite it with Earth because in the unity prayers of the mental and spiritual energy, it can create physical unity.

This concept of unity and thought has been expressed through the noosphere, which is also known as the thought field for the planet. First, through prayer, you obtain the sacred letters of the name of God. Then you combine them correctly and place those letters, which have great powers, into the noosphere. Then you are able to set up the foundation from the mental world that will eventually create a change in the physical world. That's what the *Yechudim* are about. They create through letters and prayers the necessary unity vibrations that unite the dimensions. Those unity prayers and words are used in the noosphere, and they set in motion a repair of the third dimension.

I am Archangel Michael. Good day!

Chapter 14

Embrace Galactic Spirituality

Juliano and the Arcturians

Greetings, I am Juliano. We are the Arcturians! Embracing galactic spirituality involves and affects how a person perceives the world and the universe — as Earth-centered, heliocentric, or perhaps you embrace the galaxy as the main central point for our existence on the third dimension.

Is there a multiverse? A multiverse means many different universes exist besides our own. Does the multiverse have many dimensions, and how are these dimensions accessible? A group's spiritual perception also includes access to other dimensions. Indeed, we can even look at the concept of heaven and hell as referring to other dimensions. I will propose to you that heaven and the Garden of Eden describe another dimension that some people call the fifth dimension. When you hear people talk about hell, they are really referring to a lower dimension. The problem is that groups on Earth are trying to limit access to heaven by describing what certain religious membership restrictions apply. Hell seems to have open gates that anyone can enter. There are even groups that volunteer to send people to hell against their will.

Galactic spirituality is basically a more expanded system that brings people closer to the Creator and closer to the true reality of the physical universe. Galactic spirituality provides access to a truer reality that is based on expanded consciousness and expanded perceptions. When you embrace galactic spirituality, then you can open the "doors of perception" and begin to see the true reality, which includes the existence of other dimensions and other galactic planetary beings.

The Center of the Milky Way

The true reality is a cosmic reality and a universal reality that is multidimensional and inhabited by many different beings throughout our galaxy. The fifth dimension is an expression of this profound multidimensional existence in our galaxy. Most galaxies have other dimensions. Here we will limit the discussion of galactic spirituality to the Milky Way galaxy.

The Milky Way is the galaxy that you and I reside in. It is a galaxy that is multidimensional; that is, it has various levels of dimensions. It is a huge galaxy that may be as long as 50,000 light-years wide, and you and I and other planetary beings within the galaxy are traveling around its center, the Galactic Sun. We must understand that the Galactic Sun is a multidimensional physical and spiritual point in the center of this galaxy.

Remember, in earlier times humankind perceived that Earth (or even our Sun) was the center point of the universe. Now we know that Earth and the solar system travel around the center of the galaxy! If you are heliocentric, then you believe that your Sun is the center of the universe. Are you Earth-centered? Do you believe, as did humankind in the Middle Ages, that the universe goes around Earth? Or are you galactic-centered and acknowledge that everything goes around the center of the galaxy?

We can also talk about how galaxies are in groups. The Milky Way galaxy belongs to what is known as a local group, which is approximately twelve or thirteen galaxies that are part of a nearby system of galaxies.

In galactic spirituality, we say that the center of the galaxy is the Central Sun, a multidimensional spiritual and physical energy field that is responsible for the creation of all life and all spiritual development. Therefore, when we describe the galactic alignment in 2012, we are describing both a physical alignment and a spiritual alignment. Let us look back for a moment on December 21, 2012. Perhaps in your subjective memory, this happened yesterday, but it was several years ago. This galactic alignment was the source of predictions that included mass destruction, mass volcanic eruptions, major Earth changes, and other planetary upheavals.

The true interpretation of this galactic alignment is that Earth aligned with the Central Sun, and this event brought down new spiritual energies. This alignment can be described as downloading galactic spirituality into the consciousness of humanity. The alignment began a process of bringing spiritual galactic consciousness, or cosmic consciousness, to Earth in a strong, energetic wave.

The Star Family within Galactic Spirituality

Part of this energetic wave has been introduced to you through the Galactic Kachina. The Galactic Kachina is an intermediary similar to the ones who are spirit guides and mentors to the Hopi and Navajo. These kachinas, including the Galactic Kachina, reside on the famous San Francisco Peaks near Flagstaff, Arizona. The idea of the galactic consciousness and galactic spirituality was also introduced to the New Age community through the 1990s and early 2000s. However, there was also an awareness in certain other Native groups, such as the Mayan, the Cherokee, the Plains Indians, and the Iroquois. They also had knowledge of our galactic family. You see, the star family is part of a system that is included in galactic spirituality.

One core idea in galactic spirituality and the concept of the alignment with the Central Sun says that all life forms that exist in this galaxy originated through the Source masters in the Central Sun. The Source masters in the Central Sun oversee the spiritual development and placement of higher life forms throughout this galaxy. There are certain periods in the life of a planet in which the energies from the galactic spiritual center are more intense, and when those times occur, there is an opportunity among the inhabitants of that planet for expanded consciousness, expanded perception, and expanded spiritual tools and skills. Bringing down and aligning this spiritual galactic energy does not immediately solve Earth's problems. You have witnessed this! Although you are very capable people as starseeds and you and others have been working diligently to bring down, teach, and download galactic light and galactic energy into Earth, you will agree that this process has not stopped the entropy or the self-destruction that seems to be occurring before your eyes on this planet.

Multidimensional Interaction

To explain this entropy and destruction, I want to go to another concept in galactic spirituality, which is the principle of holographic energy. Simply stated, holographic energy says that the part represents the whole, but there is a corollary to this: What happens in the whole also affects the part. In applying this to galactic spirituality and to the existence of the galactic masters and the galactic council, I want to explain the holographic principle. What happens to Earth holographically affects all parts of this galaxy.

We have talked about this through the concept of quantum cohesiveness. We know, for example, that thought forms attract similar thought forms. What is going on in the galactic council affects what happens on Earth. It is a two-way street. What's happening on Earth affects the galactic center, and what happens in the galactic center affects Earth. This sounds simplistic, but it has major ramifications because the galactic council is affected while learning from what is taking place on Earth. Earth, through many of its spiritual leaders, is trying to integrate the healing energies from the galaxy.

We now come to another important principle in galactic spirituality: Higher dimensions, specifically the fifth dimension, interact with the third dimension. There is a multidimensional interactive force. The dimensions that exist in our multidimensional galaxy interact with each other. The fifth dimension is not totally cut off or separated from the third dimension. Some of you may believe that there is a complete separation between the dimensions. Even if you have the most restrictive definitions of heaven and hell, you still have a sense of the interaction between those two levels. Heaven is often seen as a reward: If you behave in one way or if you believe in a certain person or belief system, then you will be granted permission to enter it. However, if you do not act in a certain way, then you could go into a lower dimension. Some religions even state that you only have to remain in the lower vibration or lower dimension until you are purified, and then you can go to a higher level.

What is key now is to understand the interaction that the ascended masters and the galactic council achieve by interacting with Earth. In galactic spirituality, we say that the galactic masters — including the ascended masters, angels, certain beings known as star masters, the Arcturians, the Pleiadians, and other fifth-dimensional beings — have the ability to interact with you on the third dimension. The masters have a possibility to interact with you in a deep and expanded way. This interaction has becoming more powerful because of the 2012 galactic alignment.

The galactic alignment in 2012 opened even more pathways and corridors that allow this interaction. Even though this interaction has occurred, Earth has not been healed. Earth has not been brought to the fifth dimension. There have been many of you who have come right to the edge of entering the fifth dimension during your spiritual work. This is a great achievement, a great accomplishment, and a great spiritual advancement that you should feel good about and proud of. I'm certainly proud that in the midst of this Earth chaos and polarization, you have developed your spiritual energy and focus strongly. That means that you are able to enter or work in the fifth dimension. In the holographic theories of galactic spirituality, the ascended masters are learning about Earth, just as you are learning about the fifth dimension.

I know you believe that the ascended masters know everything, are able to predict exactly what is going to happen, and have the powers to intervene on Earth events. Every part of the galaxy has a unique perspective on the Creator and on the galaxy and the development of galactic energy and galactic spirituality. This answers the questions many of you have: Why are the ascended masters so interested in Earth? Why do so many spirits want to come to Earth now? It is because Earth is unique in many ways, and the most obvious way is the existence of duality and density.

Earth Graduation

In the principle of cosmic and galactic spirituality, we talk directly about soul growth and soul expansion. We talk about graduation from Earth — specifically about learning certain lessons and completing incarnations so that you can graduate from Earth. We are not saying that you have to belong to a certain group; you don't. But you have to complete your Earth lessons so that you can elevate yourself.

Densities are also compared to evil, and the reason for the existence of evil has always been one of the most complex questions to answer. Why does evil exist? Why does such density exist on a planet as beautiful as Earth, and how is it that this density seems so powerful that it prevents the advancement of this planet into the fifth dimension? We know that Earth is capable of going into the fifth dimension.

Many of you are planetary healers and are working to bring this planet into the higher realms. The answer to why evil exists is not simple.

It has to do with complex issues and cosmic karma. This complexity is not easily explained, but there is a simple part. I am going to give you the simple answer, but I want you to understand that it's not the total answer because there are corollaries and parts of this you may not be able to understand from the Earth perspective. Remember, even as advanced as you are, you are still in Earth's perspective — even as you go into the higher realms and enter the corridors.

To achieve soul evolution and soul advancement, you must have free will; you must have free choice. To have free choice, densities must exist. You must be able to choose whether you want to go to expanded consciousness or contracted consciousness. You must be able to choose whether you are going to do good or evil. In some cases, the choice is obvious, and in some cases, the choice is not so obvious. Sometimes, the choice is cloudy because you may get immediate gratification from choosing something that is dense. (Notice the use of the word "dense" instead of "evil.")

For example, consider the buffalo hunters of the 1800s. In a simple way, they might have thought, "We can kill all the buffalo and make a lot of money from the buffalo hides." They would get an immediate pleasure. They might have become very rich from selling the hides, but overall, it might have been an evil thing to eradicate so many buffalo. It's strange because they might not have received the immediate karmic feedback, but galactic spirituality says that there is reincarnation and there is karma. The galaxy is set up so that the appropriate karmic lessons for this particular situation will be found for incarnation to occur there.

[Chants and tones: Oooohhhmmm.] Let each of your souls become purified so that all contracted energies, all of the dense energies that may be around you, are released. [Chants: Oooohhhhmm, oooohhhhmm.] In any one incarnation, you can totally purify your soul, totally purify your self.

There is a distinction between your self and your soul because, yes, the soul is already whole. The soul is already pure, but the parts of your self that experience these other realities need purification in the lower aspects so that you can allow your soul to manifest in a totally pure way in this incarnation. This purification will let your soul light come in. You see, the Creator and the galactic council are saying that we want everyone to be able to manifest their soul light in the third dimension. Why? Why is this third dimension so important? If we're on the fifth dimension, why would we even care about the third dimension? The answer focuses on coming back to the holographic principles: The third dimension affects the fifth dimension, and the fifth dimension affects the third. It's an interaction that is reflected in "as above, so below" and "so below, as above."

Open the Doors of Perception to Multiply Your Psychic Skills

We can say that the fifth dimension does have seals, or entry protections, which are necessary. You are quickly learning that the way to open those seals is to use the special skills and knowledge that are taught in galactic consciousness. The first skill has to do with opening the doors of perception. Everyone who has had the doors of perception opened will experience unity consciousness and cosmic consciousness. People with unity consciousness are more open, more accepting, more loving, and they are willing to work in a loving way for the planet. The assemblage point controls higher perceptions. When that point is opened, one can experience expanded consciousness. The assemblage point also relates to what is known neurologically and scientifically as the pineal gland and the reticular activating system. These two points within an area of the brain that is directly related to higher consciousness.

What is the relationship between the pineal gland and the opening of the doors of perception, and what is the relationship between the assemblage point and the pineal gland? What is the relationship between the third eye and the pineal gland? The pineal gland is able to secrete a neurochemical substance that sets off the reaction that opens the doors of perception. When the doors of perception open, you will see and experience expanded consciousness in a quantum way. You will see wavy lines, energy fields, and auras. When the pineal gland is open, you will have other higher powers, such as synesthesia. You will be able to see into the past and the future. You will be able to astrally travel with ease. You will see that there are thin etheric cords that attach everyone to the Central Sun!

Everyone has an etheric energy cord that comes from the Central Sun. This Central Sun is multidimensional and, energetically, the source of what's in existence in this galaxy. There is a way that the Central Sun is connected to another higher source. By opening the assemblage point and that part of the brain connected with the pineal gland, you will be able to have expanded doors of perception, and your psychic skills can then be multiplied.

The skill of bilocation is important, but understand that to go into the fifth dimension, you have to also possess expanded consciousness. With expanded consciousness, you can see everything as energy, and with that awareness, you will be able to go through the fifth-dimensional corridor. But to go through the corridors, you also will use the skill known as thought projection. Now, this is a higher principle. It is a higher spiritual skill to be able to thought project. In your galactic spirituality, you're coming to realize that this physical body is just one aspect of your true manifested self. It's not the only aspect, and believe it or not, it's not the most important aspect. But you identify completely with this aspect of manifested self on Earth. We are working with you to expand your identity into your multidimensional self. You have a portion of your self in another realm, and understanding this is an important part in your success for the ascension. Do not identify only with this physical body on Earth. You can also identify as much as possible with your fifth-dimensional self. You can learn how to travel through the corridors and not be caught up in lower, fourth-dimensional energy. If you are in any way caught up in the fourth dimension, we will train you how to remove the parasitic attachments that may become attached to you while traveling through that realm. By removing the attachments, you can move into higher light and of consciousness and toward the Galactic Center.

There are planets, such as Alano, that are more directly connected energetically with the Galactic Center and with the Central Sun. These planets have achieved a level of expanded consciousness and are directly and consciously interacting with the Central Sun. On this type of planet, you will find prophets and ascended masters interacting and appearing regularly among the inhabitants. You will find that there is incredible spiritual life on such planets. It could be described as a spiritual heaven where the planet does not have densities.

In conclusion, I want to say to you that there is a great contraction on planet Earth. This contracted energy makes your choosing the light and your choosing spiritual, galactic energy more meaningful and significant. You have been able to choose spiritual expansion in the face of this contraction. As strange as this sounds from your standpoint, this planet is serving you well, and now you and I and all ascended masters will be working together to shift the planetary consciousness to a more expanded level. I am Juliano. Good day!

Chapter 15

Anchor Fifth-Dimensional Light in Times of Darkness

Juliano and the Arcturians

This channeling was done after the tragic Bastille Day attack in France in 2016.

I am Juliano. We are the Arcturians. It is true that the keepers of the fifth-dimensional light, like yourselves, are important and valuable. It is necessary at all times to hold and anchor this light, especially when there is any darkness. Our mission today is to increase the receptivity of fifth-dimensional light onto this planet. We are here for unity meditation and harmonization and unity in higher light — unity in the light of the ring of ascension, the light of the Sacred Triangle, and the light of the Central Sun. This beautiful, healing fifth-dimensional light that transcends logic is coming to this planet. Earth is now set up to attract and hold this fifth-dimensional light that transcends all lower, dark vibrations. We have helped establish the ring of ascension, the halo of light, around Earth.

Now, I know that there are those who do not want to harmonize and merge in higher light. There are those who want to destroy the planet and its biosphere. I am aware of the recent political and social events. I am aware of the biological events such as the mining accidents in Brazil and Colorado. I am aware of numerous other events that have to do with ocean pollution, destruction of the coral reefs, and radiation leaks. Earth can still respond to humans negatively, creating more imbalance.

But we are here together for a higher purpose. We can communicate with the Spirit of Earth and influence the outcome with our positive thoughts of harmony and balance, especially in the noosphere, the thought field around the planet. Thoughts of harmony, balance, and fifth-dimensional light and energy create a vibration that affects the whole planet. Earth receives your thoughts.

You are witnessing one of the greatest periods of polarization in Earth's history, but at the same time, there is a great movement toward higher light. Many of you are seeking to attract the fifth dimension and fifth-dimensional energy to Mother Earth.

Unity Consciousness Meditation

Visualize with me, Juliano, a golden halo around Earth filled with the beautiful light you might imagine surrounds Jesus, Kuthumi, or any ascended master. Visualize this halo now around Earth.

Earth's halo is like a ring. We call it the ring of ascension. The ring of ascension attracts the fifth-dimensional masters and brings a connection to all from the higher light. You and I meet there and can interact very comfortably with the fifth-dimension. This halo has special powers that radiate light and energy to different parts of Earth. You can project yourself to it and work to attract the fifth dimension and make a force field.

Earth's noosphere is filled with both darkness and light, both negativity and positivity. But the ring of ascension is filled with the thought fields only of higher light and therefore has a great power.

Feel your energy field, your aura, your spirit, rise out of your body. As it rises, it travels to the ring of ascension. All of us are together now. Our aura bodies are sitting in a great circle within the ring of ascension. It is a wonderful feeling to be within the ring of ascension, for we are able to interact with the fifth dimension and bring higher light into Earth.

As you are in the ring of ascension, say, "I attract fifth-dimensional light to Earth. I am attracting fifth-dimensional light to Earth." All your thoughts and powers are increased because you are in the ring of ascension, and we, the ascended masters, are with you now, increasing the arcan power of your affirmation: "I am attracting fifth-dimensional light."

Now say, "I am helping to attract the fifth dimension to Earth" twice, and then pause. Say, "A time is coming soon when the fifth dimension is going to interact with the third dimension. I am working to create this intersect and bring a huge download from the fifth dimension to Earth." [Tones: Ooohhhmmm.] "I am sending fifth-dimensional light and energy to all the victims of the Nice tragedy." Many of those souls are lighting up; their lightbodies are opening up. Visualize all the entanglement, the energies of darkness and anger, removed from the victims whose energy fields are lighting up. The perpetrators will remain in darkness, heaviness, and density.

We are together in the ring of ascension where we have great healing powers. Go with me to the top of Earth, to the North Pole. You might be able to see the Iskalia mirror, a special receptor of the highest light from the galactic center. Now Earth will receive the highest light of fifth-dimensional innovation, discovery, and methods to solve the planet's problems. Send your spirit body and aura now to the Iskalia mirror, where we will sit together to increase its receptivity with our thoughts and powers . [Tones: Ooohhhmmm.]

Together we increase the attraction of the Iskalia mirror, the power of connecting with the fifth-dimensional Central Sun that will help to bring new solutions to problems on the whole planet. Around the Iskalia mirror, we attract and implement solutions. May the powers of all planetary healers be increased. May the powers of the Biorelativity exercises be strengthened. As we meditate, we ask that each of us receives an arcan increase in spiritual powers and energy.

Now we will return in our aura bodies back to the ring of ascension. As we travel together around Earth, I stop over France because there is a huge energy of unity consciousness, a huge power of healing that is focused from many different sources onto France. We, the Arcturians, see the power of this unity. May a unity come to the whole planet so that all are accepted as brothers and sisters and those who are in darkness become powerless to do more evil.

Return slowly, leaving the ring of ascension to come back into your physical body. Reenter your physical body in total harmony, and feel this enlightenment, this harmonization, as your spirit reenters your physical body in perfect alignment. Now you feel closer to the fifth dimension; you feel you can attract more of the fifth-dimensional light's delightful power in your personal life and Earth body. [Pauses.]

You are Earth healers. You are planetary healers. You are lightworkers. Now more than ever, your work in holding this energy for the planet is so important. Remember that this drama on Earth will lead eventually to the planet ascending to the fifth dimension. Those in darkness will be separated and kept from entering higher light.

We love you. The ascended masters love you. We continue to send you the power and attraction force for your fifth-dimensional work. I am Juliano. Good day!

Chapter 16

Expanded Consciousness and Quantum Healing Energy

Juliano and the Arcturians

Greetings, I am Juliano. We are the Arcturians. Expanded consciousness is very important to us. We will look at it first from the standpoint of human evolution. Our observation is that the next step in the evolutionary process is the expansion of the human consciousness. When you look at leaps in the evolution of humans, you see that they developed tools and learned to speak and walk upright, which are all examples of consciousness. Our study of the evolutionary process confirms that major steps occur during crises with such dangerous energy that the species must adapt to survive.

It is obvious to you and me and to all starseeds that there is a major crisis on Earth. It is a monumental crisis that some have called the sixth planetary extinction event. There have been five previous major extinctions in this planet's history. The most well known involved the dinosaurs, but there have been others that were just as serious. I could say it was because the dinosaurs lacked the flexibility to adapt, but other circumstances were involved, especially the meteor strike at the Yucatán Peninsula.

Humankind has to shift consciousness and be aware that it must change. It appears that the starseeds like you are in the forefront of this evolutionary change, so you understand there must be a shift toward connecting with the fifth dimension, which we have described in great detail.

The Origin and Gift of Consciousness

Any attempt to define consciousness will lead to lengthy, detailed, philosophic, and scientific explanations, and I don't believe spending a great deal of time on that is our purpose, although I certainly would enjoy the opportunity to explore that with you. However, I do want to say several things about consciousness.

Consciousness originates with the Creator, and one of the greatest and most powerful presentations in the Hebrew Bible occurs when God, the Creator, says to Moses, "I am that I am." The original Hebrew was in the future tense — "I will be that I will be" — but the key in that phrase is the key to consciousness, which is "I know that I am" and "I am." Therefore, the gift the Creator gave Adam (or the species of Adam) is consciousness. No other creature on this planet has the sophisticated consciousness of humankind.

Just having the consciousness means a great deal, but there are levels to consciousness. Some Kabbalistic rabbis, for example, talked about the small mind and the large mind — small, narrow consciousness, and wide, expanded consciousness. The small, narrow consciousness is what most people experiences in their daily lives, and it's what most people think primitive cultures experienced. That is really interesting because primitive cultures often lived in expanded consciousness because they lived in their natural environment. The Aboriginals, for example, were once totally in tune with their environment, so they were in expanded consciousness.

To Enter Expanded Consciousness, Certain Needs Must Be Met

The narrowing of consciousness is also important to your civilization's development. I don't want you to think that narrow consciousness is bad, because it has many applications. There is no way you could build spaceships or automobiles or perform surgery unless you had focus. Expanded consciousness allows an awareness of all there is in your environment and that your perceptions are open. In the analogy of a horse on the racetrack, the horse has blinders and only sees in front (narrow consciousness). In the race, you want the horse to only look straight ahead because looking left or right causes distractions that would slow it (expanded consciousness).

To experience expanded consciousness, you must have your physical needs met and you must feel safe, which an American psychologist named Abraham Maslow described as a higher hierarchy of needs.[1] He described emotional and physiological needs that must be met before you can relax and allow your consciousness to expand. Some needs are obvious (food, sleep, and security), and some are maybe less obvious (family, belonging, and respect), but you must also have the understanding that your brain, your mind, is programmed for expanded consciousness.

The Adam species DNA is programmed to expand, and there are aspects of the brain — for example, the pituitary gland and the reticular activating system — that contain codes. When those codes are opened, then the expansion, the doors of perception, open. Yes, for humanity to survive, new men and women must live in expanded consciousness. Expanded consciousness in the way I describe includes environmental awareness and sensitivity to all surrounding sounds and creatures, but it also includes the awareness that other dimensions exist. I am talking about acknowledging the higher levels of awareness and higher dimensions.

You experience deep levels of brain activity and different dimensions every time you enter the REM cycle in sleep, giving you tremendous abilities to travel dimensionally and interdimensionally. However, I am talking about having this expanded consciousness and awareness in waking life, integrating your understanding and experience of the dimensions, particular the fifth, while you are awake in the third dimension. This interaction is one of the major teachings in our work with planet Earth.

The Fifth Dimension Is Inhabited by People with Expanded Consciousness

Now, what is the fifth dimension, and why is it so important for your development? There have been references and even a song that describes the fifth dimension as being the beginning and welcoming in the New Age of Aquarius.[2] I say this jokingly, but if the chaos and confusion of the past four or five years on Earth are an introduction

---

1. Abraham Maslow, *Religions, Values and Peak Experiences toward a Psychology of Being* (New York : Penguin Books , 1970), Reviewed by Tim Knepper, 2001 (http://people.bu.edu/wwildman/relexp/reviews/review_maslow01.htm).

2. "Aquarius/Let the Sunshine In," The 5th Dimension, 1969.

to what the Age of Aquarius is like in the fifth dimension, I don't think you'd be interested in going there.

The fifth dimension is better described through the works of Jesus, Mary, Kuthumi, and other the ascended masters. The first point is that you have to be at a certain higher-vibrational frequency to experience the fifth dimension. The frequency is the vibration of your aura, which you can measure with certain tools and equipment. You might not have that readily available at this time, but there is a new branch of medicine called "vibrational medicine" that studies the speed at which people vibrate. The theory is that illness and disease are accompanied by the slowing of the human aura in certain sections of the body, which could be a symptom and even a cause of the disease. To heal, a vibrational-medicine healer would use techniques to increase the vibration. Even late-stage cancer can be cured with higher-vibrational healing techniques and interventions, but the fifth dimension requires you to be at a high vibration.

Higher vibrations include love, acceptance, and compassion, and lower vibrations include anger, jealousy, and greed. If you have anger, jealousy, and greed, you cannot enter the fifth dimension. In contracted consciousness, you might experience those, so don't think that you must be perfect or never experience any hatred, greed, or jealousy. You're human. But you can expand and go to the higher consciousness, the higher emotions.

The fifth dimension is inhabited by people who are in expanded consciousness. The fifth dimension has different rules. In the third dimension, for example, you are at the mercy of some simple rules: gravity, space, time, the space-time continuum, and linear reality; there's a beginning and an end; and you are born and then you die. You are also ruled by polarities and duality, a subject Taoists have quite adequately discussed when they say that first there was the Tao and all was in unity but that when this reality was created, so was male and female, yin and yang. For this third-dimensional reality to exist, there must be linear reality, linear time, gravity, and duality — and duality, of course, leads to polarization.

Peak Experiences Are Part of Humanity's Next Evolutionary Step

In the fifth dimension, there is no duality and no space or time the way you know them. In the fifth dimension, there is expanded consciousness; therefore, you are able to experience a unity that is almost impossible to experience on Earth. I say almost because it *is* possible, and those who have experienced it on Earth describe it as enlightenment. Maslow, who was a starseed, described the unity consciousness experience as leading to expanded consciousness, which he called "peak experience." A peak experience is rare. It's not something you would have every day, though you want to for the rest of your life. Maslow described people who've had peak experiences as being so happy and accepting that they aren't even afraid of death because they have seen and felt the true reality and the fifth-dimensional continuous unity.

Peak experiences and expanded consciousness are part of the next evolutionary step for humanity. Why is it necessary? All the great inspirations, discoveries, medicines, and technology come from scientists and philosophers who were able to connect with the fifth dimension. Even if you look at someone like Einstein, there are questions. There were other people in Switzerland and in Germany who were brighter than Einstein. Yes, he was very bright, but there were scientists who were quicker and better mathematicians. Einstein's genius was that he was able to connect with the higher dimensions and get a perspective on the dimensions that others could not.

With that perspective, you can understand that the fifth dimension contains energy that can be brought down into the third dimension. This is a very important point: Ideas, thoughts, emotions, and even healing energy from the fifth dimension are transferrable to the third dimension and your third-dimensional body, but that takes special training and techniques. Part of our Arcturian teachings is about how to bring fifth-dimensional energy to Earth.

Our examples today include Einstein, Mozart, and Beethoven, who were able to connect with higher realms and bring back ideas, music, and new formulas that were not available to anyone in contracted consciousness. As I said, there could be great scientists, but if they did not have expanded consciousness, then they would not be able to bring in new ideas. Our observation is that the fifth dimension is intersecting with the third dimension and that there are more opportunities now for connecting with the fifth dimension than at any other time in the history of this planet. Part of the reason is that the fifth dimension is more available and is moving closer.

When people talk about the Age of Aquarius, they actually refer to a time when the dimensions get closer, which is now. From an astrological standpoint, there is a shift in energy and in the solar system's relationship to the Central Sun. There are different alignments, and some are related to Earth's position to the zodiac and also to the Central Sun. In part, those ideas are accurate.

We all have a choice: We can live in duality or we can live in oneness. Is that right?

Yes, it requires a certain level of protection because remember, as Maslow said, certain needs must be met for you to be in a state of oneness. If you were attacked by a crocodile in the Outback, for example, it wouldn't help you to be in a state of oneness because then you would be one with the crocodile and be eaten. Being in a state of oneness requires a certain safety and security.

For example, you [the people at the live channeling] are safe in a beautiful building among friends with similar vibrations. This is a perfect opportunity to experience oneness. But if you were to go to downtown Los Angeles late at night, you might not want to experience the oneness because of the danger there. Once certain needs are met, then you can choose the oneness.

What is the difference between oneness and unity consciousness?

They are very similar. It's very difficult to distinguish because oneness sounds like it's a unity. Unity consciousness doesn't mean you give up your individuality. You are able to maintain the division between yourself and the universe while voluntarily giving up that separation to experience unity, knowing you will go back to the separateness. Oneness is really the state of when you're in unity.

Maslow talked about the unity consciousness as a peak experience, so on the third dimension, you have to have opposites. You have a time of unity when you peak, but you also have a time when you're not peaking. Even those who are enlightened will say they are not always in the state of enlightenment and unity. There are times when they have to be in more contracted consciousness. When you're driving a car on a freeway, you probably want to be steady in the third dimension to focus on the road.

Thought Is a Quantum Particle

Let's go into quantum energy and its relationship to healing and to the fifth dimension. The subject of quantum particles and quantum light is very deep and is beyond our limitations in this lecture, but I will make a few comments. Einstein was not a big believer in quantum consciousness, physics, and particles. The main reason is that quantum particles and quantum energy are unpredictable, meaning that in the subatomic world there are interactions and rules beyond logic and predictability — but only in the third dimension with its limited observations.

Thought is a quantum particle, and it is the fastest energy in the universe, faster than the speed of light. Using thought, you can be anywhere in the universe instantaneously, while the light, though it travels at tremendous speed of 186,000 miles per second, still requires great time. If you were to come to Arcturus, at the speed of light, you would have to travel for thirty-six years, and that's assuming your body could tolerate that speed.

Thought is subatomic particle that's not measured. Thought is a subatomic particle that no Earth scientists has observed or discovered yet. They have discovered quarks and many other things but perhaps aren't even looking for the inherit particle and composition of a thought. Is a thought a particle, for example? Quantum physicists argue about whether light is a particle or a ray. The quantum world does not follow the rules of logic in the physical world.

For Quantum Healing to Work, You Must Believe

To access quantum energy for healing, you must have and be able to receive expanded consciousness and this particle. The best example I can give you for quantum healing is a doctor with expanded consciousness talking to a dying cancer patient who is desperate for a cure.

The doctor says, "I have this new medicine I just discovered in the Outback. It's a special medicine that the Aborigines have been using for centuries, and they have given me permission to bring it into the West. I have extracted ingredients from a special plant to create this healing pill, which I am giving you."

The patient takes the pill, and all the cancer goes away. That's not logical. How could the cancer go away? The doctor was borrowing energy from the fifth dimension. Quantum energy does not follow the rules of logic in the third dimension. For the patient to receive this type of quantum healing, he or she must be receptive to the healing and prepare the mind for it. If he or she says, "This is a bunch of malarkey," it won't work. There has to be a resonance of energy between the patient and the doctor, and the doctor must believe and present this method in a very special, convincing way. The doctor only has to believe it at the moment of interacting with the patient. With the right set of circumstances and connection with the fifth dimension, there are great possibilities that are not possible in the third dimension, amounting to what would become a quantum healing experience.

Some of you are quantum healers and are able to access this kind of energy in your healing work. Now, I speak of expanded consciousness and quantum healing for individuals and for the planet. You know that some of the experiences and circumstances on this planet are so dangerous that it is highly unlikely humankind can resolve them. It's highly unlikely the oceans and many other parts of the biosphere can be cleaned up before they die if things continue at the present level. But if scientists and planetary healers like yourselves are open to connecting to the fifth dimension and quantum healing, then you can bring down techniques and energy that could miraculously heal this planet and its people.

What is the actual catalyst for healing — vibrational energy or expanded consciousness?

It's all of it. As I said, you have to prepare the consciousness and the energy field of the patient. It's not just your energy. In the example of the cancer patient, the person is desperate and will likely be thinking, "I believe in anything. I'm ready. Why not? I know I'm going to die anyway, so sure, give me that pill. I accept it, I'm ready." It's an interaction on all levels, but primarily it's you as the healer presenting it in the right way.

Omega light, the Iskalia mirror, and quantum healing light are all variations of techniques and light frequencies that can be used for this process. Also, there are power places on Earth that lend themselves to quantum healing and fifth-dimensional light. Grose Valley is one of those places, as is Lourdes, France. There are a lot of sacred places on this planet that provide the increased vibrational energy that would be just the boost needed to do the quantum healing. You want everything possible on your side, and being in a sacred place certainly helps.

We are talking about physical manifestation like cancer as a disturbance in the aura, but what about any mental disturbances?

Yes, any physical disease or imbalance is a disruption of frequencies in the aura, and you can absolutely use quantum healing to rebalance the mind. It's only been discussed in modern medicine with dire illnesses such as cancer, but it can be applied to mental imbalances as well.

Chapter 17

The Healing Chambers

Helio-ah, Juliano, the Arcturians, and Mother Mary

Greetings, I am Helio-ah. We are the Arcturians. Healing chambers exist in our fifth-dimensional ship, the Athena. There are two distinct healing chambers: the phone booth healing chamber and the healing room.

The phone booth healing chamber is a small booth with a computer in it where we can download the history of your lifetime on Earth and your whole soul journey. When we turn the computer on, we have access to the energy and information we need from this and previous lifetimes. That means we can access any memory or event you experienced. In this lifetime, for example, there could be 50,000 or more images stored in your healing chamber computer. Each experience you have on Earth creates a picture in your mind similar to how you dream. You mostly dream in pictures and images, not usually in words. Occasionally you speak, but basically the dream world is one of vivid images.

One type of healing involves bringing a person back to a traumatic event. For example, for someone who was sexually molested as a child, we could bring back the image of that experience, but then in the healing chamber, we can reshape the image and create an improved healing image. That image overrides the old memory and becomes the new one. We then reinsert that memory into the chronological order of your lifetime experiences on Earth. The future from that point forward is updated. If you had a trauma, we would create a new image based on the information you gave us, and then we would bring in a healer who would produce an image of you being rescued (as if by Archangel Michael, perhaps). Then that image would be saved in the holographic healing chamber and updated in your memory. Any part of you that was traumatized or blocked can be updated and removed or re-created so that it is not harming you.

Retroactively Remove Illness with Holographic Healing

The second part of the healing chamber is a healing room where Juliano and I work, which might address any questions you have about healing physical illnesses. Sometimes the image of the point when the illness began can be modified. Say, for example, you received a pathogen when you were on an airplane. We could take the image, find the point when the pathogen entered your body, and then create a rescue screen or filter to stop the pathogen from coming in. Realistically, illnesses begin when the immune system is lowered, but just because you are vulnerable or genetically predisposed to an illness doesn't mean you have to get it. If you do get it, we can holographically reprogram your brain and your memory.

We have a healing chamber where we do specific healing on the person, working with the etheric energy field. Even though the body manifests the illness, in reality, the illness starts in the aura. That's why vibrational medicine is so powerful. In a sense, it goes to the source, which is the energy field.

Helio-ah's Technique of Aura Cleansing

What we do is bilocate. We take the person's energy field and do an exercise where we have the person go around an Earth inner room in a circle; we call it "the merry-go-round." The aura leaves the body. I meet the person in a tunnel, and together we travel through the corridor at the speed of thought into the starship and into the healing chamber. There, I use some methods of working the energy field. The one I call the rotating chair method is similar to a type of preparation astronauts use before going into space and zero gravity: They have a reclined chair that rotates at high speeds. In my technique, a being sits in the chair, which is then reclined before I set the rotation speeds. As the person experiences higher speeds, the lower vibrations, densities, and blockages in the aura are released, and the blocked energy is elevated. As I stand over the being, I send these blockages away. Then the aura is purified.

When I do this, it's very important that I direct the energy so that it goes away from both of us. Once the aura is purified, I slowly bring the chair back to normal speed, stop it, and if necessary, make some final adjustments to the aura. For example, perhaps I would help reshape it or remove any lower vibrations still there. I might fill it with light and so forth. At that point, the aura is totally pure without any evidence of disease or imperfection.

Together we travel back from the corridor down into a position 5–8 feet above his or her head on Earth. There I ask the person to go into the body in perfect alignment, which is a very important step in this healing. You want to make sure the etheric body aligns perfectly with the physical body. Sometimes in traumas, the aura leaves the body, and when it comes back in, it doesn't do so in perfect alignment. People even report not feeling like themselves or as if they never totally returned to their bodies.

After I direct the purified aura to enter the body in perfect alignment, this purified energy updates the whole system with new energy much like you would put new programming in a computer. Say you're updating your operating system; it might take two or three hours to download all the information into the computer. Now that your aura was in the fifth dimension in my healing chamber, you might need two or three days to download the information. During the exercise, you could receive 5 or 10 percent of the programming and spend the next few hours or another day downloading everything.

In essence, we're giving you a new program, a clean aura to update. In some cases, if the body is very sick, it might take several tries to completely purify and heal.

Helio-ah, do other beings help you with the healing?

Basically, I do the healing. You can invite other beings. Your guides and teachers could come in with you in some cases, and we could even leave the chamber to go to a higher level, where we can invite other healers. Other beings use other methods, but this method is unique to us, as we were the primary developers of it. I am Helio-ah. Good day!

I go to the healing chamber quite regularly, and there are two people in my life who are not very well. Can I take them with me? What is the best method? Can I just imagine being in the healing chamber in fifth-dimensional consciousness and sending love and light to them?

This is Juliano. That's one method, but bringing ill people to the healing chambers requires explanation and preparation, part of which involves bringing their energy fields or auras to the healing chamber and removing the lower vibrations from the auras. Then you bring the purified auras back to their bodies. When you say, "I'm going to bring them," as the healer, I want you to be able to maintain your separation and not to merge with them. This is a mistake that healers often make. You don't want to merge with them in unity; you have to direct them. I am Juliano. Good day!

* * *

Bring Your Lightbody Down to Your Physical Earth Body

Greetings, I am Mary. Some of you know me as Mother Mary. I am an ascended master and a teacher, and I have a mission to oversee the healing of Earth and bringing the planet into the higher realms. I love Earth, and I have so many followers who want to work on love: loving Earth, loving life, loving the galaxy, loving the Creator, loving Jesus. You are all aware of the universal law of love. It is the greatest purifier.

The lightbody is your perfect fifth-dimensional body. If you imagine yourself in the most perfected state, you might picture yourself when you were twenty-five years old, or maybe you like yourself now and find your body is perfect for you. You can, in your lightbody, create and shape the body to your liking. Some of us imagine ourselves as wise, older beings, and some like to look young. Maybe you've seen pictures of the ascended masters, and they all look young and handsome. They created those images. You will also be able to do that when you come to the fifth dimension. You'll be able to create the perfect image. Your lightbody already exists on the fifth dimension, and for example, in your sleep state you inhabit your sleep body, your dream body. You are multidimensional, so you have a fifth-dimensional body. You can bilocate, or travel, to that body.

Jesus had multidimensional presence. He had multiple bodies and was able to bring his fifth-dimensional body to Earth. When he was on the cross, he left his physical body, and when that physical body died, he continued to live on Earth in his multidimensional body.

Each body has a percentage of soul light in it. It is a great soul accomplishment and advancement to be able to bring down your lightbody onto Earth and into your physical body. Bringing your lightbody in facilitates quantum healing, enlivening your physical body and filling it with light. When you see people who are sick, sometimes they are already trying to leave their physical bodies. The lightbody radiates, holds vibration, protects you, and allows you to visit the lightbody in the other realm.

Juliano has talked about shimmering and the ability to move and increase the vibration of our aura so that you can travel to and inhabit your lightbody. I want to teach you to become familiar and comfortable with your lightbody. In fact, at the moment of ascension, you will go to your lightbody. This is the remarkable, alchemical transformation of the ascension. You leave your physical body, travel to your lightbody, and transfer your full consciousness into it.

Let's say that right now you are 98 percent in your physical body and 2 percent in your lightbody. If you can change that percentage to be even 5 to 10 percent in your lightbody and connect those bodies, you'd bring more light and energy into this world. It works also with Earth. The planet has an aura, and you can actually bring the whole aura of Earth into the fifth-dimensional lightbody of Earth.

In working with the lightbody, we work with the aura. In working with the aura, we become aware of the state of the aura. Does the aura have holes in it, and is it the right shape? Does the aura vibrate at the right frequency and accept cohabitation of another, higher spirit within you? By yourself, you might not be able to do more with the higher energy, but with the cohabitating higher spirit, you can do more things. For example, Moses would not have been able to do miracles without Archangel Gabriel and Archangel Michael.

When we are busy working here on Earth, can we take our lightbodies wherever we go?

Yes, this is what Jesus did. He brought down the Christ light in his physical body, and he spread the light. If you connect with your lightbody — each one of you has a higher light frequency — you can bring that light frequency into Earth and then transmit and emanate that energy. The true miracle of Jesus was his ability to connect with the Christ light full time. But he was only able to do this after he reached a certain age (I believe it was thirty). He was part of the Christ light, and he was already a higher being. You are also a higher being, so you can allow your lightbody to be in your physical body on Earth.

We want to see Earth's aura healed. This is part of why the Arcturians downloaded the etheric crystals and why you have an etheric crystal in Grose Valley. It is a source of fifth-dimensional light, and those who are close to that source experience their lightbodies easier. It's a very sacred place with high energy, and if you go there, you will find your lightbodies are very comfortable in being there.

The last time we were here, we brought down the Galactic Kachina. Is she a lightbody?

You can have the Galactic Kachina cohabitate with you. You can invite the lightbody of the Galactic Kachina to be with you. Then you will be more knowledgeable about galactic energy and galactic healing. The Galactic Kachina is an intermediary, an actual spirit. When you are in your lightbody, you will be able to allow the Galactic Kachina to come into you. I encourage cohabitation. I know that many conservative preachers don't believe in a lot of what we are talking about, yet they always invite Jesus to cohabitate with them. Jesus is always speaking through them. Remember, it's a combination of whom you are and what energy you allow to come through. We do not have time to talk about negative cohabitation, but that's a big problem on this planet now because people allow lower spirits to come in and cohabitate. It is one reason that there is so much violence now.

I bless each of you in the light of my father, in the light of Yeshua ben David. In the light of the lightbody may you walk with great powers of emanation and healing. I love you all. I am Mary.

Chapter 18

The Principles of Planetary and Personal Holographic Healing

Helio-ah and the Arcturians

Greetings. I am Helio-ah. We are the Arcturians. I want to talk to you about holographic energy and the principles of holographic healing. You have to understand our perspective and that the principles of holographic energy occur in both a positive and negative environment. I know you all love to hear about positive planetary holographic healing.

You're experiencing worldwide terrorism and war. I want to address the terrorism from the perspective of holographic energy. The main principle of holographic energy is that a part can affect the whole, or a part is a representative of the whole. If you affect an energy field from one part, that energy field can affect the whole. The typical example is holographic photography in which you take a slice of something, such as an apple, and from that slice, a holographic picture of the full apple can be attained. As another example, somebody with the proper technology could take one skin cell from someone and actually clone and reproduce an exact duplicate of that person. You don't have this technology at this point, but these are examples of holographic energy.

The Importance of Permeability

If you introduce one pathogenic mutation into a human system, that system would require an immunity to the mutation to stop it. If there was no immunity and that one cell was powerful enough, it could overwhelm and take over the whole system of the human body, permeating it. Now, I want you to take note of the word "permeate" because it is important in the discussion of holographic energy. When I say things permeate something, I mean that they can go through many different systems.

Remember the example of the mutating cell in the human body. I suggest that there are certain immunities within the body that can block invasive cells, and those cells might mutate to overcome those immunities. The effectiveness of the mutation depends on whether it can permeate those immunities and get into the whole system. One of the principles of holographic healing is permeability.

Let's look at the reverse of mutations. Imagine you are going to send a positive, strong, loving, spiritual message. Can that message permeate the world in the same way? Would that beautiful event have the ability to permeate and affect people globally? In our observation of Earth civilization and technology, there are only a few events that seem to strike a chord that would enable them to permeate the whole civilization, the whole consciousness of the planet.

Let's look at a positive event. We are struck by the fact that positive events do not seem to carry the same permeability as negative events, but there have been some exceptions. The first exception seems to be sports. Sports events, such as international soccer or American football, baseball, or basketball championship games seem to permeate the entire world. I realize that many of you are not sports fans, but please stay with me, as sports do have global permeability, so they are worth discussing when looking at holographic energy and, in particular, planetary healing. Another global event we found was the death of Princess Diana. This was a very powerful event that seemed to move a lot of people. Of course, the terrorist events of September 11, 2001, moved people on a global scale.

Let us now look at other examples of global events that had the power to holographically affect the planet. There was the appearance of what some call "the Son of Man," which is a designation of the highest order of the ascended master. This term has many different definitions, but in galactic spirituality and from our perspective, it means a person who is able to holographically affect an entire world and move that world into a positive direction toward peace, harmony, and unity consciousness. Jesus's appearance is an example of how one person can holographically influence 2,000 or 3,000 years of a civilization.

What type of person can affect an entire civilization and an entire planet? A person does not have to be the most powerful or the wealthiest, but there is a certain power contained in knowing how to permeate the holographic system on the planet.

Find a Point of Maximum Effect

Another principle that applies to planetary work and planetary healing is accessibility, and it's particularly applicable in holographic planetary healing. The first principle, permeability, means that what you do has the ability to affect and permeate many different systems on the planet. The second principle, accessibility, means that you must enter Earth's system at a point of maximum effect. For example, Jerusalem has the potential for maximum impact and accessibility for holographic work. I'm sure that's why Jesus emerged in Jerusalem. There were many different places on the planet that he could have come to. There certainly were other civilizations on this planet that he could have emerged from where he would have been received in a more humane and safe way. But his mission of holographic planetary healing and of affecting humanity was done through a point of maximum accessibility, which at that particular time was Jerusalem. Even today, Jerusalem provides a point of accessibility that holographically can affect the entire planet.

Let's look at Jerusalem from a logical standpoint. When we look at the size of the city, the population, and the number of armaments, you might say, "There is no way that an area of that size could affect the entire planet and this whole civilization." Don't miss the point. Jerusalem isn't a point of maximum accessibility because it has the most armaments or the most powerful leaders but because it is an access point where an intervention would have maximum permeability: The energy could permeate the whole planet and all the systems on it.

There are other access points on the planet. Jerusalem is not the only one. One of the tasks of the Arcturians is to expand the access points so that there are other places on the planet that have the powerful effect of holographic healing with permeability and accessibility. An intervention done from one of those points would have maximum holographic impact on the planet.

This leads to the twelve etheric crystals. There are twelve special places on the planet that have magnificent beauty and energy. These twelve points are all beautiful, but they don't have the power of Jerusalem. How could working from these etheric crystal points, such as Lago Puelo or Volcán Poás or Mount Shasta, create a holographic event that would affect the whole planet in a positive way? I agree that Mount Shasta certainly does not have the energy of Jerusalem by itself, and it probably would not be able to affect the whole planet in a positive way. If Jesus/Sananda returned today and went on top of Mount Shasta and gave a lecture, would it affect the planet? Probably not. However, if Jesus/Sananda returned to the Temple Mount and gave a lecture, it probably would affect the entire planet.

Access points are power spots. Mount Shasta may have the necessary power to amplify the influence of an event, but the planetary healing is based on the principles of interaction. This interaction network includes the twelve etheric crystals and the planetary Tree of Life. In this concept of the planetary Tree of Life, we have twelve spheres, or energy points, that interact with each other so that they lend energy to one another. They are a network of light, sending energy and influencing the planet so that one access point can have the power and energy of twelve. Juliano and I have been working toward finding ways to teach this principle to you and ways to coordinate exercises that would harmonize and bring the twelve points together into one sphere.

Why would we not just use Jerusalem? The answer to that is complex. Number one, the idea of a galactic, spiritual, extraterrestrial ascended master is an idea that is not accepted by traditional religion, even though the great ascended masters, including Moses, had extraterrestrial contact. Moses in particular went on top of a mountain and was ascended. He was transferred to a higher level of consciousness and to a higher place among the masters that he could not possibly have experienced by himself. He did not have the shielding ability to protect himself and remain intact as an individual without some of the technology that was offered by the higher beings who took him to higher places.

This may sound strange to you, but Moses did not want to come back even though he knew what his mission was. If you were in a higher state of being in a beautiful dimension, you probably would not want to come back and suffer and struggle through certain difficult Earth events. In fact, some of you don't even want to stay here now and see some of the suffering and struggling on this planet. I'm sure you would much rather be back on a higher planet.

I don't feel — and Juliano agrees with me — that Jerusalem now is the most receptive place for a galactic holographic event. We still keep and hold Jerusalem in high energy, and there will be points of intervention there in the future. Clearly, the energy of Jerusalem must be protected so that it doesn't explode. A positive event could permeate the access point in Jerusalem. A negative event also would have no trouble permeating Earth, and such an event could holographically affect the whole planet immediately.

Create New Multidimensional Portals

The Arcturian planetary Tree of Life helps to create other access points and corresponding holographic events. These access points are etheric, multidimensional crystals. The Temple Mount in Jerusalem is multidimensional. Prophets went there in altered states and were able to go to different dimensions from there. We know that there is a great access point at the Temple Mount, but that area is not accessible to everyone. There is also the threat of violence there now because of the polarization and conflict among the groups who are trying to guard that energy.

Think about multidimensional points that have Arcturian etheric crystals, such as Lago Puelo and Mount Shasta. What does it mean that a point is multidimensional, and how does that apply to holographic energy? A multidimensional point or place can bring in special energies from higher dimensions. For planetary events, we look for powerful places on Earth. We also look to create new powerful places, and frankly, we want to create more of them. That is why we are working with you on the planetary ocean reserve project and the planetary cities of light project. We don't want to limit the number of power spots that have accessibility and permeability.

You and the Groups of Forty have the ability to create new multidimensional portals that could holographically influence this planet. Recently, we worked with Joatinga, which is a small beach approximately one-kilometer square and seventeen miles south of Rio de Janeiro. This beach and this work of making that place sacred illustrate the holographic principles of planetary healing that I speak of. Group of Forty lightworkers were able to gather about twenty people to perform a beautiful sacred ceremony there. Also they chose a place that had a certain higher energy already. Finally, they did an activation ceremony in which the Arcturians and the lightworkers connected fifth-dimensional energy to the sacred place.

Now that place has the power to holographically influence other parts of the ocean. This is the reverse of terrorism. Terrorism is trying to poison everyone through a negative act. In planetary holographic healing, we heal everyone from a small intervention in a very positive place. We elevate the sacred place and the consciousnesses of those who work with us to a very high point. This protocol is also true of the ladder of ascension. There is a mountain near Reno, Nevada, called Jobs Peak, that several of our Group of Forty members visited and brought a great healing force to. They were able to hold sacred energy there. It takes a long time to hike up to the peak, but they went to open the portal so that it could connect to other points of ascension.

Holographically, our work includes connecting Earth to other dimensions. In particular, we are connecting Earth to the fifth dimension. There are points where the fifth dimension can enter into the third dimension and begin to spread the power of healing and balance throughout this planet. Again, you might say, "How is it that one small point, like Joatinga Bay or Jobs Peak, can affect an entire planetary system?" What happens in a small part can affect the whole in holographic thinking.

Look at the reverse: How can Fukushima affect the whole ocean? It's only a small area where these nuclear power plants were destroyed and melted down. It is still not discussed, but it was a total meltdown, and what occurred in that one small area will affect the whole ocean for centuries. We can work together and send a powerful positive energy into the ocean by making small areas of the ocean sacred. This work is called the Planetary Ocean Reserve of Light project, and it uses the same holographic principles: A small area is chosen and made sacred, and it sends fifth-dimensional energy and light through the entire planet and the ocean.

You as starseeds have the power to create spiritual events. You can create planetary healing energy by going to power spots. Work with these holographic principles of accessibility and permeability. Maybe the spiritual event that you create will not have global publicity. This is one of the peculiarities of the media; that is, they seem to focus more on negative events. Whether or not the media recognizes the spiritual event does not diminish its effectiveness. However, we want you to achieve global consciousness and awareness because the more people are aware, the more they contribute.

Holographic Personal Healing

One of the ideas in personal healing in holographic work is to create the proper set [instructions] and use the correct setting. We already talked about the setting in our discussion about these power places and doing holographic healing interventions for the planet.

First, you would want to go to a power spot, such as the twelve etheric crystals or Jerusalem or Jobs Peak, or the ladders of ascension, such as Mount Tomaree or Grose Valley in Australia (which has a tremendous access point to planetary work) or Bell Rock in Sedona, Arizona. The set and the setting are important. For personal holographic healing, you want to use a power place. If you don't live near one of these points, you could go to a sacred place in your yard. Send light around your house, and put crystals in the four corners of your yard. The planetary cities of light are special places that have energy that can hold fifth-dimensional light. These cities are ideal settings for healing work. The setting includes when you set up the work and what time you do it.

You might want to do it at a power time, such as on a full moon when certain healing energies are available. Certainly, one of the principles of holographic work is doing the intervention at the right time. There is an interesting power alignment right now [December 5, 2015] with the Moon, Mars, Jupiter, and Venus. This is a time of great polarization, a time when some of the war energies on this planet are getting stronger. At the same time, spiritual warriors are getting stronger.

In fifth-dimensional holographic healing, we also use the setting of the holographic healing chamber on the starship Athena. The holographic healing chamber is a special energy field that we have created. You can enter it after your entry in the etheric world. You are transformed into multidimensional beings, and you can look at your entire self. On Earth, you have one aspect of your self, this Earth personality. But the truth is that if you look at your Earth self from the perspective of your higher self, you will see that you have had many lifetimes on other planets and you have had many lifetimes on this planet. Each lifetime seems to access or manifest a part of your self. In this lifetime now, each of you might have many aspects of your self manifested. You want to be in a setting where you can comprehend, balance, and interpret all these parts of your self. You don't want to be overwhelmed, either.

One of the problems with or side effects of accessing different parts of your self can be distortion and mental instability. If you look at the concept of multiple personality disorder, for example, one of the observations we have is that in this illness, mental stability breaks down. Those who suffer from it are not able to distinguish between the selves of their past lives and that of their current life, and they lose memory between each one. You might have been a warrior in another lifetime, but at this point, most of you would not want to be warriors. You wouldn't want to get into that side of your self without guidance or protection. There needs to be a certain higher, expanded consciousness where you can integrate and process the holographic aspects of your self.

There are certain planets in the galaxy that have good access to holographic energy of the self. Some planets are not as powerful and don't offer you that freedom, but Earth has the ability to provide holographic access to your past lives and your lives on other planets. You need to have the mental stability to deal with all this. Integrating the holographic parts of your self is very important. The final aspect is to send a healing balance to all the parts of your self.

While integrating past lives, people might believe that they have to heal every part of themselves in every lifetime. You might have had your energies taken away because you were a shaman when people didn't like shamans. There are many different reasons you might have unfinished business in other lifetimes. In truth, you could not complete all the unfinished business in all of your lifetimes even if you worked twenty-four hours a day on it. One of the other aspects of holographic healing is the necessity for a therapist, guide, or teacher to work with you. It's hard to heal yourself, and one reason is the risk of mental instability. You need to have somebody to anchor you.

A technique we use is to simply send a balancing and unifying energy to all parts of your self in all lifetimes that need healing, including in this lifetime. There might be parts you are not able to finish resolving in this lifetime. Perhaps you were not able to forgive someone or resolve your feelings. These are all serious issues.

There is a holographic healing technique in which you send back to all parts of your self a healing energy. You send this energy to all those parts that were unfinished, unresolved, or unbalanced and may have been traumatized. These parts will receive healing energy, healing unity, and balance. After such a healing, you could have a new attitude of acceptance that all is as it should be and that all those things, even though they were unfinished, contributed to a new state of balance within you. Then you could go back with a new perspective and look at some of these other events in this and previous lifetimes. You can forgive yourself, and you can even reshape some traumatic memories so that they do not interfere with your current level of functioning. The important thing in personal holographic healing is to send the healing energies to those parts of you that have been traumatized. Then allow those parts to use that energy for the highest good for your healing. Sometimes the holographic healing on a personal basis might be different from what you, in your third-dimensional consciousness, would expect.

In conclusion, holographic healing is both personal and planetary, and we will give you future lectures on how to use these principles for planetary and personal work more effectively. I am Helio-ah. Good day.

Chapter 19

Maintain Your Energy Fields with Spiritual Technology

Juliano and the Arcturians

Greetings, this is Juliano. We are the Arcturians! I want to speak about the Arcturian spiritual technology in relation to the third dimension and what is going on now in this dimension. I think that each time period has different spiritual technologies, so if you were living in Jerusalem in 800 or 500 BC, that spiritual technology would be different from what it is now. The spiritual technology at that time would be considered appropriate. It's amazing today to consider that animal sacrifice was widespread in Israel and Jerusalem in 590 BC. But today that certainly would not be considered appropriate. The circumstances of this reality now have particular needs, and there must be different spiritual techniques that will help you today to have the highest spiritual resonance, the cleanest aura, and the most openings in all four of your bodies. You must have openings and clearings in your emotional, spiritual, physical, and mental bodies.

Some of the techniques that were used in 600 BC might still be appropriate. For example, they had great abilities to do sound vibrational work and other advanced spiritual techniques. To evaluate which spiritual practices are necessary now, we must take into consideration the core situation occurring on this planet.

When Galaxies Collide

The third dimension and the fifth dimension are moving closer together now, and they are beginning to interact in very interesting and complex ways. The dimensions have not yet touched each other, but they are coming close. Let's compare the intersection of the dimensions to two galaxies intersecting or colliding. For example, let's use the neighboring galaxy known as the Andromeda galaxy and our galaxy known as the Milky Way galaxy. Our galaxy might be as far as 5 million light-years from the Andromeda galaxy. That is a huge distance, but in terms of the measurement of distances in the universe, it is not a great distance. Consider that some galaxies are between 10 and 12 billion light-years away. The Andromeda galaxy is on a path that eventually is going to collide with the Milky Way galaxy. This collision is going to occur sometime in the future.

There are examples in modern astronomy of galaxies colliding. These collisions look quite beautiful and have very interesting light patterns. If you were in a galaxy in a particular star system and a star from another galaxy collided with yours as the two galaxies collided, you might not have the same opinion.

Galaxies are huge, and when two collide, neither is totally destroyed. However, some interesting explosions might occur from the interaction. The resulting intersection of the two galaxies might create a supergalaxy unlike any galaxy in this section of the universe.

Visualize the spiral galaxies of both Andromeda and the Milky Way. They are far apart now, 5 million light-years. It will take millions of years for this collision to occur. Thus, it will not happen in your lifetime. However, the Andromeda galaxy is the closest galaxy to the Milky Way, and we consider the Andromeda galaxy our sister galaxy.

Some of you starseeds have lived on the Andromeda galaxy in other lifetimes. There are different civilizations and different patterns of growth and evolution in the Andromeda galaxy. Intersecting these two galaxies might produce a superintelligent, highly evolved galactic civilization. As I said, it could also produce some explosions and collisions.

With this analogy, let us take this into the existence of the third and the fifth dimensions. I look at the third dimension as a gigantic sphere. (It's difficult to give you a description of a whole dimension because it does not have the confines of lines.) It is extremely difficult to come up with a third-dimensional shape of a dimension. If you were to ask for a description of the shape of the universe, it would also be difficult because the universe is infinite, so there is no outer line. But due to your limitations, we will use the example of the third-dimensional sphere and apply it to the fifth dimension.

There are attractor forces of unknown origin throughout the universe. Galaxies are attracted to each other. Our galaxy is part of a system or group of galaxies that are bound by an attracting force, and this collection of galaxies is called the local group, which consists of twelve, thirteen, or fourteen different galaxies. There also exists a force attracting the interaction of the third and fifth dimensions. This type of interaction was not happening in 500 BC in ancient Israel or in ancient Greece or during the Roman Empire. This new interaction is in part why there must be more advanced and specific spiritual methods and technologies developed for the current situation. These two dimensions are getting closer.

To summarize, the intersection of a collision of the Andromeda galaxy with the Milky Way galaxy could result in some interesting and highly evolved interactions. Some civilizations might become super-civilizations. On the other hand, there could be some explosions and destruction as large bodies, suns, and star systems come close to other bodies. It could create all kinds of unknown and aberrant gravitational fields that could throw things off. This aberrational gravitational field pattern has been suggested within the Milky Way galaxy and even in your solar system.

Reversal of Your Evolutionary Process

The intersection of the fifth and third dimension is going to produce highly evolved energy, new spiritual technologies, and many advancements. Also, it will cause disruptions and aberrations, unusual thought patterns, and unusual energy fields. To assimilate and process the intersection of these dimensions and the energy it brings, you must do certain spiritual practices and techniques.

One of the spiritual techniques needed is the ability to be receptive to different energy fields. You have to be open to such things as vibrational energy, auras, thought projection, bilocation, shimmering, the cosmic egg, and the Arcturian temple and the stargate. These are just a few of the technologies that will help you to receive, assimilate, and work with fifth-dimensional energy. If you are not open to the vibrational energy fields, the thought fields, and the aura work, then the incoming energy from the higher realms will be experienced as disorganized and chaotic.

The effects on your thought and emotional patterns could cause a regression of the evolution of humanity. When you are in a confused or chaotic energy state, for example, it is known in your modern psychology that you could revert to an earlier time when you had unresolved issues. You could use coping mechanisms that are quite primitive. Does this sound like what you're seeing now on the third dimension?

In many ways, you're seeing reversals of your evolutionary process. You're seeing the increase of primitive energy, and this is partly due to the high frequencies coming in and the inability of many people to process them. The Arcturian spiritual technology is being offered for this period to help you with this particular reality. Our spiritual exercises and techniques are offered to assist you in this time and in this unique environment. No matter what happens now, no matter how much chaos there is or how much regression in thought forms and activity, you can still hold on to your spiritual centeredness for balance.

Humans' Subtle Energy Fields

Computer technology is a continuation of the mental mind of humanity. Many of the Arcturian terminologies and processes relate symbolically to your computer technology. These terms especially have meaning when we describe the human evolution, the human brain, and the mind. One of our favorite terms is "updating." Do you update your computer software? Have you downloaded the latest additions to your antivirus software? Do you have the latest antimalware on your computer? You might notice these updates happen frequently, sometimes daily. Why is that? The reason is that many people on this planet have negative energy and try to do bad things. One of the bad things people like to do is harm computer systems.

You have to continually update your spiritual energy field. One of the Arcturian spiritual technologies updates your aura and energy field based on the new configurations and energies in existence. It can be a dynamic task to upgrade and update your energy field. Please do not think that once you have achieved an adequate understanding and protection that you are finished with your energy work. No! The Arcturian spiritual technology also helps you to update your energy field to be in alignment with the new shifts.

Some of you are experiencing the recent magnetic storms that occurred on the Sun last week [**Author's Note:** On January 2, 2016, there was a coronal mass ejection on the Sun] and the release of negative energies that have come from certain blockages in Earth's meridians. There has also been a downloading of higher frequencies. Earth's energy field is shifting dramatically on a daily basis, and you are all encouraged to update your shields and your energy fields.

Because things are changing so quickly, it is now required to update all four bodies (physical, emotional, spiritual, and mental). This is something that was not necessary in 500 BC. There were many changes in the social, economic, and political arenas, and there were wars at that time in the ancient world, but the situation wasn't complex in regard to humans' subtle energy fields. In contrast, even the radio wave energies today on this planet are shifting people's subtle energy fields.

The radio frequencies and the electromagnetic energy field of this planet are shifting dramatically. The recent solar coronal magnetic emission dramatically affected the electromagnetic energy field of the planet. Some of you probably felt this shift, and maybe you found yourselves a little confused, tired, or disoriented. This reaction is on top of all the other events occurring on this planet.

You are in a highly accelerated period that is remarkable for its immediate and long-lasting transformations. Changes are occurring on this planet that normally would take 20,000 to 30,000 years or even longer. You are seeing these changes happen, in some cases, in three months or even less. That means that in terms of evolution, a 20,000-year period would be needed for a climate change to occur. In 30 or 40 years, you've seen climate changes that normally would take thousands of years. How has your energy field adapted to these dramatic climate changes?

Your immune system has to be updated when there are dramatic climate changes. You have experienced changes in your electromagnetic energy field that have been so rapid that you might have had difficulty upgrading your system. There's been a lot of difficulty in electromagnetic shielding. Your immune system is under a lot of stress because of the dramatic transformational changes you are witnessing on Earth.

The fourth dimension is a lower dimension, and it has lower vibrations. There are different levels of the fourth dimension: the lower, middle, and upper fourth dimensions. There are some very high beings on the fourth dimension. But the lower fourth dimension contains ghosts and other negative spirits who can often be mischievous. Some of these beings are parasitic, and they attach to people on the third dimension. This is a time on Earth when people's auras and energy fields are especially susceptible and vulnerable, particularly due to high drug usage. The strength of the human aura has weakened overall, often resulting in confusion and disorganization.

There have been some military experiments and activities that have damaged the protective, etheric layer between the third and fourth dimensions, creating holes in Earth's energy fields. I'm referring to specific examples of high frequency radiation activities (HAARP). Some of the recent wars used techniques that severely damaged the core etheric energy field of countries in the Middle East. This happened in the Iraqi War where the military used certain secret weaponry that disoriented and damaged the Iraqi soldiers, and it also damaged Earth's aura in that area. Negative forces from the lower fourth dimension are attaching themselves to you and creating violent acts in that area of the Middle East. All of these events make it necessary for you to upgrade your aura.

Energy-Field Upgrade Meditation

Visualize your aura as four layers. You have the spiritual layer, the emotional layer, the mental layer, and the physical layer. They are all separate energy fields. Command your aura and four bodies to take the shape of the cosmic egg. Command that they all interact and merge in balance. Your spiritual energy is in balance with your mental energy, your mental energy is in balance with your emotional energy, and your emotional energy is in balance with your physical energy. Let them all respond to this rhythmic tone. [Tones several times: To to to to toooo.]

Let the four bodies come into balance in your aura as they all go into the shape of the cosmic egg, and see a smoothness around each system. Know that if one system goes out of balance, then the others will help bring it back into balance. Your emotional system can go out of balance due to a negative event. This may induce fear or anxiety. Your spiritual body is especially strong, and it can loan your emotional body the energy it needs to heal itself. Your emotional body is receptive to the high spiritual energy and the high spiritual light quotient you are carrying with you now.

Say these words: "My spiritual body is so strong that it can heal any imperfections in my emotional body now." *Repeat:* "My spiritual body is so strong that it can heal any imperfections in my emotional body now." *Meditate on that statement. We will go into silence. [Pauses.]*

I, Juliano, am sending an upgrade of light and energy into each of your crown chakras. This energy light will go into your spiritual body. [Tones several times: Ohhhhhh.] There is a golden fifth-dimensional light coming into your crown chakra and going into your spiritual body. You are able to store much higher light in your spiritual body. This higher light can be used for healing your mental, emotional, and physical bodies.

Let that energy now flow into your other three bodies. We'll go into silence now. [Pauses.]

Earth Is Struggling for Balance

Earth's energy field also experiences these dramatic energy changes. You are planetary healers working hard to interact with the spirit of Earth. Earth is making a very intense effort to update its feedback loop systems so that it can hold its balance. But Earth is having trouble. Some of the expressions of this trouble will be seen as more violent reactions, such as fierce weather patterns, geological shifts, and an overall climate change.

Earth as a spirit really wants to hold, to the best of its ability, the systems' balance that will allow humanity to exist. Earth is struggling and is now out of balance. Earth wants to hold the existing temperatures and weather patterns that are most advantageous to humanity. Earth doesn't want global warming or to see humanity destroyed. As I said earlier, it is a great honor for a planet to have high beings on it.

You are working as planetary healers sending light and thoughts to the noosphere. You are working to increase the number of planetary cities of light. You are doing many other things that are extremely helpful. You are helping to update and work intensively with Earth's spirit. Earth has a planetary spirit, and updates are necessary. This is why it is so important to continue to rapidly increase the planetary cities of light, because they help in the updating process to bring sacred light and a new balance to Earth. Each one of you is open to this new balance.

Use Spiritual Tools to Maintain Your Energy Field

It is important to update your immune system, and many of these updates can be done by bringing down fifth-dimensional energy. One of the greatest tools that we teach is to access your multidimensional presence through thought projection. Many of the updates that you need are in your fifth-dimensional body, so when you bilocate and shimmer and go to the crystal lake, you will meet and interact with your fifth-dimensional body. As you stay in your fifth-dimensional body, you can receive these updates, and then you can etherically bring the energies with the updates back into your aura and back into your body . This is one of the most effective tools in updating.

A similar method is bilocation. Bilocation is a slight variation from thought projection. Bilocation is described as being in two different places in the physical world. In essence, using bilocation you send yourself through thought projection to another place. Shimmering is another technology that helps you to heal the aura. In shimmering, you accelerate the pulse of your aura so that your aura moves into a higher alignment with the fifth dimension.

Get comfortable, take three deep breaths, and feel a golden light gently descend around you. It is a protective ball of light that has an opening to a fifth-dimensional corridor above you. Allow your spirit body, your aura, to rise. Your etheric double goes into this corridor and travels with me at the speed of thought to the Arcturian temple. [Chants: Ta ta ta ta ta ta ta ta ta ta ta ta.] At the speed of thought, you immediately arrive at the crystal lake. Look down to find your fifth-dimensional body sitting there in a comfortable position. Some of you will see that body in a yoga pose; others will see your fifth-dimensional body sitting in a chair or even standing. Find your fifth-dimensional body.

Helio-ah and I worked with your fifth-dimensional bodies before you came. To use a modern computer term, we have updated your energy field with the latest "firmware." These updates will result in your highest functioning on the third dimension now.

Enter your fifth-dimensional body now. Again, the highest technique for increasing your immune system, for updating all four bodies, including your emotional body, is found in your fifth-dimensional body. Enter your fifth-dimensional body and receive these new updates for your system. We will go into silence now as you receive these new updates. [Pauses.]

These updates include information on how to keep your aura stronger and how to protect your immune system. I know some of you are concerned about certain insects and mosquitoes carrying diseases. For example, this is a concern now in Brazil.

These updates are critical for your immune system. They will improve your emotional body and your mental body. You must have the most advanced thoughts and the most advanced ideas for this dimensional interaction and how it affects so many people. [Chants: Ohhhhhh several times.] The updates are finished.

Now release yourself. Flow upward from your fifth-dimensional body, rise to the top of the crystal lake, and take my hand as we travel at the speed of thought back into your physical Earth body. [Chants: ta ta ta ta ta ta ta ta ta ta ta ta ta.] You are in direct alignment now with your physical body and your etheric body with all this new information. These new updates will help you to function with the changing environment, the changing energy fields, in the dramatic events that are unfolding on this planet. You will be able to maintain your unified energy field. Go into perfect alignment three feet above your physical body, and at the count of three, reenter. One, two, three! Your spirit body has reentered your physical body with all of the updates.

It will take approximately forty-eight hours to download all of this information and the updates. Even though we were only on the fifth dimension for several minutes, the amount of information, energy, and updates you received were very high because of your receptivity to get higher information and higher programs. You will feel little surges of energy and light throughout the next forty-eight hours.

* * *

I bless each one of you. Know that this technology is helpful, especially now. You will find an increase of so many of your skills now, particularly your planetary healing skills. I am Juliano. Good day!

Chapter 20

Fifth-Dimensional Consciousness

Juliano and the Arcturians

Greetings, this is Juliano. We are the Arcturians. It is our belief that the next step in the evolution of humanity is to obtain fifth-dimensional consciousness. We can look at the evolution of the human species and see that during many different crises, adaptations and changes were made in the genetic structure and the manifestation of the physical body on Earth. These changes were necessary for humanity's survival on Earth. Now humanity is again at a crisis point of great magnitude. The change necessary for humanity to survive and evolve to a better place requires a specific, directed shift and expansion of consciousness. Humanity now exhibits a narrow consciousness.

Consciousness is very difficult to describe. It is something that everybody can recognize when they are aware of it. A simple and modified definition of consciousness is awareness and self-awareness. The evolution or expansion of fifth-dimensional consciousness means that the human being can become aware of the existence and the energy of the fifth dimension and the thoughts and vibrations there. In fact, communications continually stream from the fifth dimension to the third dimension. Fifth-dimensional consciousness is a heightened state that is part of your inherent genetic structure, and it affects all four bodies it exists on: the emotional, mental, physical, and spiritual. To ascend, one must have fifth-dimensional consciousness.

The Emotional Body

As we have mentioned, to enter the fifth dimension, you have to refine and move your emotional body to a higher plane. For example, jealousy, hatred, and violence are not fifth dimensional. People who experience the lower vibrations, or the lower emotional feelings, will not be able to enter it. You cannot bring those emotions into the fifth dimension. You have to be at a higher vibration — one in which you experience love, unity, and acceptance. Those who act out of hatred and commit terroristic acts are not allowed.

I know that many of you are doing very serious work to clear and heal your emotional bodies. This clearing and healing work is one of the personal tasks in life for all beings who come to this planet. It is a noble and highly regarded task. I am convinced that your work will be sufficient to allow you to enter the fifth dimension. Entry into the fifth dimension does not require perfection. If you cannot purify your emotional body 100 percent, do not worry, because you are committed and working toward that level of purification, and your intent is important. The fact that you are working on these issues carries a great deal of weight for those higher beings who guard the fifth dimension and make decisions on who can enter it.

How does your emotional body react to the cosmic drama that is now occurring on Earth? This cosmic drama contains many tragic aspects, and even as I briefly summarize them, I am sure it will evoke emotional reactions, such as sadness and confusion. This planet has dying oceans, polluted air, and contamination in all aspects of the biosphere. This planet is now in the middle phase of its sixth mass extinction. Mass extinctions have also occurred on other planetary systems throughout the galaxy. I call this a cosmic drama because the themes that are playing out are common throughout this section of the galaxy. In fact, some of these themes are purposely manifesting at this time in hopes of purification and resolution. I am sure that everyone has an emotional reaction to what is now occurring on this planet.

When I talk about the ascension, I often tell starseeds that you must develop a response of detachment from what is occurring. At the same time, there is a paradox because being detached does not mean that you are indifferent or that you stop trying to help Earth or its society. This is one of the most difficult concepts to explain regarding fifth-dimensional, emotional evolution. How could one be detached yet still be deeply involved? This is not a time for you to live in a cave and try to ignore what is going on.

Equanimity as a Form of Higher Detachment

One of the higher states of being for the emotional body is referred to as "equanimity." This high state of consciousness is even classified as a fifth-dimensional emotion. In reality, you may have jealousy, anger, fear, love, and other strong emotions. This is a natural occurrence in the third dimension. Equanimity is defined as being even-tempered or unaffected by what is occurring. It implies that even if someone is insulting you, your attitude, self-esteem, and feeling of well-being are not affected. You are able to maintain this state, which I call emotional balance. The few people who have attained equanimity are still able to do valuable service to this planet, for themselves, and for others. This state of equanimity is a type of higher-level detachment. In fifth-dimensional consciousness, there is great value and importance to equanimity.

Detachment means that you are not affixed or tied to the outcome on Earth and you could let everything go. Some starseeds have complained about this description. They have responded that they want to return to Earth after their ascension. Many say that they have already made the decision to come back to Earth. To me, this is a sign that they are still connected and are not totally detached from the outcome of Earth's drama. I understand this, and I'd like to point out that your identity, your self-esteem for the most part, is tied to your Earth self. We are trying to work with you to broaden your identity to include your fifth-dimensional self, but frankly, the third-dimensional self has more power and gets your attention more often.

Let us again look at the concept of equanimity as a form of higher detachment. Surely you who are working for the ascension have a commitment to this Earth, and you might choose to continue your work on Earth after you ascend into the fifth dimension. I honor that commitment. You are working toward attaining this equanimity as part of your preparation for the ascension. This is a more evolved detachment that will allow you to leave Earth with a higher level of spiritual energy. The idea of an attachment is often defined as sticking to Earth, sticking to the third dimension. You have family, you have children, you have pets, and you might have financial interests that are extremely attractive to you. To be detached means you are willing to let those things go.

For example, you might be committed to your Earth family, and the idea of leaving your loved ones behind during the ascension is extremely difficult. Often, family members do not share in your fifth-dimensional evolution and your desire to work on your fifth-dimensional consciousness. That is why I am expanding this discussion into attaining equanimity. Equanimity affects both how you look at the planet and the planetary drama as well as how you look at your personal life, your Earth family, and how people treat you. Working on fifth-dimensional consciousness often provokes anger, criticism, and other negative comments. The majority of the population still generally feels that speaking about the ascension, spiritual evolution, and fifth-dimensional consciousness is verboten. Many people in society think that only crazy people perform fifth-dimensional spiritual practices. To make matters even more difficult, there are people who want to exploit and control starseeds who are working so hard to evolve.

Ego-Centered Consciousness and Protecting Vulnerabilities

This brings me to the next aspect of the emotional evolution toward the fifth dimension: the ego. The ego is a subject of much debate in the history of psychology, philosophy, and religion. It is a state of consciousness. The ego is basically more focused on the animal instincts that are within humanity — self-satisfaction, self-control, greed, and domination, all of which are now strongly coming to everyone's attention on Earth. It is helpful that these are coming to a global awareness because that makes it more difficult for people to hide this part of themselves, especially in the political world. Those people who are egocentric and wanting to dominate are being revealed to everyone.

The ego is more connected to aspects of the animal self, which were necessary for survival in the past. But what was necessary for survival yesterday in the jungle sometimes can be a hindrance to what is necessary for survival today in the modern world. The ego is individualistic, focused on making gains for the self, and is not necessarily for humanity.

Egocentric consciousness often is the opposite of unity consciousness.

Unity consciousness is a higher fifth-dimensional aspect that is of a more evolved emotional state. Unity consciousness is difficult to achieve when you live on a planet dominated by self-centeredness, greed, and control. There are certain vulnerabilities for everyone who is on the fifth-dimensional evolution track. You must be aware of your vulnerabilities, and you must have certain levels of protection.

Now let me compare this again to evolution. If you look at the evolutionary steps and gains that have been made by humankind, you will see that they weren't always immediately successful. I'd like to point out that the Cro-Magnon might have been physically weaker than the Neanderthal, yet the Cro-Magnon had higher intellectual functioning. This is not to say that the Neanderthal were stupid. This species was also relatively intelligent. The Cro-Magnon were able to overcome vulnerabilities and use their higher intellectual powers for protection, and eventually, this species was able to dominate, control, and even contribute to the extinction of the Neanderthal. There are many people who now believe that the genetic structure of the Neanderthal still exists in humanity, as there was cross-fertilization between the two species. How were the Cro-Magnon able to protect their vulnerabilities? Through their intelligence, they learned to use fire, develop tools, and create boundaries. The Cro-Magnon were on a higher evolutionary tract, both emotionally and intellectually, than the Neanderthal.

Now you starseeds who are fifth dimensional and working on fifth-dimensional consciousness also have vulnerabilities and sensitivities. There are people who laugh at you. There are people who do not pay attention to you, and there are even people who want to dominate and control you, as you are a small minority on this planet. This, then, leads to the discussion of vulnerability, protection, and boundaries. As I said, the Cro-Magnon had to develop boundaries, and this was one of the keys to their success because it was done in a very effective way. I have suggestions on how to apply this to modern starseed vulnerabilities.

Empathy Is a Vulnerability with Advantages

First, let's talk about why you might have vulnerabilities. The first point is that you are very sensitive. Some people have called many of the starseeds "empaths." Empaths are people who sense other people's feelings and receive thought waves and energies. They are directly affected by what other people think and feel. There are some advantages to this. This ability is usually a first step toward psychic gifts, such as telepathy.

One of the problems with being so sensitive is that you can pick up information and energy that you don't want or are not able to deal with. On Arcturus and other fifth-dimensional planets, everything is telepathic; there is no hiding of thoughts or feelings. In the evolution of fifth-dimensional emotions, there is no need or desire to hide thoughts. Being totally open in this way would not work on the third dimension, as you know. Some of the starseeds even complain, saying, "I wish I weren't so sensitive. I wish I were not picking up all of these feelings. I'm picking up too much energy. I don't want to know what everybody is feeling."

Also, on a planetary basis, these people are so sensitive that they pick up negative energy from a variety of sources. Some of the negative energy could be coming from galactic sources. Some of it could be from extraterrestrial sources that are invading or intruding on the planet, and some could even be from fourth-dimensional sources.

The veil between the fourth and third dimensions has been weakening on planet Earth. There are various reasons for this weakening. Some of it has to do with military experiments that have led to destruction of parts of the veil or holes in Earth's aura. Some of this has even resulted in holes in people's auras. Negative spirits pass through these holes. This is a complicated and easily documented observation. For example, many acts of totally illogical violence are occurring on the planet. These acts show the negative results of when a lower spirit enters and cohabitates negatively with a vulnerable person.

Cultural Upbringing and Sensitivity

The second point about vulnerability has to do with your cultural upbringing. You are a starseed, and many of you are awakening to your fifth-dimensional awareness, work, and consciousness later in life. When you were young, you were exposed to common Earth traumas and psychological constraints of being raised in an Earth family, and for the most part, your spiritual sensitivity was not encouraged. That usually means you had to grow up hiding your true nature. There have been continual global dramas and catastrophes since your childhood. These events and wars proliferate, causing numerous traumas. It is difficult to deal with sensitivity, spiritual awareness, and fifth-dimensional energy when you are traumatized.

Spiritual sensitivity can be developed during traumatic experiences, but it requires assistance and persistence and usually counseling from higher beings to help you through those events. Trauma in youth often means you end up constraining and contracting yourself, and this includes constraining your consciousness. Generally, if you and your valves of consciousness were totally open, then you would see reality as an energetic vibration. It might even be entertaining to see the world in that way. Some of you have had that experience with psychedelic drugs — for example, seeing energetic waves, auras, and even thought patterns. But needless to say, you were probably overwhelmed, and it would be difficult for you to function in daily life on that level. For a person to function on that level and be able to see all these energies and vibrations (including being able to read thoughts and continually maintain empathic feeling levels), he or she would need special training and boundary techniques for protection.

Now, as an adult, you can continue to develop your sensitivity. You need it because it is your sensitivity that is allowing you to go into the fifth dimension and to feel and receive fifth-dimensional impressions and light frequencies. But be aware of some of the dangers and the necessity for boundaries, protection, and shielding.

You Are a Vessel Holding Light

Let's compare needing boundaries to the creation of the universe. In early mystical thinking, it is said that the higher spiritual energy light was brought to this universe, but the vessels that were to hold this light shattered. This is an interesting metaphor for you, because I want you to think of yourself as a vessel of light. You are in a state of evolution. You are on the forefront of evolution for humanity. You might not be able to hold all this energy and may need to moderate it to protect yourself. You might need to close down the perceptual valves at times so you don't feel as much. Some of the lower beings entering Earth might even try to dominate and control you. I say this honestly because one of the big lessons on Earth is how to live in spiritual brother- and sisterhood with everyone.

Earth has a history of control and domination when it comes to religious and spiritual work. If you are a student of history, you know about all the religious wars that have been fought on this planet. Even today, you see clashes of cultures and religions that have led to terrible and tragic consequences. It is difficult to hold equanimity in the face of these outrageous, destructive, and tragic interactions. Polarizing wars are exactly the opposite of the unity consciousness that is necessary for moving into the fifth dimension. But you can protect yourself. This is the beautiful thing about fifth-dimensional consciousness, because it includes protection for the emotional, mental, physical, and spiritual bodies.

Discover a New World Consciousness

I want to explore the other three bodies and how they relate to your evolution as fifth-dimensional beings. Reaching the fifth dimension is comparable to the discovery of the New World in 1492. It is amazing that the people in Spain at that time did not know of the Americas before Columbus landed, and they discovered the New World with new energy and new ideas. It is interesting that they immediately tried to control it, setting off a chain reaction for domination of the Americas. Vast majorities of the native peoples were killed, and there was greed and spiritual constriction. I look at the fifth dimension as a New World. This is a time when there are great connections through corridors to the fifth dimension. The interaction of the fifth with the third dimension can be used to solve Earth's problems.

There are people who might want to take advantage of the fifth dimension, exploiting it for personal gain and ego purposes. This is exactly why there is a certain vibrational frequency that is necessary; it is so that only those on that level can enter into the fifth dimension. At this time on Earth, it is necessary to bring in more fifth-dimensional energy because third-dimensional belief systems and thinking are based on logic and finite energy patterns. Many people are using the third dimension for greed and domination. Fifth-dimensional thinking and belief systems can shift such attitudes, and some of these higher energy belief systems need to be instilled in the third-dimensional consciousness. Some of these belief systems can be instilled through the noosphere and planetary subconscious.

Some of these higher principles actually need to be taught, including unity consciousness, quantum healing, and quantum light, as well as the idea that Earth is a living spirit and planet that has self-regulation methods. Another fifth-dimensional observation is that Earth can be communicated with through spiritual intervention such as Biorelativity.

Manifestation Follows Consciousness

There are many paradoxes now operating on Earth. One of these paradoxes is that people who seek to control the planet have more power than starseeds and fifth-dimensional beings. This leads me to an important principle. Manifestation follows consciousness. I repeat: Manifestation follows consciousness. When you are in the fifth dimension and you want to manifest a temple or a crystal or even a spaceship, you work on this first through consciousness. Since you will have more powers on the fifth dimension than on the third dimension, you can directly manifest what you think. It must come into your consciousness first, and then you will be able to manifest it.

All of you are probably trying to manifest higher energy on the third dimension. You want to manifest your fifth-dimensional energies on the third dimension, but you are finding that there are blocks and time constraints to manifestation. Your thoughts, even though they are of a high vibration, do not seem to manifest immediately, and in some cases, they may take years to fully manifest. I have heard these complaints. Why aren't your acts and thoughts immediately manifesting? The answer is complex and paradoxical: Earth is slowed down. This means that Earth is a slower and denser environment for thinking and manifestation. Earth is a school, and when you're in school, there are classes and certain restraints set up to allow you to make mistakes. School must be structured with room for mistakes. You have to allow students to make mistakes, but do it with kindness and compassion.

Compassion is another important aspect of higher, fifth-dimensional emotions. We also accept strictness, judgments, and constraint when these traits are expressed with compassion. At this time on the planet, when compassion alone doesn't always work for many people, they will continue to abuse and dominate Earth. There is a need for exhibiting justice and strength with compassion. Because Earth is a school that slows manifestation, you need more patience. You have to be more consistent, and you also have to learn some of the tricks of manifesting.

One of the tricks is to work together in large groups, which can often counteract the resistance to change and manifestations on the third dimension. Please do not get discouraged with this process. You are living in a slower energetic environment, namely the third dimension. There is a certain level of purification that you must accomplish in your thinking and in your work as a "manifester" on Earth. You need to learn how to think and how to manifest properly. This is preparation for your fifth-dimensional work. If you decide to continue to work on Earth after you ascend, then you can return as an ascended master and provide great teachings and demonstrations.

There is also manifestation of fifth-dimensional energy in the physical body. Some can be accomplished through diet, vibrational medicine such as Reiki, or body-healing techniques that are emerging.

There are new energy patterns coming to Earth that have dramatic healing abilities. A hundred years from now, people are going to look back and be shocked at how primitive and dangerous many of your medical techniques are. But there is a way to bring your body into vibrational healing and your mental body into higher belief systems that are in alignment with the fifth dimension. The best advice for you is that you need to learn to connect and expand your identity to include your higher self and your fifth-dimensional body. You've been trained in your upbringing to only think of yourself as this third-dimensional being. It is time to expand your consciousness.

I honor you in your great work [chants: Oooo]. Seek now equanimity. Create the necessary shield around your vibrational energy field that only lets in higher light, higher vibrations, and those energies that lower energies cannot penetrate. Allow your emotional, mental, and physical bodies to evolve into fifth-dimensional levels. Let your higher spiritual body come into your Earth body. You, as a vessel, can hold higher light on Earth. Visualize now your fifth-dimensional body. Connect with that body, and let it bring you the strength to protect all of your vulnerabilities and all of your sensitivities. Be able to live with equanimity, strength, and spiritual unity, and please know you are on the forefront of this next step in human evolution — fifth-dimensional consciousness. I am Juliano. Good day!

Chapter 21

Tools for Dimensional Shifting

Juliano and the Arcturians

Greetings, this is Juliano. We are the Arcturians! Today, I am going to introduce a new topic called dimensional shifting. This term has some important implications for your ascension and for maintaining your higher perspective on Earth during this time of dramatic change and crises. Dimensional shifting relates directly to your ability to go into different dimensions with your consciousness. Each of you enters another dimension every night when you are in the sleep state. In the sleep state, you go through several different states of consciousness. Eventually, you enter the dream state, which is characterized by rapid eye movement, or REM. At that point, you officially enter the fourth dimension, which has different systems classified as its lower, middle, and higher levels. During the sleep state, you enter, or shift into, another dimension. Dimensionally shifting is a natural ability in humans. It is part of the normal course of the workings of human consciousness.

Dimensional shifting is a key concept in your ascension. You want to be able to shift your consciousness into the fifth dimension at the point of ascension. You must begin the process of shifting your consciousness now. Every night, you practice how to shift your consciousness in the dream state. Think about how many days there are in a year and how many years you have been alive, and multiply those numbers to determine the number of times you have experienced or practiced going into this dream state of consciousness.

I realize that not everyone goes into the dream state with ease, but basically you've all had that experience. Now, how often have you shifted into the fifth-dimensional consciousness? Why do I use the word "shift"? There is a new spiritual technology we offer based on the teachings of the Arcturians and the ascension. This new spiritual technology includes basic exercises for dimensional shifting, such as shimmering, bilocation, and thought projection. These exercises are based on the concept of the energetic vibrational aura.

The Intersection of the Dimensions

Dimensional shifting involves a basic change in your perception. In bilocation or thought projection, we help you move your astral body into the fifth dimension. In this exercise called dimensional shifting, you stay in this reality and perceive the interaction of the fifth dimension in the third dimension. The reason this is possible relates to the intersection of the dimensions. We view each dimension as a total and separate sphere. Perhaps we could even use the analogy of a ball. The third and fifth dimensions are separate spheres that are beginning to interact.

Compare this to the gravitational fields in astronomy. All the planets are affected by the larger bodies, such as the stars, because of gravitation. Even though the planets might be separated by great distances, their gravitational fields still affect each other. This is also true in the description of the dimensions. We are approaching a point that I call the intersection of the dimensions, when the attraction between the two spheres increases because the two dimensions are coming closer. The intersection of these dimensions will cause a dramatic influx of spiritual energy and spiritual consciousness, as well as the ascension.

The energy of the fifth dimension is different. It operates on different principles. You can break the laws of physics in the third dimension into four types of forces: electromagnetic, strong, weak, and gravitational. But these forces are not applicable to fifth-dimensional energy. Also, the whole concept of space-time in the fifth dimension is dramatically different than space-time in the third dimension. What you might be experiencing now is the closeness of these dimensions, which is helping to expand your abilities.

The fifth and the third dimensions have not intersected yet. However, beings of light (ascended masters) have gone to the fifth dimension and returned to the third. Many of you are studying to be ascended masters. You are focusing on your teachers in the fifth dimension, and many of you are doing this very successfully. I'm very proud of you. You are following your intuition. Sometimes you do this alone because more conservative and orthodox people on this planet are not open to the ascended masters and their teachings. Because the fifth and third dimensions are closer, there are more opportunities now to receive and interact with fifth-dimensional energy and light.

Shimmer to Increase Your Spiritual Power

There are many advantages to dimensional shifting, such as how the shifting affects your physical, mental, spiritual, and emotional bodies. To help you understand this concept, I will discuss mechanics. Let's use the transmission of an automobile as an analogy for dimensional shifting.

The basic automobile has a transmission and an engine, and we have the concept revolutions per minute (RPMs). In the past, primitive automobiles had three gears, so the transmission shifted from first to second to third. Transmissions in newer cars have five speeds: first, second, third, fourth, and fifth! I hope you can see the analogy already. In dimensional shifting, we are talking about the ability to shift to higher functioning and higher movement. I still see the gasoline engine as a primitive engine; nonetheless, we are talking about an improving technology because now the modern gasoline engine functions with five speeds. It can function at a higher performance. Also, the engine will not wear out easily because it has additional gears.

Now, if you go up a hill or run into resistance, you have to shift to a lower gear, and in that lower gear, the engine and the transmission work harder and the RPMs increase. This analogy is also true on the third dimension. When you see blocks and a lot of resistance, you have to work harder to overcome them. When you see a lot of lower energy, you might experience a feeling similar to going up a hill and your engine working harder.

Now for this discussion, let's change RPM to FPS (frequency per second). As a vessel in this energy field called the third dimension, you are required to work at a certain frequency-per-second vibration. The third dimension is at a lower frequency vibration than the fifth dimension.

If you want to understand and experience the higher frequency, you need to be able to change gears. You have to practice shifting your consciousness and your perspectives to do what I call dimensional shifting. If you only have three speeds in your transmission, then you are able to function at a certain level and might have some problems maintaining your engine. A modern car, such as the Honda Accord with its six-speed transmission, is able to go up mountains maybe in fourth gear and sometimes even in fifth gear. This is because of the sophistication of the transmission and the engine. I hope you can see these parallels and the application because I want to help you understand how to change your dimensional gears and perceptions.

Shimmering is a spiritual exercise that increases your aura's FPS. Imagine that you are going up a hill and you need more RPMs. The engine can adjust and provide the power you need. Shimmering can give you more spiritual power.

When you go up a hill and it is hot outside and you haven't changed your radiator fluid in a while, you might find that you have a blockage somewhere in your cooling system. Your engine could overheat. The overheating could happen even though you're in the right gear and you have the ability to shift. Compare this to the work you have to do to keep your cooling system in your vessel clear. You have to practice the frequency-per-second vibrational speed exercises, and you have to purify yourself to make sure that there are no blockages, just as you need to clean the radiator system and removing any impurities or obstructions. Flushing to remove particles or blockages in the system ensures that the cooling is sufficient even when there is resistance, which you encounter when you drive up a hill.

You are at a point on this planet when there is a lot of resistance as you "drive uphill." You might have to go to a lower gear to get up that hill. You might have to go to a lower frequency-per-second vibration to continue your spiritual movement through the third dimension. But your systems are sophisticated. You have been studying fifth-dimensional energy and the Arcturians. You have had multiple incarnations on planetary systems. You are older, experienced souls, and you possess very sophisticated transmissions so that you can adjust your frequency per second. You can expand your perceptual field based on the circumstances.

Remember, you can always shift into the fifth dimension; you don't lose that. You have to practice with dimensional shifting, though.

One of the problems I have seen in working with many of you is that you get stuck in one gear on the third dimension, such as the third gear. It is easy to lose your higher perspective. You might even lose your confidence in shifting into a higher gear. When you shift into a higher gear, you can begin to see the significance of all events from a higher perspective, such as from the mental, physical, spiritual, and emotional bodies. Now, shimmering is an exercise that works with your aura and your energy field. Shimmering uses frequency-per-second vibration in a direct way. This exercise helps you to immediately increase your frequency by increasing the vibrational speed of your aura so that you can prepare yourself for thought projection and bilocation to be in the vibrational energy of the fifth dimension.

As we have said, entering the fifth dimension requires a certain vibration. People who commit terrorism cannot enter the fifth dimension because that is exactly the opposite vibration, a lower vibration. They also enter lower karma that requires many incarnations to bring them to a point of being able to enter the fifth dimension.

"Normal" people like you might have certain aspects that need improvement. Each of you is going through purifications now on Earth. You have to clean the cooling system in your automobile, and so it is you have to purify your belief, emotional, and thought systems, even your physical body. As you rise in your personal purifications and your frequency increases, the remaining blocks are sometimes stubborn and require a particular intervention or a particular tool that you might not have considered before. There are many new healing modalities coming from the fifth dimension, including one of our favorites, which is called vibrational medicine.

The Cosmic Egg Exercise

Become aware of your aura and see a blue line around it. This will be the line separating your energy field from the universe. You can draw the line with your mind. It has a powerful reality because you enclose your energy system in this line. The enclosure of the energy system is now in the shape of an egg, and we call this shape a cosmic egg. It is an archetypal shape of spiritual light and energy. When you bring your energy field into this archetypal shape, it allows you to do the spiritual exercises more easily and effectively. You can create protective fields and directly improve the functioning of your mental, spiritual, and emotional bodies.

As you see your energy field with the line around it, become aware of how many inches away this line is from your physical body. Don't try to change that distance. It could be seven, eight, or twelve inches. The most important thing is that it is a distance you are comfortable with in which you know that you can have a direct influence and control of the energies. As we have said earlier, I would much rather have you go eight inches out and feel more confident and have a greater effectiveness than to go fourteen inches out. Go eight inches out and then go into the shape of a cosmic egg. As you do, you will feel (I hope) a greater sense of organization in your four bodies.

It is easy to be confused. There are so many different influences that pull on your energy field, including the effects of radiation and other electromagnetic energies. The effect of these energies can be described as disorganization in your energy field. (Disorganization can also be caused by drug use, particularly illegal drugs. Not all drug use is bad, but severe drug abuse can create feelings of disorganization in the energy field.) When you put your aura in the shape of a cosmic egg, you can experience a sense of organization and control.

One of the major issues on this planet now is the intrusion of lower-vibrational energies into people's auras. This is the case in what I call a cohabitation of negative spirits, or what you call ghosts. The cosmic egg provides a protective field so that lower energies cannot penetrate and gain control of your energy field.

As you visualize this cosmic egg and the blue line, see it now filled with Arcturian blue spiritual light. See it like a balloon at your crown chakra. You are receiving a special download in this beautiful tube of blue spiritual Arcturian light, and it is filling up your cosmic egg like a balloon. You will find the inside of the aura is getting stronger and more vibrant, and you have the ability to pulse. I will go into silence for just a minute while you visualize this.

[Chants: Oooommmm.] The tones I'm using now are like cleaning your

spiritual radiator system of any blockages. The cooling system in your spiritual engine can operate at its highest performance. [Chants: Oooommmm, oooommmm.] Some of the variations in the sounds are for particular blockages that are more difficult to remove than just a simple tone. You will hear an example of a tone with a distinct variation that is able to remove more sophisticated or stubborn blocks in this one. [Chants various tones.]

Now your energy in the cosmic egg is filled with this blue light, and it has a high vibrancy. You're ready to shimmer. See the pulsing of the aura, the blue line, going at a relatively even rate. You want the pulsing to be at an even pace so that when we go at higher speed, it maintains the same harmonic balance. I will give you a tone or model to follow for the pulsing of your aura. [Chants: Ta, ta, ta, ta, ta, ta, ta, ta, ta.]

I know everybody wants to vibrate his or her aura faster, but it's just as important to be able to have your aura equally balanced in frequency. When we look at a radio scope to analyze a signal, for example, we can see the shape of the frequency. A harmonious signal appears smooth and round, and it has no distortions.

[Chants: Ta, ta, ta, ta with increasing speed.] You're now ready to do dimensional shifting. Shift into the fifth-dimensional perspective now! Your aura, your cosmic egg, supports your shift. It is beautiful to have the ability to be in fifth-dimensional consciousness and to have fifth-dimensional perceptual skills while you're in the third dimension. We will go into meditation and silence for a few minutes now. [Pauses.]

Slowly come back into verbal consciousness. You are still in fifth-dimensional consciousness. You have successfully shifted into fifth-dimensional consciousness.

This is an ideal way to shift your consciousness. You can also do the cosmic egg exercise using the instructions I just offered to enhance your dimensional shifting abilities. There will be times when you can't do this exercise in such detail. The second part of this exercise will link, or anchor, your ability to do a dimensional shift.

Begin this exercise by placing your right hand on your third eye chakra, and say, "Dimensionally shift now!" Then slowly remove your right hand from your third eye, and feel the expansion of your third eye chakra.

We'll do this one more time. We are anchoring this as a link to make it easier for you to enter the shifting experience. That means when you are in a situation on the third dimension and need to be in this higher consciousness and perception, you can place your right hand over your third eye. Do that now.

If possible, place the palm of your hand (the point that is the energetic center of the palm is called the lao gung *point in Chinese medicine) over your third eye, and then say out loud, "Dimensionally shift now!" and slowly remove your hand from your third eye.*

This anchoring can be used in an emergency situation or when you don't have the luxury of time for the entire dimensionally shifting exercise.

Dimensional Shifting and the Four Bodies

When you are dimensionally shifting, you can have an expanded mental body and belief system, look at the idea of infinity and of time being circular, and see past and future incarnations. You can work with more complicated ideas about soul development or work with sophisticated ideas of protective layers in the aura and of the dimensions. By doing this dimensional shifting, you will find an increase in your ability to have more expanded belief systems. You will find the ability to use more positive affirmations. The belief systems from the fifth dimension are powerful. Many new belief systems will be introduced to you, so the time will come when we will work more directly with your belief systems.

Now, you can also use the dimensional shift on the physical body. You might have certain illnesses, allergic reactions, inflammations, or even cancers. For example, your body may have blockages. You might be unable to absorb treatments or tolerate interventions. But when you do the exercise and say, "Dimensionally shift now," you open your body to what I call quantum healing, or healing that transcends logic. Fifth-dimensional healing can also be received. Perhaps another way to look at this is to say that your body opens to the possibility of a miracle. We could also use the terms "quantum light" and "quantum healing," but maybe a term that is more acceptable in your belief system now would be "miracle." It is helpful to use a positive affirmation about your physical body, and then dimensional shifting will help it more effectively. For example, you can say, "My body is open now to the fifth dimensional energies for healing."

Dimensional shifting also works for the emotional body. The emotional body is a primary body that many of you are here to learn about. Higher fifth-dimensional emotions are compassion, acceptance, and understanding. Setting limits to sharing your emotional energy with others is also a higher-fifth-dimensional concept. Setting limits with compassion, for example, would be one way of understanding how dimensional shifting can affect the emotional body. Shifting to a higher perspective with your emotional body will help you gain a greater understanding of why people act certain ways. You still might become angry with others, but you can be angry and have compassion, and you can choose to respond with compassion.

Finally, we have dimensional shifting in the spirit body, and you are probably more open to this. Shifting with the spirit body includes practicing thought projection and moving the spirit body. Through dimensional shifting, you can also vibrate and strengthen the spirit body to bring it into the higher realms.

I don't expect that you can do dimensional shifting and immediately affect all four bodies. You want to just use one body first, and choose which one depending on the situation you are in. You don't use fifth gear for every place you go in your auto. Sometimes while you are driving, your car requires third gear. Sometimes you have to go back into the third dimension and contract a little bit as you meet resistance or go up a hill. That is okay. Know that you have the ability to expand and to use the higher gears. Know that you have the ability to dimensionally shift, and this ability will help you on your path on planet Earth. Blessings, I am Juliano.

Chapter 22

The Four Energetic Worlds

Juliano and the Arcturians

Greetings, I am Juliano. We are the Arcturians! You are very aware of the fifth dimension and the many joys and expansive energy that exist there. You are waiting with great expectation for your ascension. Many of you would choose to leave the third-dimensional life for the fifth-dimensional life immediately. Of course, there are some exceptions. Some of you have attachments and personal work that keep you on the third dimension. I say this without any judgment. You are waiting for the ascension, yet you are faced with being here on the third dimension.

Many wonder how to make or direct the fifth-dimensional energy into your third-dimensional lives. You want to know how to use expanded consciousness and the awareness of higher light so that you can download and use fifth-dimensional light to improve your third-dimensional lives. To facilitate this discussion, the application of fifth-dimensional energy is divided into four areas: the mental, physical, emotional, and spiritual. Those who study the Kabbalah know this as the four worlds, and there are specific Kaballistic descriptions and designations of these four worlds.

These four areas also refer to the four etheric bodies that are energetically attached to you: the mental, emotional, etheric, and physical bodies. When you are in an expanded state of consciousness, you can see those four bodies. When you depart this planet, primarily the spiritual body leaves; however, all four of the bodies interact. For the purpose of this discussion, we separate the four bodies, but they also interact in unity. The spiritual body in particular carries imprints of the other three bodies.

Planet Earth (also called Gaia or the Blue Jewel) has four bodies. There are specific exercises and energy work that you can do to help download fifth-dimensional energy to all four of her bodies or even one or two of her bodies. Many of my recommendations can be applied to Earth with some modifications.

The Mental World

The mental body contains the world of thought. It is the world of belief and of your self-talk and conversation. The universal mental world is the construct that keeps the third dimension cohesive. The third-dimensional reality is composed of a thought field. Its reality can be described as an agreed-on group-thought energy. You have been acculturated, trained, and educated to participate in this thought field.

Many tools are being used to help solidify and hold the mental thought field together. Some of the powers are involved in education and through the media (such as TV or the Internet). Some of them are inherent beliefs in your collective unconscious being transmitted to you from your subconscious. In fact, the subconscious is a powerful source of thought-field energy, and some of the education and control of the thought field is occurring on a subliminal, or below the conscious, level. The subconscious of the planet — the subconscious of humanity — needs to be cleansed and purified.

Examples of fifth-dimensional thoughts include "We are all one. The true reality is eternal. My soul is eternal. There are multidimensions, and I am able to participate and receive information from the higher dimensions as well as the lower dimensions." I believe that you have the idea now. Thought can open doorways into your consciousness. Belief in the Creator is a thought that can lead to powerful expansion of your perspective on this reality. Additional powerful thoughts are, "All things are for the good" and "There is a higher purpose to all that is occurring." These fifth-dimensional beliefs can be brought down into the third dimension to use daily in your application and understanding of life and its events. Beliefs and thoughts are perceptions and energy that you can control.

Earth is a freewill zone, which has many meanings. On one level, you could go where you want and do what you want, but we all know that there are restrictions. Sometimes people live in repressive societies or situations. What is always true is that you have the freedom to think and believe what you want. Try to incorporate fifth-dimensional beliefs, ideas, or thoughts into your mental body. Even modern psychology will tell you that what you think affects what you feel, even physically. The more you work with higher thoughts, the more in harmony you will be. You can also teach others fifth-dimensional thinking.

The Emotional World

There are fifth-dimensional and third-dimensional emotions. Fifth-dimensional emotions are often demonstrated from great prophets, gurus, or spiritual leaders. They include but are not limited to loving kindness, acceptance, grace, understanding, and of course, love in general. Fifth-dimensional emotions are extremely powerful. It certainly shows a higher fifth-dimensional consciousness when you can truly experience the depths of these emotions.

You can apply these higher emotions to your personal self-talk. You can express loving kindness toward yourself and others, and you can also feel acceptance. This is difficult to do at times because of the war, conflict, destruction, and polarization you witness. It is not easy. Loving kindness and acceptance in the fifth dimension must also include discernment.

There is a greater system of reincarnation, and those committing atrocities and destructions now on planet Earth will have to deal with the consequences of their actions. When you see the destruction occurring now, it is still possible to regard the people doing this with loving kindness and acceptance, but please understand that there will be judgment, a consequence, for their actions. Unfortunately, you might not see the consequences happen, but taking a fifth-dimensional perspective elevates you. You will be able to see the future consequences for those who commit evil acts. It doesn't make what they do right, and it doesn't excuse what they do.

The higher, fifth-dimensional perspective shows you there will be a reaction in their soul journeys. It might be easier and perhaps more acceptable to see the consequences immediately. In some cases, there is a direct effect on people who commit evil, and people suffer the consequences of their actions. You who are more accelerated in your soul development see consequences for your actions more quickly, and in some cases, there are accelerated consequences now. In the fifth-dimensional perspective, we integrate loving kindness with judgment.

The hardest thing for everyone to understand now is the extent of destruction this planet can endure. It is hard to see a dear and special planet that is so precious be needlessly destroyed. It takes a fifth-dimensional perspective to see that there is a greater plan for Earth, and those people who are doing the negative actions to the planet will suffer consequences.

I love to speak about Albert Einstein because he had the ability to connect with the fifth dimension. Another mathematician you likely have not heard of is Aryeh Kaplan, a famous Jewish Kaballist and physicist. Kaplan did his greatest thinking and problem solving in his bathtub. He reported that he would fill the bathtub up with warm water and become very relaxed, and then he would let his mind be free. Instead of an academic approach, he would try to solve mathematical problems by opening his mind up to the higher realms to let the solution appear. He said that he received great information in this way.

Albert Einstein used a similar process to free his mind. He created thought experiments in which he would free his mind to solve problems that he created. There is little chance Einstein could have come up with his fantastic theory of relativity solely on his training and education. He was a bright man with special abilities, but frankly, there were other scientists and mathematicians who were brighter than he was. So how was this man able to come up with one of the most complex and comprehensive scientific theories known? The answer is that he had to release his mind and connect with higher dimensions.

Of course, you would need to know how to transfer what you receive from the fifth dimension into a language or symbols that can be used on the third dimension. Another example of a great person receiving fifth-dimensional energy is Mozart. When composing music, Mozart was able to connect with the angelic realm. He had the mental ability to write down the notes of what he was hearing in the fifth-dimensional realm. If he did not have that ability, then he would not have been able to transcribe this higher, beautiful music, which we, the Arcturians, love very much.

Meditation to Solve Problems in the Fifth Dimension

Think about any problem you have on the third dimension, either emotional or mental. Maybe you are working on trying to solve something, such as radiation pollution or solar technology. Maybe you're trying to create a new motor or an engine. Maybe you're trying to figure out a difficult personal relationship you are experiencing. Maybe you have emotional depression or a lack of energy.

Close your eyes, and take a deep breath. Feel relaxation and the freedom to experience your emotional and mental bodies. Know that both of these bodies have high abilities to connect to the fifth dimension. Think about your problem from the third-dimensional perspective, describing it in one sentence in your mind. Connect with your emotional body, and describe the emotions.

Each of the four bodies has the shape of your physical body, much like an etheric double. The top of your mental body is called the crown, which has an etheric antenna that goes up to the fifth dimension. Your fifth-dimensional mental and emotional bodies exist above you in this higher plane. You have the ability to connect and receive information from those bodies.

See and feel your etheric antenna from your crown extend upward. [Tones: Oooohhhh, oooohhhh.] Visualize the antenna extending upward into the higher realms, into a higher plane. It goes up and up and up, out of the third dimension and into the fifth dimension, where it is able to receive higher light and information. Do not worry about receiving information in direct verbal language. This will come in the next part. Just receive whatever energy there is for you.

Do not evaluate or in any way judge what you receive. Your antenna is at a very high place connected to the fifth dimension, and you are receiving information mentally in ideas or thoughts and emotional energy. The emotions might be feelings of acceptance and kindness, but also know that there can be judgment involved.

Now bring your antenna down from the higher realms with this information and energy. As you bring the antenna down, allow words to formulate.

Remember, I said Mozart had the ability to put the music he heard in the fifth dimension into notes. You have the ability to bring down the emotions and the higher thoughts you experienced into words so that you can evaluate, understand, and store the information. One of the goals in fifth-dimensional work is to store it so that you can use it.

Take a moment to allow this process to occur as your antenna comes down. We will take one moment in silence so that you can translate this information. [Pauses.] Feel and know that you have successfully downloaded and stored the information. You received from your antenna higher emotions and higher thoughts. You will be able to return to this higher energy whenever you need to.

The Physical World

How can you use fifth-dimensional energy to change the physical body and the physical planet? The physical body has a role to play in your karma. Therefore, how you treat your body is important. You have all heard the statement that you must treat your body as a temple. It is your receptacle and your receiver of energy and light. There are many protective patterns you can use for your body. This includes protecting your body energetically with certain shields, and it also means protecting your body from pathogens, such as the Zika virus or the Ebola virus, as well as cancers. You might already have some of these conditions, and there are ways of strengthening the body, even if you have these problems. There is a way of healing yourself.

At this time on the planet, all people, even those in the highest light, are being exposed to certain viruses and higher doses of radiation. It is important to build up your immune system and your energy field. We do not suggest living in a cave to avoid being exposed to these conditions. There are certain precautions that you can take that even include the food you eat.

You might find that fifth-dimensional energy and fifth-dimensional thinking can directly influence your food intake and what vitamins you use. Some of you are sensitive to gluten, and you might decide that you need to stop eating food that causes inflammation in your system.

Some of you might decide your body doesn't need meat, and you might stop eating it, or you might decide not to eat genetically modified food. Unfortunately, there is not one prescription for everyone. However, there is a way to connect to your higher truth, your inner healer on the fifth dimension, who will give you directions and recommendations on what is best for you.

This is found in another very important thought, which is an integration of fifth-dimensional thinking of the mental body with the physical body and manifestation of physical energy and physical healing. It goes like this: "I can attract the healers that I need to bring me back into balance. I can work with, find, and learn from the healers. I am now sending out the call to bring those healers into my life so that they can help me." Part of downloading healing from the fifth dimension includes your ability to reach out to those who have the healing abilities you need. Never before on this planet have there been so many high-level healers at one time.

The Spiritual World

There are healing modalities from the fifth dimension being downloaded daily from many powerful sources. Some of the sources are sound healings, crystal healings, thought-form healings, sacred geometry healings, and vibrational medicine healings — the ability to use vibrations to kill disease and pathogens. Ultimately, there will come a time when someone will develop a radio wave shielding, almost like microwaves. The best way to describe it is as a device similar to a metal detector. It takes something similar to a picture using radio waves. Imagine that your healers are close to developing a type of frequency-healing energy that can be transmitted through a similar device. So when you have certain pathogens, such as HIV, Zika, or Ebola, you could walk underneath the device, and it would kill the pathogens.

Each pathogen has a vibrational signature that will respond to a certain radio frequency. This level of healing will be available in the future. Some people are so advanced in their healing abilities that they can emit the radio frequency necessary to destroy pathogens from their hands. There are healers in China who practice a method of chi gong (qigong) healing called chi-lel. This is an ancient practice of healing in which several people join in a group, and with special training, they send healing energy vibrations through their hands to destroy a tumor. This is true higher-vibrational healing. Reiki healers and other healers of light are beginning to approach this level of healing.

For the next exercise, you will go into a state of relaxation. *Clear your mind, and visualize your etheric antenna going up. Tell yourself that you want to attract to your life what you need to be more physically healthy. Be open to receiving that which you need, and ask to be guided to the healer or healing exercise you need. Maybe there's something you need to change in your diet, or maybe there is a certain exercise you need to do. We go into silence as you open to that energy. [Pause.]*

Retract that antenna now, and know that you received the information you need. You know who you need to contact. The person will appear or come into your life soon because you are using fifth-dimensional light and energy and asking that this higher energy come toward your healing. Asking the higher energy to come toward you is a key part of downloading fifth-dimensional energy into your third-dimensional life. This opens you to new healing techniques and new healers.

Some of those healing techniques, such as vibrational medicine, totally depend on your openness to them. Vibrational medicines might not work if the person's mind is closed to it. Someone said in reference to vibrational healing, "I might not understand this method, but I don't even think about it logically anymore. I'm open to it because I believe it can work. I'm not going to block it." Be aware of your logical mind. You should remove all your discrimination and logical thinking. It is equally important to not block energy healing that comes from higher levels.

Synergistic Healing

Earth has the same four bodies as the fifth dimension — mental, physical, emotional, and spiritual — and Earth is also receptive to the physical expression of higher, fifth-dimensional energy. This is why we downloaded the twelve etheric Arcturian crystals into Earth, and this is why many of you still use etheric crystals in different sections of your countries. You also download fifth-dimensional energies for the planetary cities of light and for the planetary ocean reserves of light. The creation of medicine wheels is an example of downloading fifth-dimensional energies into Earth.

There are things that you are doing for planetary healing that relate to creating sacred physical spaces on Earth. With the creation of sacred spaces on Earth, fifth-dimensional energy can more easily be transmitted throughout the planet. You might think that it is overwhelming because you are only one person or maybe in a group of four or five people. You wonder how you can change the whole planet with only a few people.

Here's an example the channel saw on a TV program recently. There was a young person, perhaps twenty-one years old, who was living in Hawaii. He decided to clean up the plastic bottles in the ocean near shore. He came up with a system using a boat and a net and collected the plastic from the water. A TV interviewer asked the young man, "Well, this is wonderful. You are a true angel to do this, but what makes you think that your one boat and your one practice is going to save the ocean?"

He responded, "Well, we have to start somewhere. One person can start a whole movement."

I tell you this story for a very simple reason: Each of you has a sphere of influence in your environment. Maybe more people in Hawaii will begin to clean up the plastic after seeing this example. We hope that will be the case. Your karmic influence and your mission lie in doing what you can in your own sphere of influence. You can bring down fifth-dimensional energy and light to your sphere of influence. It is possible that large parts of this planet will become destroyed, yet the practice of creating sacred places like the planetary cities of light will still remain on Earth.

We see the need for an increase in your spiritual power, and this can be accomplished through the unification of large groups to increase effectiveness. We have exercises to make many places sacred, and we have observed exercises from other cultures and systems that are creating sacred spaces. There has even been a successful attempt to create an Arcturian temple in Brazil, for example. This Arcturian temple holds sacred space. I encourage these activities.

In dealing with a large planet, it is important to connect with a group to increase the power and effectiveness. Remember, spiritual energy is held in a receptacle that can be described as a sacred space or sacred time. You are doing a great job in connecting with the spiritual energy of the fifth dimension. You are beginning to recognize the many methods of downloading this fifth-dimensional energy into your third-dimensional reality. This is Juliano. Good day.

Chapter 23

The Arcturian Stargate Experience

Juliano and the Arcturians

Greetings, I am Juliano. We are the Arcturians. The Arcturians are meant to be the overseers, guardians, and protectors of the stargate. There are three stargates in the Milky Way galaxy. This section of the galaxy has one stargate, and we oversee it. One of our missions is to explain what the stargate is and how to use it. It can be described as a portal or corridor, but it is really greater than those things. It is like a train station on the fifth dimension. Consider the main entrance of a train station. You can see entranceways to many cities in your country, and you have the ability to choose where you want to go. You buy a ticket and go to the proper terminal. When the train arrives, you board it and travel to that city. In a similar way, you can imagine that when you complete your Earth incarnation, you are able to travel to the beautiful interdimensional station called the stargate. You will enter the stargate through a beautiful doorway and see a remarkable view of entry portals to different fifth-dimensional planets throughout the galaxy. There, you are a free soul with no attachments to the third dimension or Earth. You have earned the powerful choice to go to any fifth-dimensional planet. Only those of highest-vibrational energy can pass through this stargate.

At the stargate, you will notice many familiar planet names: the Pleiadians and their planet Era, the Arcturians and our planet Arcturus, the Lyrans and their planet Lyra. There is Alano, the moon-planet near the Central Sun. There is Sirius, the star system that is made famous by its connections and interactions with the Egyptians. There are even entranceways to galaxies nearby, such as the Andromeda.

You will have the choice to go to whichever fifth-dimensional planet you wish. You will also sense your home planet. Your home planet is where you originated in this galaxy. How will you choose? All planets in the fifth dimension will look inviting, and certainly, they are in a higher state, which means that each has higher consciousness, fifth-dimensional light, and advanced spiritual evolution.

When you enter the stargate, you will meet many of your spirit guides and teachers. You will have the opportunity to ask their advice on which fifth-dimensional planet is in your best interest. In fact, the stargate has special powers. When you look down the corridor of the train station in the stargate, you can see your future life in that fifth-dimensional planet. You will retain your consciousness and all of your memories from past lives. This is different from being on third-dimensional planet Earth. When you come to Earth, for example, you also enter a corridor. You enter Earth with third-dimensional consciousness. But there is a difference between entering Earth in the third dimension and entering a fifth-dimensional planet from the stargate.

Before you come to Earth, memories from other star systems, past lives, and soul experiences are temporarily erased. You forget who you are. This is done purposely so that when you enter this third-dimensional Earth, you have a clean slate. You have some memories of soul impressions, but the soul memories are pushed back. It is possible to recover those soul memories and experiences from other planets; however, it requires a particular technique.

Adults in Western cultures do not in any way encourage young children to remember their past soul experiences. This is very different from entering the stargate and the fifth-dimensional planets. Past-life memories are encouraged there. While in the stargate, you will choose the next planet that you go to, and you will enter that planet fully conscious with full memory. Your memory will not be repressed. Also, you will be able to see what you'll be experiencing in that lifetime on the fifth-dimensional planet.

Your Home Planet

The stargate represents an important transition in your soul journey

— graduation from Earth. It also represents a completion of all your Earth lessons and an elevation of your soul into higher interdimensional realms. The soul is eternal. Your soul existed before the Big Bang. (Conservatively, this universe began with the Big Bang 13.7 billion years ago. But this was not the beginning of your soul.) Your soul existed before this universe began. Your soul decided to begin a series of incarnations in the Milky Way galaxy. Earth is approximately 4.5 billion years old, so Earth is not as old as the galaxy. Some of you have had soul experiences and incarnations only on Earth. There certainly has been enough time on Earth for many incarnations.

You are starseeds, and one of the definitions of starseeds includes the experience of incarnations on other planetary systems. There are 5,000 planets in this Milky Way galaxy that have advanced life similar to Earth, meaning that there is consciousness, religion, spirituality, and even space travel. As starseeds, you have most likely had incarnations on other planets besides Earth. We use the term "home planet," and I know each of you is eager to learn the name and location of your home planet.

What does it mean to have a home planet? The home planet is the first planet you incarnated on during this cycle of the universe. Your soul might have had experiences and incarnations in other universes. For our purposes, we are only referring to this universe and the fact that your soul incarnated first on a planet in this galaxy.

You might remember your soul records of that home planet. I know you yearn to return. Many people have only had incarnations on Earth. You starseeds are advanced because you have incarnated at earlier times on other planetary systems. This indicates you have a greater soul advancement. This also indicates that you are more understanding of the stargate and the ascension, and you can recall and integrate your knowledge and experiences from these other planetary systems. As starbeings (starseeds), you remember many experiences from your home planet or from other planets.

You might also have had what I call multiplanetary incarnations. I have often used the words "cosmic karma," "cosmic archaeology," and "cosmic anthropology." Cosmic anthropology is the study of civilizations in this galaxy to advance the knowledge of the incarnational cycle.

That means that there are starseeds who incarnated on their home planets, and there are also starseeds who have chosen to incarnate on several other planets. This can be compared to visiting four or five different countries. Those who are advanced starseeds have had multiple experiences on other planets, and some of you have even given up your allegiance or connections to your home planet, feeling as if you are a citizen of the galaxy, which is, of course, fine and beautiful.

In the stargate station, you can choose where you want to go in your next incarnation. Incarnations do not happen immediately, and in some cases, people might wait for long periods before they incarnate. In other cases, people might choose to incarnate immediately.

Ascension Opportunities

Let's look at the relationship of the access to the stargate and the ascension. Access to the stargate depends on several factors, and it is not available all the time. There are certain alignments that must occur for the ascension to happen and for access to the stargate to be granted. These alignments can be compared to a solar eclipse. For a solar eclipse to happen, there has to be a specific alignment of the Sun, the Moon, and Earth, which only happens at certain times. Sometimes it happens once a year; sometimes it happens once every two or three years. A solar eclipse is not visible everywhere on Earth. Sometimes it is only visible in Australia, and other times it's only visible in North America or Africa.

If you are a true scientist of the stars, then you will probably visit certain parts of the planet to observe a solar eclipse. There are scientific opportunities that can only be tested and observed during the solar eclipse.

Using the solar eclipse model, we can illustrate the alignments necessary for the ascension and for accessing the stargate. Several important alignments have come to the forefront with regard to the ascension. Earth has come into alignment with the Central Sun, and this is an important alignment for accessing the stargate and the ascension.

A complicated alignment is difficult to explain without maps of the galaxy. This occurs periodically when the Sun, your star, comes into a particular alignment with the center of the galaxy, known as the Central Sun, which is multidimensional. You might have read that the center of the galaxy is a black hole, but that reality is just one third-dimensional aspect of its properties. The Central Sun is multidimensional and exists in higher realms as well as having a link to the black hole at the center of this galaxy.

Other Earth alignments include the precession, or Earth wobbling on its axis. One wobble occurs approximately every 26,500 years. That wobble creates a unique alignment. Many of you came to Earth in this time because you knew these alignments would give you access to the stargate and the ascension.

So if you knew that there would be a solar eclipse visible in Australia in October 2017, then you might buy a plane ticket to be there. Similarly, if you knew there were going to be powerful and important alignments on Earth between 2010 and 2018 that would give you specific access to higher dimensions, you might decide to incarnate on Earth then to have these higher experiences.

Some starseeds on Earth now are ready to ascend. There may not have been opportunities to do so before now. For example, there were no opportunities in 1920 or 1830. However, there were opportunities during the time of the Atlanteans and the Lyrans. There have been periodic opportunities for the ascension and access to the stargate throughout the galaxy, but they were in different epochs and other centuries.

The Intersection of the Third and Fifth Dimensions

The intersection of the third dimension with the fifth dimension is more difficult to observe scientifically. It's not something that happens every year but rather in different epochs and in different parts of the galaxy. When the third dimension approaches the fifth dimension, there is greater access to the stargate. Other channels compare the stargate to a corridor or portal to spaceships or other systems on different dimensions. The Arcturian stargate is more than a portal; it is more than just a corridor. You use a portal or a corridor to reach the Arcturian stargate, but the Arcturian stargate has greater functions.

The stargate has an opening that I call a vestibule, which is typically a small corridor. You must pass through this room to go into the stargate. From your point of view, it would seem quite large. You would see it as a large garden with a beautiful pond or lake. You can visit this garden, or entryway, in your meditations. The guardian of the stargate is Archangel Metatron, and he has the highest authority over who enters. He has a corps of workers assisting him.

The codes of ascension are like a password used to enter the stargate, which is the famous expression, "Holy, holy, holy is the Lord of Hosts." (*Kadosh, Kadosh, Kadosh Adonai Tsevaot.*) This is a high-vibrational phrase, and when you say or think this phrase, you are vibrationally ready to enter the stargate. However, you must be at a vibrational frequency that includes the following:

You have no ego attachments left on Earth, and you have completed all Earth lessons to the best of your ability.

You are able to experience higher, fifth-dimensional emotions and push aside lower emotions, such as jealousy, hatred, and attachments.

You must have consciousness and awareness of your soul journey. You must understand that you have multiple soul incarnations and have earned the right to consciously choose where and when you incarnate again in this galaxy.

You Will Have Help to Raise Your Vibration

It's possible to incarnate from the stargate to another galaxy, such as the Andromeda galaxy. The entranceway into the stargate appears like a gigantic door, and the light behind this door is intense. Even when pushed open a only crack, the light that pours through the stargate is so strong that it is enough to immediately elevate you into the fifth dimension. However, the door can only be opened to those who have completed their Earth incarnations. This is why Archangel Metatron guards the gate. He makes sure you have achieved the right vibrational frequency required for entry. He can read your soul history and your aura, and he can see whether you have vibrationally completed all that you need to on Earth. Everything is recorded in a vibrational imprint on your aura. No one is expected to be 100 percent vibrationally ready. If you were perfect, you would have already ascended.

This ascension is filled with grace. People trying to the best of their ability to go to higher light will be given the opportunity to go through the ascension process. Sometimes people seeking entrance are evaluated, and they are given the opportunity to go to a special training in human evolution. They are given the chance to process and resolve unfinished experiences. Some of you are already going through that review process to resolve experiences from this lifetime and other lifetimes on Earth. Now you seek to heal these experiences.

Part of the healing involves understanding your Earth experiences. Other parts involve releasing pain and anger. You will see the higher purpose of all that you have done. The healing lessons in these mini areas of learning are available at the entranceway for those who need further advancement. The guides and teachers will be there to help you. You will go through the necessary learning to complete all incarnational lessons on Earth in an accelerated way. We will provide you with whatever is necessary to have the higher consciousness and higher vibration to enter the stargate, and Archangel Metatron will allow you to pass.

Passing through the stargate is an experience that can only be described as filled with ecstasy and extreme joy! You'll be free of all earthly burdens. You will feel close to your guides and teachers, surrounded by the ascended masters you love, including Sananda, Archangel Michael, and Chief White Eagle. You will feel a sense of timelessness. Most important, you'll have the beautiful choice of where to go in your next incarnation.

Some of you will want to return to Earth, and there is a portal from the stargate to do just that. Returning to Earth would be very different from your previous incarnations. First, you will not lose your memory or your knowledge or your skills. You will not have to start from scratch if you choose to reincarnate to the third-dimensional Earth again.

Stargate Meditation

Visualize a blue corridor over you. I, Juliano, place a powerful blue corridor over each of you. This corridor is directly linked to the entranceway of the stargate. Take three deep breaths. Give permission for your spirit to rise out of your physical body into the blue corridor above. [Chants: Ooooo, ooooo.]

At the speed of thought, travel with me to the stargate entrance. Your astral cord is securely attached to your third-dimensional body. Immediately and surprisingly, you are at the entranceway to the stargate, and you find yourself sitting in a beautiful garden with a sunset of orange and golden light.

We sit together in the presence of Archangel Metatron, and a sense of well-being, compassion, and expansion fills your consciousness. We go into silence as you feel this joyful and peaceful light.

Archangel Metatron cracks open the stargate doorway one inch. As the doorway opens, you feel and see a huge expanding light unlike any you've ever seen or experienced. This light cleanses and purifies you. It heals you, and it brings you into a beautiful sense of balance. Archangel Metatron closes the door, but even with the door closed, the light is still in the room. You absorb it into your astral body on a deep cellular level, and when you return to your physical body, you will transform this ascension light from the stargate into your third-dimensional body.

We come together and reenter the corridor that brought us here to journey back into our Earth home. [Chants: Ta ta ta ta ta ta taa, ta ta ta ta taa, ta ta ta ta taa.] We travel at the speed of thought. You find your Earth body and position yourself six feet above it. Tell yourself that you will reenter the physical body in a state of perfect alignment. All the higher light and energy will be absorbed into your physical body in a healing way. One, two, three: Reenter your physical body. You now feel a great healing and a great sense of peace and balance.

At the right time in the future, you will easily find your way to the Arcturian stargate. I am Juliano. Good day.

Chapter 24

Human Intervention Can Help Rebalance Earth

Juliano and the Arcturians

Greetings, I am Juliano. We are the Arcturians! You can improve your abilities to work with Earth's feedback loop system. It is perhaps surprising to some that Earth's energy system operates under somewhat similar circumstances as a human being's system. Many of you are very dedicated to being planetary healers. One of the core principles of Biorelativity and effective planetary healing is learning how to work creatively and directly with Earth's feedback loop system.

The human body also has a feedback loop system. This includes the ability to regulate your internal temperature, your blood pressure, your sugar levels, and numerous functions in your sympathetic and parasympathetic systems. These systems allow you to be alive and to self-regulate. The key to a personal feedback loop system lies in its ability to self-regulate, and you will see that same principle operating on planet Earth.

Meridians in the Human Body

The human body has a very complex feedback loop system. The Chinese and the Taoists have identified hundreds of acupuncture points that seem to correlate with a personal feedback loop system that maintains balance in the human body. In Chinese medicine, the energy channels that flow throughout the aura and the body are referred to as meridians.

There is a well-known principle in Chinese medicine that an illness of any sort is a reflection of a blockage in one of the meridians. When the body is unable to overcome a blockage, it often responds through inflammation or other reactive measure, such as the creation of antibodies, to combat the intrusion and blockage of the body's natural energy flow. Acupuncture stimulates the blockage to lend energy and support. With the energy feedback of the needle or even just pressing on the acupressure points, the body can self-regulate and begin to heal.

What do I mean by self-regulate? In essence, you are communicating with your immune system. You can communicate with the self-regulating system through the needles and tell your body you need more support and energy in a particular area to rebalance. It is as if you are sending a message to the self-regulating systems, nervous systems, lymph node systems, and other systems to become directly involved in this blockage. You are telling your body to bring forth more energy and more healing at the blockage point.

The human body self-regulates. In fact, your body is constantly working to remove blocks. Your body is constantly creating new antibodies and is continually working to flush out toxins, but the world you live in is extremely complex because of the toxins, pollutants, and radiation levels.

You are living in a stressful time, and I emphasize the word "stress." It is hard to describe how much stress you are under. The reason is that your total physical experience often blocks the stress experience so that you can operate efficiently and happily. Oftentimes, what your body is experiencing as stress will not come into your consciousness. Under stress, the immune system and the feedback loop system of the human body can deteriorate.

You are experiencing new stressors, toxins, and pollutants that your body is not trained to deal with. There are many reasons why blockages happen to your body. Healing through acupuncture and acupressure points can greatly assist in reawakening and activating your immune system. By using acupuncture, you ask your immune system to rebalance itself. Most importantly, you achieve this by encouraging the blockages to be removed from your body so that positive energy can flow.

We see Earth as a living organism that even includes immune and feedback loop systems. We call this planetary organism the Blue Jewel. You often call it Gaia, the spiritual name for planet Earth. It is still controversial to call Earth a living organism, but I want to point out three obvious factors:

Earth has a feedback loop system that is analogous to the feedback loop system of all living organisms.
Earth has a unique planetary balance that it must maintain for humanity and all of its living inhabitants. The balance for the biosphere maintains the life force energy field. The biosphere must keep the oxygen at a certain level, the nitrogen at a certain level, and numerous other planetary systems stable.
Earth's systems are extremely complex. They include a variety of earth, geological, and weather-like occurrences such as ocean currents, winds and jet streams, and tectonic plate systems. Forests directly affect the oxygen content in the atmosphere, which includes a very complex and interactive electromagnetic shielding system.

Cosmic forces and radiation are continually bombarding Earth; therefore, Earth needs a sufficient electromagnetic shielding atmosphere to block the harmful effects of radiation waves. Even the Sun constantly sends dangerous waves to Earth. The filtering in the atmosphere allows the biosphere to maintain its successful balance that supports the comfortable existence of humans and other life forms.

The lymphatic system of the human body filters out toxins and infections; Earth has a similar system. Earth has a system comparable to your nervous system. There are many undiscovered parts of Earth's living systems that have not yet been fully exposed and explained. Nonetheless, humankind must eventually learn to assist Earth so that it can regulate and hold its balance. This regulation occurs through the working of the feedback loop system.

Earth's Energy Flow

Remember, I said that the human body has meridian points, meridian channels, and energy channels. There are various estimates of how many meridians there are on a human body. Likewise, Earth as a living organism has many energy pathways and channels. When there is a blockage in the meridian system, a human becomes ill. This blockage could be in the lung, liver, or heart meridian. Earth also becomes ill when there are blockages in its energy system. The term "ill" is being used as a reference point, and the term "well" will be used to describe a continuum of wellness on Earth.

Maximum health and wellness on Earth is measured by how well Earth can sustain its biosphere so that humanity can live comfortably. There are extremes in temperatures, rainfall, and geological actions that make living difficult and even unbearable. When the atmosphere becomes too clogged with carbon dioxide, it is unbearable to breathe and will cause death.

It has been documented that large parts of the ocean are dying. There is an area in the Gulf of Mexico around Louisiana and Mississippi where tremendous amounts of fertilizer have washed down the Mississippi River and out into the Gulf of Mexico. That area is filled with toxic fertilizers that are killing the Gulf and smothering the oxygen from the ocean. There are large areas around the Gulf in which fish and other organisms cannot live because there is no oxygen in the water. This area of the planet is sick. How do you help Earth rebalance a dead ocean? A specific response from Earth is necessary.

One possibility for healing a dead ocean area is to create lots of rain to increase water in that area. If an area of the ocean is dying, Earth's feedback loop system senses that blockage and attempts to correct it. It is the same when you have an infection and your body responds by sending antibodies to it. But after a point, you might find your body has sent all the forces it can muster and is still not successful.

There is a blockage of life force energy at the Gulf of Mexico, as well as other areas, and there needs to be some kind of intervention. With a blockage in the human body, you can use acupuncture and place a needle in that area to remind the immune system to create the necessary feedback to open up the energy flow. However, the self-correction of planet Earth is much more complex.

There are two points I want to make: (1) Earth tries to correct itself when it is out of balance, and (2) this means that Earth knows where humanity and all life forms are living on her. Earth attempts to maintain a balance and will self-correct to achieve balance for its life forms.

An example of a planetary self-correction is adding more rain to the

Gulf of Mexico to dilute the fertilizer. Another example is to cause damage to a fertilizer plant that's on the Mississippi River. That might sound quite radical. There was even some suggestion that droughts or fires in Canada were related specifically to the oil drilling that was particularly damaging to the environment. There was a very severe fire near the sand oil operations in Alberta, Canada, where there also has been extreme drought. You don't know all there is to know about Earth and how Earth responds to certain intrusions in the biosphere.

It is noteworthy to observe the extreme drought and a severe fire near the areas of this dirty oil drilling in Alberta. This drilling could have been causing harm to the environment. Is it a coincidence that Earth had this response, or is it due to some other reason? My answer is that you have to be open to all factors. At this point in Earth's development, these coincidences are not accidents; they are teaching and pointing to serious and damaging circumstances. You need to pay attention and keep your minds open to all possibilities. You must work together on helping Earth's feedback loop system correct itself.

Following are some suggested interventions that can be used to help Earth rebalance. Some you are already using, and some are yet to be developed. All relate directly to Biorelativity, which you impart as a telepathic communication to Earth's feedback loop system to balance and correct irregularities and imbalances in Earth's biosphere.

Conduct Sacred Ceremonies

Conduct ceremonies and sacred work at sites near or on ley lines, or Earth's meridians. Native people have often used this intervention. It is an important method of communicating with Earth's feedback loop system. It encourages shifts or changes in Earth's self-regulation patterns. There are a variety of ceremonies that can be used, such as a medicine wheel ceremony, talking circles, and drumming.

Ceremonies for ill people are effective methods of strengthening the human feedback loop system. You might be aware of the tepee healing ceremony and the sweat lodge. There are many possible variations on this theme that can be used for personal healing and development.

Recently, a beautiful attempt was made by a Native American named Blue Thunder to create medicine wheels along Earth's ley lines.

This is wonderful, but it requires a strong level of coordination. The idea is equivalent to how Chinese medicine views the human system of self-healing.

You as modern people have the advantage of obtaining images of Earth from the Moon, and you can estimate where Earth's ley lines are. There need to be new insights, discoveries, and drawings of the ley lines. Ley lines are similar to meridian lines. Often ley lines and meridian lines follow river paths. Ley lines run along the Mississippi River in the United States, the Ganges River in Asia, and the Río de la Plata River in Argentina and Uruguay, as well as the Amazon River in South America. Many rivers are life force meridians. In Earth's case, humankind has mistakenly blocked these ley lines, so you have a serious situation.

Your body sets up blockages to bring forth antibodies and to fight off illness. On the other hand, humanity has erroneously built dams, polluted oceans and rivers, and allowed deadly fertilizer into Earth's channels of energy, blocking these vital pathways. This has occurred numerous times. The reasons for the dams are justified as a need for hydroelectricity. In addition, there are nuclear power plants built on ley lines. Some faults such as the San Andreas Fault and the Ring of Fire are also major Earth ley lines.

Humanity does not yet have complete maps of Earth's ley lines and meridian channels. If you agree that the San Andreas Fault represents a ley line and a powerful energy meridian line for this planet, then you should be shocked that humanity has built a nuclear power plant near it. Earth is sensitive to radiation exposure. The Fukushima nuclear power plant is on a ley line. However, there are examples of ley lines that are not blocked. There are ley lines through Greenwich, England. There is one on the equator, and there is a ley line from the North Pole to the South Pole.

One method of encouraging Earth to keep the energy flow going is to have ceremonies on the ley line pathways. This can be a very complex process. You might not be able to go to the Amazon River and perform a ceremony there because it can be very difficult to travel there. On the other hand, you might be able to do ceremonies along the San Andreas Fault because the area is close to major population centers in California.

I commend the medicine wheel work throughout the North and

South American continents as a beautiful effort to open up channels. It's a monumental task. Maybe if at some point the Group of Forty is able to strengthen its membership and its operational capacity, then they will be able to help with this work.

Build Sacred Structures

Another intervention to help Earth strengthen its feedback loop system is to build sacred structures. Examples are the pyramids in Egypt and the Maya and Aztec structures. The Maya had a particularly strong understanding of Earth's ley lines and how to work with this energy in a sacred way. You can use sacred buildings to connect with cosmic energy and cosmic light. Connecting with this energy and bringing it into certain points on Earth's energy system is one of the strongest healing techniques available to humanity. We know that the Nile River is on a ley line energy system, or meridian system. The pyramids are not built exactly on the Nile, but they are close.

The ancient Egyptians were very much in alignment with the Sirians. They were aware of the relationship between the Sirian energies and Egyptian civilization. There is speculation that several of the pyramids were built in direct alignment with Sirius, and because of that alignment, the Egyptians were able to do powerful cosmic energy work that strengthen their civilization and their part of Earth and opened interdimensional corridors between ancient Egypt and the Sirians.

The Maya also built cosmic temples, which they related to the center of the galaxy. There are many examples of how humans built sacred energy sites (churches and temples) on powerful meridian lines. Another good example is Stonehenge, where there is a deep meridian line the ancient people of England used for multiple purposes. That ley line is still as powerful as it was then, and a lot of Earth healing can happen now at these points.

Through Biorelativity or Earth healing exercises, you can enter a ley line and send energy to release a blockage point. To get into a ley line and into the meridian system, it is better to enter at a strong point. This is why many of you have been so attracted to going to the pyramids and Stonehenge. You sense their power for Earth healings. Doing Earth healing exercises near the Ring of Fire can be very powerful. Remember that we established an etheric crystal at Volcán Poás, which is on the Ring of Fire near San José, Costa Rica.

Use the Bypass Meridian System

Unfortunately, there are so many blockages on Earth's meridian system now that it might be beyond humanity's ability to repair all its blockages in the short time that is needed to complete the healing. I like to use the example of bypass surgery for this intervention. A surgeon might look at your heart and say, "Well, we can't repair 'this' vein, so we are going to put in a bypass. The energy is still flowing, and it will be just as strong as before. We are using a vein from your leg to bypass the blockage in your heart."

I use this example because we have downloaded twelve etheric crystals along certain pathways around this planet. These pathways are partly on existing ley lines. Volcán Poás is on one of the pathways for the twelve Arcturian etheric crystals and also on the Ring of Fire. Mt. Shasta is on the Ring of Fire as well as Mt. Fuji. We have established a system of strong points in these areas that is like bypass surgery for the planet. You can create a powerful flow of energy and light by using the twelve etheric crystals as a ley line in this new and emerging meridian system.

This is a meridian system superimposed by the Arcturians. It is necessary to develop this new bypass system because at times you are not going to have the power or the ability to remove all the blockages in the existing meridian system on Earth. So the third intervention in strengthening the feedback loop system is to use this bypass system.

By using these types of meridian systems (the Mississippi and the Amazon Rivers, the Arcturian crystal grid, or the Ring of Fire system), you can communicate more powerfully to Earth's feedback loop system. Again, I make the comparison to the human body. Let's say you have a problem in your lung area, and you go to the lung meridian. You unblock the area in the lung meridian, and then you can heal yourself. There are problems around the Ring of Fire and in the Gulf of Mexico. You might find it necessary to go to the closest ley line, or meridian, and do the exercise from there. I realize that because of limitations, you may not be able to do that. However, you might be close to another Arcturian etheric crystal, such as the one at Bodensee (Lake Constance), Germany.

That could be your entry point into communicating more directly into the feedback loop system for Earth's healing.

Dance in the Rain

Another simple example for Earth healing is the rain dance that the Native Americans use in a ceremony to ask Earth to bring rain to an area. The Natives send that thought to a particular place. This is similar to accessing Earth's meridian system. You can go to a place close to the Ring of Fire and say, "We want to balance Earth. Please send the energy of tranquility through the geological plates. Please send rain to the drought-stricken areas." In other words, you are giving directions to Earth on how to rebalance.

Your body's system could also become confused. Your human system may not know how to rebalance itself, and you have to tell it. When doing acupuncture and putting the needle in the acupuncture point, you're essentially saying, "Okay, nervous system, lymphatic system, and muscle system, let's rethink this. Let us expand and relax, and let's put in a new energy source, a new paradigm." Your body will respond. It is the same with Earth. Earth could be blocked, and Earth might not know how to rebalance or realign itself. At these points, you give Earth these instructions: "We need more rain in California, Venezuela, and Sao Paulo."

Activate the Ring of Ascension

Crop circles are examples of cosmic energy that has come into Earth. Crop circles communicate on a deep level to Earth's feedback loop system. There are many factors involved in balancing and holding together the planet, including Earth's biosphere, ocean currents, weather patterns, and fault lines. But some of Earth's systems are not obvious. I call these cosmic interdimensional forces; they are involved in keeping this planet and the biosphere balanced. These mysterious cosmic forces are immeasurable.

There are no scientific facts available to describe or measure the effects of the interdimensional cosmic forces on this planet. Yet our observation is that these mysterious forces have an effect on the overall biosphere and the feedback loop system on Earth. Therefore, interventions on one part of the planet can affect other parts of the planet. Thus, crop circles in one area of the world can affect the whole planet!

The interdimensional cosmic effect comes from powerful galactic forces, such as alignment with the Central Sun, bringing down cosmic light from certain systems such as Arcturus, and activating the ring of ascension. The ring of ascension was created as interactive so that starseeds could feel the effect of interdimensional light. This helps starseeds apply the interdimensional healing light to Earth's feedback loop system for balancing Earth. The ring of ascension downloads light from the fifth dimension that can be used for special Earth healings.

I will conclude our brief lecture today with a meditation: *Visualize the ring of ascension as a fifth-dimensional light around Earth. It appears as a halo of golden light. Know that the golden light of the ring of ascension has cosmic healing powers. Visualize this ring of ascension also as a golden, electromagnetic source, highly charged with healing and balancing energy. As the ring of ascension light goes around the planet, see Earth's meridian system light up. See the Mississippi River or the Amazon River fill with fifth-dimensional light. Visualize the meridian lines on Earth as open and flowing.*

Now visualize a halo of light above your crown chakra. Visualize a small circle of light as a small duplicate of the ring of ascension. It is placed above your crown chakra. Let that light be downloaded into your energy system now, opening up all of your meridians, removing any blocks, and increasing your life force energy flow. [Chants: Oooo, aaaa.] Let this light healing force strengthen your immune system and your energy field. May all of your body's meridians be opened and fully charged.

I am Juliano. Good day.

Glossary

Abraham Maslow — An American psychologist who described a hierarchical structure of physiological and emotional needs. To safely enter expanded consciousness, base needs must first be met.

Adam species — The term Arcturians use to refer to human beings.

Adonai — Hebrew word for God in the Old Testament. It literally means "My Lord." It is also the galactic word for God.

Adonai Tzevaot — Hebrew for "Lord of Hosts."

akashic records — An etheric collective library in the higher dimensions that contains all the information, thoughts, and events of all beings throughout the galaxies and their lifetimes, including past and present experiences.

Alano — An Arcturian moon planet located near the Central Sun.

alchemical dimensional transmutation — A concept that references work to advance to the fifth dimension using alchemical and quantum energies.

altered (higher) states of consciousness — A term in modern psychology used to describe different states of consciousness. This includes the dream state, trances, meditation states of consciousness, and heightened states of consciousness in which one has a higher perception of reality. This state is usually described as a condition in which one can see ultimate truth and experience the present more fully. In the 1960s, this term was also used to describe drug-induced changes in consciousness, such as what one could experience with mind-altering drugs.

Andromeda — A large spiral galaxy 2.2 million light-years from the Milky Way. Andromeda is the largest member of our local galactic cluster. It is commonly referred to as Earth's sister galaxy.

Andromedans — An advanced, higher-dimensional race of beings from the Andromeda galaxy. A specific group of Andromedans is currently working with the Arcturians in their effort to facilitate the planetary ascension process of Earth.

arcan — Thought-form energy described as traveling in an arc wave. In Biorelativity, we use etheric crystals implanted within our arcan energy to increase the power of prayers and intentions.

archangel — A term that applies generally to all angels above the grade of angel. It also designates the highest rank of angels in the angelic hierarchy. The Kabbalah cites ten archangels. They are considered messengers bearing divine decrees.

Arcturian crystal lake — A fifth-dimensional lake on Arcturus set up to interact with Earth and the third dimension.

Arcturian etheric crystals — Fifth-dimensional crystals that originate from the etheric world and interact directly with the planetary noosphere. These crystals are great vessels for fifth-dimensional light. They can hold the unity consciousness from the fifth dimension amid the duality and polarizations of this planet. The crystals hold special codes and programs for planetary ascension.

Twelve etheric crystals were brought down, each corresponding to a certain sphere on the map of the Tree of Life. The Arcturian crystals are located in Mount Fuji, Japan; Istanbul, Turkey; Bodensee, Germany; Montserrat, Spain; Serra da Bocaina, Brazil; Poás Volcan, Costa Rica; Lake Puelo, Argentina; Lake Moraine, Canada; Copper Canyon, Mexico; Mount Shasta, California, United States; Grose Valley, Australia; and Lake Taupo, New Zealand.

Arcturian Tree of Life for Planetary Healing — An updated version of the Kabbalistic Tree of Life with the added characteristic of balancing the spheres specifically for healing and helping Earth connect with the fifth dimension. The Arcturian Planetary Tree of Life has been designed to correspond to twelve sacred areas on the planet, and it is now helping to establish a healing energy system. Each designated sacred area has been downloaded with a fifth-dimensional Arcturian etheric crystal to help it become more receptive to higher healing light.

Arcturus — The brightest star in the constellation Boötes, which is also known as the Herdsman. This is one of the oldest recorded constellations. Arcturus is also the fourth brightest star seen from Earth. It is a giant star, about twenty-five times the diameter of the Sun, and one hundred times as luminous. It is a relatively close neighbor of Earth's, approximately forty light-years away. High up in the sky in the late spring and early summer, Arcturus is the first star seen after sunset. One can find Arcturus easily by following the Big Dipper's handle away from the bowl.

ascension — A point of transformation reached through the integration of the physical, emotional, mental, and spiritual selves. The unification of the bodies allows one to transcend the limits of the third dimension and move into a higher realm. It has been compared to what is called "the Rapture" in Christian theology. It has also been defined as a spiritual acceleration of consciousness that allows the soul to return to the higher realms and thus be freed from the cycle of karma and rebirth.

ascended masters — Spiritual teachers who have graduated from Earth or teachers on higher dimensions, including archangels, higher beings from the galactic world, and prophets. A spiritual guide from any Earth religion, including Native American traditions. They have graduated from the Earth incarnational cycle and ascended into the fifth dimension.

Ashtar — The commander of a group of spiritual beings who are dedicated to helping Earth ascend. The beings Ashtar oversees exist primarily in the fifth dimension and come from many different extraterrestrial civilizations.

assemblage point —

1. A concept that appears in the shamanistic world. The assemblage point is a point in the aura. Some people think it is in the back below the neck. That point is like a valve. When that point is opened, you have an input of higher perception. That means you can see the dimensional worlds; you can see the spirits that are around us all the time.
2. The place where things come together and, through their resonance of frequencies, the whole becomes greater than its parts. The amazing thing is that there are many assemblage points (of frequency) within the Hebrew letters that relate to the Sephirot (spheres) in the Tree of Life. Once you have come to an assemblage point and know that frequency, you resonate with it and internalize it until the unity in resonance leads to entrainment. Also, the assemblage point can spread and expand on this entrainment. Assemblage points are necessary for interdimensional interaction.

astral plane — The nonphysical level of reality considered to be where most humans go when they die.

Atlantis — An ancient advanced civilization that reportedly was in existence 10,000 or more years ago. It was reported in the readings of Edgar Cayce, and there were vague references to such a civilization by Plato. There has never been historical or scientific confirmation of this civilization.

bilocate — The ability to be in two places at the same time: physically in your body and mentally or spiritually in another dimension.

Biorelativity — A technique that encompasses the use of mental telepathy and thought processes to interact with Earth and the spirit of Earth. The downloading of energy through corridors can be viewed as an acceleration of Biorelativity. When you connect in a group consciousness with a Biorelativity exercise, you create a powerful interactive force. When you are accessing a corridor, that connection is incrementally increasing the abilities of your telepathic communications. On the more advanced level, the corridors and accessing the energy of the corridors are combined with Biorelativity techniques.

Biorelativity techniques send healing energy to the planet in a practice similar to group. Native Americans know how to pray to the Earth as a group, often asking for rain, for example. In Biorelativity exercises, groups of starseeds around the planet send healing thought to specific areas in the world. Storms, hurricanes, and even earthquakes can potentially be averted or diminished.

biosphere — A term used to describe the whole environment of Earth, including the oceans, atmosphere, and other necessary ingredients that keep and support all life.

Blue Jewel — The name Arcturians use to describe planet Earth. This is also a name of a movie made by German film producer Oliver Hauck on planetary healing, which features David K. Miller.

butterfly effect — The concept that small causes can have large effects. In chaos theory, a small change in a state can result in a large difference in another state. In weather and Earth changes, the flapping of the wings of a distant butterfly could have a significant outcome on global weather patterns.

Central Sun — The fifth-dimensional spiritual center located in the center of the Milky Way galaxy from which high spiritual energy is emitted. Earth came into direct alignment with the Central Sun in 2012.

chakras — Energy centers of the human body system. These centers provide the integration and transfer of energy between the spiritual, mental, emotional, and biological systems of the human body.

channeling — The process of entering a meditative trance to call forth other entities to speak through you. See *trance channeling*.

Chief White Eagle — A fifth-dimensional Native American guide who is very connected to Jesus and other fifth-dimensional beings.

codes of ascension — Cellular keys for the ascension sometimes described as the Keys of Enoch. The codes of ascension are contained in certain sounds and tones that can activate energy fields to open to the fifth dimension.

cohabitation — A Kabbalistic term for occupying another soul's energy in one's aura. This can be done for positive purposes, in which case a positive, highly evolved energy, such as Archangel Michael, can coexist in a person's energy field. This allows the person to accomplish, perform, and enhance his or her ability to achieve greater and more positive tasks in life. This is referred to as positive cohabitation (*Ibbur* in Kabbalah). There is also negative cohabitation, which is the occupation of the Earth energy of a person by a negative lower spirit, such as a ghost (*Dybuk* in Kabbalah). Negative spirits occupying an energy field can cause a person to act irrationally and even commit crimes and violent acts.

collective unconscious — This term, in part developed by the Swiss psychiatrist Carl Jung, is used to describe the ancient Earth archetypes and symbols used in each culture around the globe.

consciousness — "I think; therefore, I am" (a statement from Descartes) is the foundation of Western consciousness, which implies consciousness is based on thinking. "I Am That I Am" is a newer interpretation, which means, "I am aware of my being."

corridor — A pathway or etheric tunnel on Earth that leads to a higher dimension. Corridors can be found in high-energy places such as sacred sites on Earth. The Arcturians believe that we can establish corridors within our meditation areas on Earth.

cosmic drama — A term used to describe standard conflicts that different planets experience during their evolutionary cycles. Some soul groups come from other parts of our galaxy and then incarnate on Earth to try to resolve their conflicts.

cosmic egg — The optimal shape of your aura for health benefits. When your aura is in the shape of an egg, you are expressing maximal energetic possibilities. The egg is a universal shape of wholeness, and thus it is also referred to as the cosmic egg.

cosmic memory — Energies and events that people are attracted to that are related to previous experiences locked in their cellular structures. In the theory of cellular memory, you tend to attract situations that were important to your soul development, whether positive or negative.

Council of Elders — A group of spiritual leaders who seek to lead Earth toward a higher spiritual plane.

Cro-Magnon — Early modern humans from Europe. They lived as early as 43,000 years ago. They are considered ancestors of modern Europeans and coexisted with the Neanderthals.

crystal temple — An etheric temple on the fifth dimension that has been made available by the Arcturians. The crystal temple contains a lake more than one mile in diameter that houses a huge crystal half the size of the lake itself. A huge glass dome encloses the entire lake and surrounding area, allowing visitors to view the stars.

dimension — Refers to the level of frequencies of energy. For example, etheric energy expands to higher-dimensional levels, including the fifth dimension. Awareness increases and energy progresses upward through the dimensions. This increasing energy frequency on the fifth dimension helps one experience a greater unity. That is to say, as one goes into higher dimensions (such as the fifth dimension), one experiences a greater unity — a unity that is not experienced on the third dimension, where duality and conflict are usually experienced.

dimensional bleeding — A process that can occur when there are not sufficient protections between dimensions. Many of the acts of violence, distortion, and strange events occurring on Earth are because of the bleeding of the lower fourth dimension into the third dimension. In many cases, because of these leaks, lower fourth-dimensional beings are able to come down into the third dimension and cause great mischief. These areas in the lower fourth dimension often have lower spirits, ghosts, and generally lower energy beings.

dimensional boom — The sonic boom that occurs when a spaceship comes from hyperspace and reenters close to a planet. The planet that is being reentered can be thrown off balance by a dimensional boom.

dimensional shifting — The ability to move one's consciousness from the third dimension to higher dimensions.

dimensional waves — Pre-ascension fifth-dimensional waves of light coming down to the planet usually experienced by starseeds. You can call on the dimension energy wave to help you experience more fifth-dimensional light.

doppelgänger — A German word describing the astral double of a person. "Doppelgänger" means that there is a double, or duplicate, of your body. Your astral body energetically forms a duplicate of your physical body. When you visualize during astral travel, you work with the doppelgänger. Your etheric duplicate has powers and abilities far beyond the physical body. The physical body has limitations because it is in the third dimension, but the etheric body can bounce around, travel remotely, go through doors, and do all kinds of fun things.

Earth homeostasis — A maintained balance of certain levels of oxygen and nitrogen, as well as many other chemical factors, in the biosphere.

Earth lessons — A term in soul psychology that relates to what lessons one has to learn during this incarnation on Earth.

El Na Refa Na La — Hebrew for "Please God, heal her now!" This is a famous Kabballah healing chant.

etheric — A term used to designate the higher bodies in the human system. In India, "etheric" is used to describe the unseen energy and thoughts of humans.

etheric crystals — Invisible crystals that contain fifth-dimensional energy that have been sent to Earth by the Arcturians. The purpose of these etheric crystals is to provide healing energies to Earth's meridians.

etheric energy — The vibrational frequency that is one level higher than physical reality. Etheric energy is often referred to in terms of etheric energy bodies, which can be described as vibrational energy frequencies around objects and people that sometimes can be seen by people who have psychic abilities.

feedback loop system of Earth — Earth's self-regulating mechanism that holds the biosphere in balance. It receives input from the planet and then makes adjustments accordingly.

fifth dimension — A higher dimension of existence that transcends the circumstances of the third and fourth dimensions. It is the realm of infinite energy and love and can be compared to the Garden of Eden. In the fifth dimension, one transcends (ascends) the incarnational cycle and graduates from Earth. Jesus is one of the ascended masters residing in the fifth dimension.

galactic cultural anthropology — The study of how societies develop on other planets.

Galactic Kachina — The intermediary between the Central Sun and this planet. In Native American Puebloan folklore, a kachina is an intermediary between the higher spirit world and this world.

galactic spirituality — A spiritual philosophy that accepts the existence of higher beings throughout the galaxy and the understanding that spirituality and planetary evolution are part of a galactic family of civilizations.

grace — A reprieve from negative karma due to good deeds . This reprieve can be brought as a blessing from spirit guides.

grid lines — Another name for energy lines that run through the planet. In Chinese medicine, energy lines that run through the body are called "meridians."

Group of Forty — A concept of group consciousness suggested by the Arcturians to aid humans in the ascension process. According to the Arcturians, 40 is a spiritually powerful number. The Arcturians emphasize the value and power of joining in groups. A group of 40 consists of 40 members located worldwide who focus on meditating together at a given time each month. Members agree to assist each other in spiritual development. These groups assist in Earth's healing and provide a foundation for the individual member's ascension.

Gurhan — An ascended master from the seventh dimension in the Andromedan galaxy.

harmonic light — Fifth-dimensional light often appearing as gold balls of etheric energy. This light can be transmitted through the noosphere (the collective unconscious) and can spread energy of balance and harmony wherever it is directed. It can be directed by the thoughts and prayers of starseeds around the planet.

Helio-ah — An Arcturian female ascended master who is the partner of Juliano. She specializes in discussing holographic energy.

Heylang — An ascended master from the Andromedan galaxy.

higher self — In Kabbalah, the self that relates directly to higher dimensions, transcending the ego.

holographic work — Described scientifically as a part of any image created through a laser that reproduces the original whole image. In fifth-dimensional work, holography is the ability to access all universal energy from any spot in the universe. Holographic healing is based on the assumption that humans can access their greater selves through holographic energy.

intermediaries — Refers to guides between the third and fifth dimensions who are here to help with the ascension.

Iskalia mirror — An etheric mirror the Arcturians helped place over the North Pole. Visualize a gigantic mirror a mile or two in diameter in the etheric realm above the North Pole and in special alignment with the Central Sun. The purpose of the Iskalia mirror is to act as a magnifier, allowing a pure energy field to reach Earth from the Central Sun.

Juliano — The main Arcturian guide and ascended master working to help activate Earth and Arcturian starseeds for ascension.

Kabbalah — The major branch of Jewish mysticism. The Hebrew word "Kabbalah" is translated as "to receive." The study of Kabbalah can raise one's level of consciousness to new heights and assist in unlocking the codes for transformation into the fifth dimension.

kachinas — Intermediaries for the Native Americans who bridge the gap between this third-dimensional world and the spirit world. The kachinas have a home in the San Francisco Peaks outside of Flagstaff, Arizona. Katchinas are also masked dancers embodying such spirits as well as carved dolls representing them.

Kadosh, Kadosh, Kadosh Adonai Tzevaot — Hebrew for "holy, holy, holy is the Lord of hosts." This is a sacred Hebrew chant used to unlock the keys of ascension.

Kuthumi — One of the ascended masters who serves Sananda. In a previous life, Kuthumi incarnated as St. Francis of Assisi. He is generally recognized as holding the position of world teacher in the planetary White Brotherhood-Sisterhood. An extensive record of his teachings can be found in the works of Alice Bailey.

lightbody — Higher etheric spirit body that is connected to the highest soul energy.

lightworkers — A term used to describe people who have spiritual interests in the higher dimensions, including studying and receiving energy from the higher dimensions. The energy from the higher dimensions is often referred to as "light" — hence the term "lightworkers."

lower self — A description in the Kabbalah of humans' animalistic nature, including instincts.

Lyrans — A group of advanced beings who lived near the constellation Lyra in the Milky Way galaxy.

medicine wheel — A circular pattern of rocks and crystals created on the ground by Native Americans. It is used for ceremonies, including communicating with the earth.

Merkavah, Merkabah — the term Hebrew for "chariot." In modern spirituality, it refers to a chariot in etheric form that is used to take spiritual seekers to higher dimensions. In Kabbalah, the term means God's throne-chariot, referring to the chariot of Ezekiel's vision. It is also used in describing a branch in the Kabbalah called "*Merkavah* mysticism."

Metatron — Tradition associates Metatron with Enoch, who "walked with God" (Genesis 5:22, KJV) and ascended to heaven and was changed from a human being into an angel. His name has been defined as "the angel of presence" or "the one who occupies the throne next to the Divine Throne." Another interpretation of his name is based on the Latin word *metator*, which means "a guide or measurer." In the world of the Jewish mystic, Metatron holds the rank of the highest of angels — that of an archangel. According to the Arcturians, Metatron is associated with the Arcturian stargate and assists souls in their ascension to higher worlds.

Michael — The name is actually a question meaning, "Who is like God?" He is perhaps the best known of the archangels and is acknowledged by all three Western sacred traditions. He has been called the Prince of Light, fighting a war against the sons of darkness. In this role, he is depicted most often as winged with an unsheathed sword, the warrior of God and slayer of the dragon. His role in the ascension is focused on helping us cut the cords of attachment to the Earth plane, which will allow us to move up to higher consciousness. In the Kabbalah, he is regarded as the forerunner of the *Shekhinah*, the Divine Mother.

monad — The original, elemental creative force. Each one of us contains a portion of that force at the center of our true essence.

multidimensional presence — Existence on several different dimensions. The Arcturians are trying to help humans become aware of their existence not only on the third dimension but also on the fifth dimension.

multidimensional self — A view of the self existing on different dimensions, including the dream world and the fourth and fifth dimensions. Aspects of the self can exist in other dimensions.

multiple personalities — In modern psychiatry, a mental illness that is described as a person having several personalities at the same time. Each personality is neither conscious nor aware of the other personalities.

Neanderthal — An extinct species of humans, possibly a subspecies of *Homo sapiens*. Neanderthal are closely related to modern humans. They lived in parts of Europe from 350,000 years ago to as recently as 32,000 years ago.

noosphere — The thought field of the entire planet. The noosphere has many levels and can, in some ways, be compared to the akashic records. It interacts with Gaia as well as the dimensional levels and stability of the planet. The noosphere is part of the etheric energy field, which is having quite a dramatic effect on all of the events manifesting on Earth.

omega light — A fifth-dimensional light that has high healing properties. The light can help transcend the world of cause and effect; thus, it can help produce miraculous healings. The effects of this healing light can be increased by toning the sounds "omega light."

Orion — A superb, highly recognizable constellation. The most striking part is the belt, which consists of three bright stars. No other constellation contains as many bright stars.

Orions — An extraterrestrial culture that descended from another ancient civilization near the constellation Orion. The Orions have been extremely influential in the genetic makeup of the current human being, reflected now in human beings sharing physical, emotional, and mental traits.

P'taah — An ascended master and spirit guide from the Pleiades star system.

parallel lives — The idea that people live simultaneously in other universes and worlds while living in this third-dimensional world.

peak experiences — Described by Abraham Maslow as periods of heightened states of awareness and perception during which one has feelings of well-being and even ecstasy. These are experiences of expanded consciousness that result in altered states of consciousness. During these peak experiences, you can see the third dimension through a new perceptual lens. Thus, concepts difficult to understand (such as unified energy, unified field theory, or luminous strands of light theory) suddenly make sense. You can solve problems that previously might have seemed impossible.

planetary cities of light — Cities that have been activated with fifth-dimensional energy. A planetary city of light is also part of a global network of other planetary cities of light on Earth.

planetary cities of light project — A project working toward planetary healing and balancing by establishing cities of light around the planet. Each city of light has a fifth-dimensional energy field that contributes to the higher unified energy field for Earth. The key is that the planetary cities of light become united in a network. To achieve planetary ascension, Earth must have a powerful network of planetary cities working together on an interactive basis.

planetary healing — Exercises used to rebalance Earth and help the biosphere become healthy again. Planetary healing exercises can include medicine wheel ceremonies and Biorelativity meditations.

planetary mission — In soul psychology, the view that people come and incarnate on Earth to do special soul work to help the planet.

Pleiades — A small cluster of stars known as the Seven Sisters in some mythologies. Some Native Americans believe that they are descended from the Pleiades. This system is near the constellation Taurus, about 450 light-years from Earth, and is the home of a race called the Pleiadians, who have frequently interacted with Earth and her cultures. It is said that the Pleiadians have a common ancestry with humans.

portal — An opening at the end of a corridor that allows beings to go into interdimensional space. This could allow beings to go into the fifth dimension.

quantum light — Healing light from the fifth dimension that transcends the normal cause-and-effect energy on the third dimension. Such light can create miraculous healings.

resistance — A term in modern psychology describing a defense mechanism in which one prevents oneself from seeing a truth or does not want to learn new ideas or approaches because of a fear of change.

ring of ascension — An etheric structure that was downloaded with the help of the Arcturians and ascended masters to aid Earth's ascension. The ring downloads fifth-dimensional energy into the third dimension.

Sacred Triangle — The teachings of the Sacred Triangle focus on the unity of three spiritual paradigms. Each paradigm (galactic spirituality, the White Brotherhood-Sisterhood, and the Native people teachings) on its own is not strong enough to manifest the fifth-dimensional energy necessary to heal Earth, but all three working together can bring a powerful healing energy to Earth.

Sananda — Known to many as Master Jesus. His galactic name, Sananda, represents an evolved and galactic picture of who he is in his entirety. Sananda is known as Joshua ben Miriam of Nazareth, which can be translated as Jesus, son of Mary of Nazareth.

San Francisco Peaks — A 12,000-foot mountain range near Flagstaff, Arizona, that is the sacred home of the Navajo Indians. The kachina spirits are said to live there.

self-talk — A term in modern psychology that describes the ongoing private conversation one has with oneself in the mind. Self-talk can be either positive or negative.

shimmering — Representative of an energy field on telepathic interactions between the third-dimensional starseeds and lightworkers and fifth-dimensional energy. The shimmering light is a telepathic etheric force field that is accelerated through etheric crystal work. It can be described as a circular energy field that is distributed around the planet.

The evolution of humankind is represented by new abilities and new energies. These new abilities and new energies are related in part to shimmering energy, a methodology and force in which third-dimensional objects, people, and even weather are upgraded into a fifth-dimensional modality. On a personal level, shimmering allows your auric field to vibrate at a frequency that enables the aura to shift the electrons. The atomic structure of your cells transmutes into a vibratory energy field that elliptically shifts the cellular structures into the fifth dimension, causing a back-and-forth or "shimmering" modality. This back-and-forth shimmering modality actually affects the atomic and quantum levels of your cellular structures.

This shimmering energy is the precursor to the ascension. The ascension is an accelerated and enhanced shimmering energy in which we elevate ourselves into the fifth dimension permanently. The energy that we are now working with in shimmering is a powerful and necessary prelude to the fifth-dimension ascension. This shimmering is a force-field vibration. The global network is the scale that we are working on in terms of group ascension of the planet. The shimmering energy is also enabling powerful streams of energy to be distributed throughout the planet.

soul groups — Like-minded people who come from the same soul root or soul branch. One can often feel deeper connections with people who come from the same soul group. The term "soul group" refers to people who belong to the same soul family and soul origin. Often soul groups reincarnate together on Earth and form groups. At other times, people on Earth might incarnate alone and away from their soul groups. People in the same soul group often have similar feelings, thoughts, and inclinations. When a person is with members of his or her soul group, that person feels deeply connected. It's like being with family.

soul lessons — In soul psychology, life lessons that a person specifically came to Earth to learn in this lifetime.

soul psychologist — A term used to describe a therapist or counselor who uses information from past lives, karma, life lessons, other dimensions, and spirit guides or mentors to help heal clients. Methods used by soul psychologists can include past-life therapy, channeling of guides and teachers, and life-between-lives therapy. Personal problems presented to soul psychologists are viewed in the perspective of a person's soul history, which includes other lifetimes. This perspective transcends the traditional realm of modern Western psychology practices. Please note that the term "psychologist" as used in this context does not refer to the traditional practice of psychology in the twenty-first century.

space-time continuum — The four-dimensional continuum of one temporal and three spatial coordinates in which any event or physical object is located. When you collapse space, you also collapse time.

spirit guides — Teachers from the higher realms who are guides and mentors. They give spiritual advice and recommendations and also offer insights into the higher worlds and higher consciousness.

spiritual light quotient — A term used by the Arcturians to indicate how well developed a person is spiritually. A person with a high spiritual light quotient, for example, can understand and use higher spiritual concepts such as meditation, unity consciousness, and ascension. One's spiritual light quotient can rise with age.

star family — A group of higher masters and teachers and similar to the Galactic Council from planetary systems related to Earth. The star family oversees the evolution of Earth energies as well as other planetary energies throughout the galaxy.

stargate — A multidimensional portal into higher realms. The Arcturian stargate is very close to the Arcturus star system and is overseen by the Arcturians. This powerful passage point requires that earthlings who wish to pass through it complete all lessons and Earth incarnations associated with the third-dimensional experience. It serves as a gateway to the fifth dimension. New soul assignments are given there, and souls can then be sent to many different higher realms throughout the galaxy and universe. Archangel Metatron and many other higher beings are present at the stargate.

Many people are now using the term "stargate" to refer to openings on Earth to higher dimensions when, in fact, they are describing corridors. The stargate is a magnificent, temple-like, etheric structure that can process and transform many souls.

starseeds — People who have been born with the awareness of galactic consciousness. Starseeds may also have memories of past lifetimes on other planets and feel connected to civilizations from other planets such as the Pleiades or Arcturus. Some starseeds have come to Earth at this time to assist in her evolutionary transformation.

supermind — The higher part of the mind that connects with universal and galactic consciousness.

tachyon — A small particle that travels faster than the speed of light. A tachyon stone is an object that contains tachyon particles and is used for healing in much the same way that one uses crystals.

third dimension — The Earth plane where humans now live. There are higher dimensions beyond Earth.

thought projection — The ability to put one's mind and awareness into one's thoughts. This awareness can be in the present, past, or future. In thought projection, one can send awareness to other realities, to other locations on the third dimension, or even to other dimensions. In its highest form, thought projection can be used to send one's astral body to distant locations, either on this dimension or the fifth dimension.

Tomar — An Arcturian ascended master who specializes in using and describing Arcturian temple energy.

tones or sacred sounds — Sounds producing a vibratory resonance that helps activate and align the chakras.

trance channeling — Automatic speaking from a light trance or hypnotic, almost somnambulant, state. Trance is a type of hypnosis in which you put yourself into an altered state of consciousness. Deep trance is the way Edward Cayce used to channel. In light trance channeling, you are still awake while bringing through messages.

Tree of Life — In Jewish mysticism, the Tree of Life is a galactic blueprint for the creation of this reality. It includes ten energy emanations placed in spheres in the shape of a tree. Each sphere has a specific energy and a sacred name of God associated with it. These spheres are used for individual and planetary healing. The three spiritualties of the sacred triangle are included in the Tree of Life. The Tree of Life is not flat; rather, multidimensional and holographic with paths for manifestation.

unification — A spiritual process in Kabbalah. One unifies different energies in an attempt to bring healing or repair to the world or to oneself. There are unifications within a person's personal system and life that need to be completed. A unification is an alignment and bringing together of energies so that they are harmonious.

White Brotherhood-Sisterhood — A spiritual hierarchy of ascended masters residing in the fifth dimension. "White" is not used here as a racial term. It refers to the white light or higher frequency that these masters have attained. The masters include Sananda, Kuthumi, Mother Mary, Quan Yin, Sanat Kumara, Archangel Michael, Saint Germain, and many other ascended beings.

Vywamus — A fifth-dimensional soul psychologist known for his insight into the psychology of Earth problems and resolution of issues related to starseeds incarnated on Earth.

About the Author

David K. Miller is the director and founder of an international meditation group focused on personal and planetary healing. He has been the director of this global healing group, called the Group of Forty, for more than fifteen years. David has been developing groundbreaking global healing techniques using group consciousness to help heal areas of Earth that need balance, restoration, and harmony. The technique he uses with his group work is called Biorelativity, which uses group consciousness work to restore Earth's feedback loop system, a complex planetary system that maintains the correct balance of our planet's atmosphere, ocean currents, and weather patterns.

David's meditation group has more than 1,200 members worldwide. In addition to his lectures and workshops, David is also a prolific author, having written ten books and numerous articles on Earth healing techniques. Several of his books also have been published in German and Spanish.

David works with his wife, Gudrun Miller, who is a psychotherapist and visionary artist. Together they have conducted workshops in Brazil, Germany, Australia, Mexico, Argentina, Costa Rica, Spain, New Zealand, Belgium, and Turkey. David's foundation for this work lies in his study and connection to Native American teachings and his intense research in mysticism, including the Kabbalah. He also has an avid interest in astronomy and Earth's relationship to the galaxy. To learn more, go to www.GroupofForty.com.

Light Technology PUBLISHING Presents

TO ORDER PRINT BOOKS

Visit LightTechnology.com, Call 928-526-1345 or 1-800-450-0985, or Check Amazon.com or Your Favorite Bookstore

BOOKS THROUGH DAVID K. MILLER

Arcturians: How to Heal, Ascend, and Help Planet Earth

Go on a mind-expanding journey to explore spiritual tools for dealing with our planetary crisis. Included in this book are updated interpretations of the Kaballistic Tree of Life, which has now been expanded to embrace fifth-dimensional planetary healing methods. Learn Arcturian spiritual technologies.

$16.95 • 352 PP. • Softcover

978-1-62233-002-7

Biorelativity: Planetary Healing Technologies

Biorelativity describes the ability of human beings to telepathically communicate with the spirit of Earth. The goal of such communication is to influence the outcome of natural Earth events such as storms, volcanic eruptions, and earthquakes. Through the lessons contained in this book, you can implement planetary healing techniques right now, actively participating in exciting changes as Earth and humanity come together in unity and healing.

$16.95 • 352 PP. • Softcover

978-1-891824-98-2

BOOKS THROUGH DAVID K. MILLER

Connecting with the Arcturians

Who is really out there? Where are we going? What are our choices? What has to be done to prepare for this event? This book addresses all of these questions in a way that we can easily understand. It explains what our relationships are to known extraterrestrial groups and what they are doing to help Earth and her people in this crucial galactic moment.

$17.00 • 256 PP. • Softcover
978-1-891824-94-4

Expand Your Consciousness

Now more than ever, humankind is in need of developing its higher consciousness to heal itself and Earth and to experience life in a much more meaningful way. By expanding in consciousness, we can see the connections and unity that exist in all reality, and we might see objects with sharper colors, hear sounds with greater clarity, or even experience two sensations simultaneously! In this book, you will explore the fascinating multidimensionality that is yours for the taking.

$16.95 • 288 PP. • Softcover
978-1-62233-036-2

Light Technology PUBLISHING Presents

TO ORDER PRINT BOOKS

Visit LightTechnology.com, Call 928-526-1345 or 1-800-450-0985,
or Check Amazon.com or Your Favorite Bookstore

BOOKS THROUGH DAVID K. MILLER

Fifth-Dimensional Soul Psychology

"The basic essence of soul psychology rests with the idea that the soul is evolving and that part of this evolution is occurring through incarnations in the third dimension. Now, to even speak about the soul evolving is perhaps a controversial subject because we know that the soul is eternal. We know that the soul has been in existence for infinity, and we know that the soul is perfect. So why would the soul have to evolve?

"The answer to this question is complex, and we may not be able to totally answer it using third-dimensional terminology. But it is an important question to answer because the nature of soul evolution is inherently connected to your experiences in the third dimension. The soul, in completing its evolutionary journey, needs these experiences in the third dimension, and it needs to complete the lessons here."

—Vywamus

$16.95 • 288 PP. • Softcover
978-1-62233-016-4

Kaballah and the Ascension

"Throughout Western history, channeling has come to us in various forms, including mediumship, shamanism, fortunetelling, visionaries, and oracles. There is also a long history of channeling in Kaballah, the major branch of Jewish mysticism. I am intrigued by this, especially because I believe that there is now an urgent necessity for entering higher realms with our consciousness because of the impending changes on the planet. Through these higher realms, new healing energies and insights can be brought down to assist us in these coming Earth changes."

— David K. Miller

$16.95 • 176 PP. • Softcover
978-1-891824-82-1

All Our Books Are Also Available as eBooks on Amazon, Apple iTunes, Google Play, and Barnes & Noble.

Light Technology PUBLISHING Presents

TO ORDER PRINT BOOKS
Visit LightTechnology.com, Call 928-526-1345 or 1-800-450-0985,
or Check Amazon.com or Your Favorite Bookstore

BOOKS THROUGH DAVID K. MILLER

New Spiritual Technology for the Fifth-Dimensional Earth

Earth is moving closer to the fifth dimension. New spiritual ideas and technologies are becoming available for rebalancing our world, including native ceremonies to connect to Earth healing energies and thought projections and thought communication with Earth.

$19.95 • 240 PP. • Softcover
978-1-891824-79-1

A New Tree of Life for Planetary Ascension

This is the second book David Miller has written about the Kabbalah. His first book, *Kaballah and the Ascension*, introduced basic concepts in the Kabbalah and linked them to the ascended masters and the process of ascension. In this book, David teamed up with Torah scholar and Kabbalist expert Mordechai Yashin, who resides in Jerusalem, Israel. This book is based on unique lectures and classes David and Mordechai gave over an eight-month period between 2012 and 2013. These lectures on Jewish and Hebraic lessons were held in open discussion groups and offer a truly unique perspective into the Kabbalistic Tree of Life and how it has been expanded.

$16.95 • 336 PP. • Softcover
978-1-62233-012-6

All Our Books Are Also Available as eBooks on Amazon, Apple iTunes, Google Play, and Barnes & Noble.

BOOKS THROUGH DAVID K. MILLER

Raising the Spiritual Light Quotient

The spiritual light quotient is a measurement of a person's ability to work with and understand spirituality. This concept is compared to the intelligence quotient (IQ). However, in reality, spiritual ability is not related to intelligence, and interestingly, unlike the IQ, one's spiritual light quotient can increase with age and experience.

$16.95 • 384 PP. • Softcover
978-1-891824-89-0

Enseñanzas del Sagrado Triángulo Arcturiano

Este paradigma es necesario para ayudar en la transición de la humanidad hacia la próxima etapa evolutiva. La humanidad debe realizar esta próxima etapa de la evolución, para asegurar su sobrevivencia por los cambios climáticos globales, la guerra y la destrucción del medio ambiente. ¿Cuál es la próxima etapa? Esta involucra la expansión de la consciencia del ser humano y está representada por el símbolo de este nuevo paradigma, el Sagrado Triángulo Arcturiano.

El guía de la quinta dimensión, Juliano, proveniente del sistema estelar galáctico conocido como Arcturus, trabaja junto a David en un papel prominente en esta introducción de la energía del Triángulo Sagrado en la Tierra. David le ofrece al lector un entendimiento del alma, su naturaleza evolutiva y como la humanidad esta avanzando hacia esa siguiente etapa evolutiva.

$19.95 • 416 PP. • Softcover
978-1-62233-264-9

Light Technology PUBLISHING **Presents**

TO ORDER PRINT BOOKS
Visit LightTechnology.com, Call 928-526-1345 or 1-800-450-0985,
or Check Amazon.com or Your Favorite Bookstore

BOOKS THROUGH DAVID K. MILLER

Teachings from the Sacred Triangle, Volume 1

The first book of the Sacred Triangle series explains how the Arcturian energy melds with that of the White Brother-Sisterhood and the ascended Native American masters to bring about planetary healing.

Topics include the Sacred Triangle energy and the sacred codes of ascension, how to create a bridge to the fifth dimension, what role you can play in the Sacred Triangle, and how sacred words from the Kaballah can assist you in your ascension work.

$16.95 • 272 PP. • Softcover
978-1-62233-007-2

Teachings from the Sacred Triangle, Volume 2

Our planet is at a dire crossroads from a physical standpoint, but from a spiritual standpoint, it is experiencing a great awakening. Never before have there been so many conscious lightworkers, awakened spiritual beings, and masters as there are on this planet now. A great sense of a spiritual harmony emanates from the many starseed groups, and there is also a new spiritual energy and force that is spreading throughout the planet.

$16.95 • 288 PP. • Softcover
978-1-891824-19-7

Teachings from the Sacred Triangle, Volume 3

Learn how to use holographic technology to project energies in the most direct and transformative way throughout Earth. It will not be necessary to travel to distant places. When you interact with the part of Earth you are familiar with, you can affect the entire planet. Any part of the whole that has been distorted can be transformed into a fifth-dimensional holographic energy.

$16.95 • 288 PP. • Softcover
978-1-891824-23-4

All Our Books Are Also Available as eBooks on Amazon, Apple iTunes, Google Play, and Barnes & Noble.

FILM FEATURING DAVID K. MILLER

The Blue Jewel

$17.00 • DVD • 96 minutes • ASIN: B00D5S5UTA

We live in a time of great change and transformation. Some of these challenges include global climate change, economic and financial fluctuations, and the shifting of our personal relationships to our daily work lives.

Structures that have held so far seem to be crumbling, and we begin to question them. As a result, a lot of society's structures have become imbalanced. The film *The Blue Jewel* proposes new solutions to restore this balance. This equilibrium is so important to live in peace, which is what each one of us strives for: peace with oneself, peace within one's relationships, and last but not least, peace with our Earth, the planet we share. Meet planetary healers who provide solutions that restore planetary balance. What starts out as a journey over the planet to restore Earth's balance turns into a journey within.

This award-winning documentary film offers a method to bring personal and planetary balance into your life.

With David K. Miller; Pepper Lewis; Gudrun Miller; Ruben Saufkie Sr.; Dietmar Born, PhD; Roger Nelson; and Johanna & Ignaz Leitner.

Light Technology PUBLISHING *Presents*

TO ORDER PRINT BOOKS

Visit LightTechnology.com, Call 928-526-1345 or 1-800-450-0985,
or Check Amazon.com or Your Favorite Bookstore

Books through David K. Miller

Connecting with the Arcturians 3

The themes of this book focus on the evolution of humanity, the next stage of our planetary development, the planetary crisis in general, and how we, as spiritual lightworkers and starseeds, can prepare for our future and for the ascension. We look at the relationships between such complex subjects as quantum physics and spirituality and New Age physics to learn how that relates to the higher dimensions and healing techniques that use new terminology such as "quantum healing" and "omega light."

$17.95 • Softcover • 6 x 9 • 272 PP. • ISBN 978-1-62233-063-8

Connecting with the Arcturians 4

During this time of planetary crisis, the Arcturians explore how we starseeds can cope with these dramatic changes, such as by updating our immune systems and dealing with electromagnetic energies and energy fields.

The Arcturians present a model based on their observations that precipitating events of ascension occur when the third dimension and fifth dimension intersect. At the time of that intersection, a powerful spiritual energy will download into Earth's energy field that can uplift those who are at the highest vibrations and prepared for ascension.

$17.95 • Softcover • 6 x 9 • 352 PP. • ISBN 978-1-62233-078-2

All Our Books Are Also Available as eBooks from Amazon, Apple iTunes, Google Play, Barnes & Noble, and Kobo.

Light Technology PUBLISHING Presents

TO ORDER PRINT BOOKS
Visit LightTechnology.com, Call 928-526-1345 or 1-800-450-0985,
or Check Amazon.com or Your Favorite Bookstore

BOOKS THROUGH DRUNVALO MELCHIZEDEK

THE ANCIENT SECRET OF THE FLOWER OF LIFE VOLUME 1

Once, all life in the universe knew the Flower of Life as the creation pattern, the geometrical design leading us into and out of physical existence. Then from a very high state of consciousness, we fell into darkness, and the secret was hidden for thousands of years, encoded in the cells of all life.

$25.00 • 240 PP. SOFTCOVER • ISBN 978-1-891824-17-3

THE ANCIENT SECRET OF THE FLOWER OF LIFE VOLUME 2

Finally, for the first time in print, Drunvalo shares the instructions for the Mer-Ka-Ba meditation, step-by-step techniques for the re-creation of the energy field of the evolved human, which is the key to ascension and the next dimensional world. If done from love, this ancient process of breathing prana opens up for us a world of tantalizing possibility in this dimension, from protective powers to the healing of oneself, others, and even the planet.

$25.00 • 272 PP. SOFTCOVER • ISBN 978-1-891824-21-0

LIVING IN THE HEART

Includes Heart Meditation CD

"Long ago we humans used a form of communication and sensing that did not involve the brain in any way; rather, it came from a sacred place within our hearts. What good would it do to find this place again in a world where the greatest religion is science and the logic of the mind? Don't I know this world where emotions and feelings are second-class citizens? Yes, I do. But my teachers have asked me to remind you who you really are. You are more than a human being, much more. Within your heart is a place, a sacred place, where the world can literally be remade through conscious cocreation. If you give me permission, I will show you what has been shown to me." — Drunvalo Melchizedek

$25.00 • 144 PP. SOFTCOVER • ISBN 978-1-891824-43-2

All Our Books Are Also Available as eBooks on Amazon, Apple iTunes, Google Play, and Barnes & Noble.

Light Technology PUBLISHING Presents

TO ORDER PRINT BOOKS

Visit LightTechnology.com, Call 928-526-1345 or 1-800-450-0985, or Check Amazon.com or Your Favorite Bookstore

BOOKS THROUGH RAE CHANDRAN

DNA of the Spirit, Volume 1

The etheric strands of your DNA are the information library of your soul. They contain the complete history of you, lifetime after lifetime; a record of the attitudes, karma, and emotional predispositions you brought into this lifetime; and a blueprint, or lesson plan, for your self-improvement.

$19.95 • Softcover • 384 PP.
ISBN 978-1-62233-013-3

DNA of the Spirit, Volume 2

This companion book to *DNA of the Spirit, Volume 1* originated with the intention and desire to bring forth understanding to support humanity. Go through this volume while holding a sacredness inside of you, asking that the material be imprinted there so that it may become an experience that you will be able to live.

$16.95 • Softcover • 192 PP.
ISBN 978-1-62233-027-0

Dance of the Hands

Dance of the Hands is for everyone, not just people who are spiritually advanced. It is for any layperson, regardless of religion. This material is for those who have an interest in bettering themselves or improving their well-being — practitioners, teachers, masters, the spiritually advanced, neophytes, and children.

$16.95 • Softcover • 160 PP.
Wire-O bound
ISBN 978-1-62233-038-6

Partner with Angels

Angels are the Creator's workforce, and in this book, individual angels describe their responsibilities and explain how they can help you with all aspects of your life — practical and spiritual. All you need to do is ask.

$16.95 • Softcover • 208 PP.
ISBN 978-1-62233-034-8

Angels and Ascension

Angels are available with all kinds of help. This must become part of your reality. Set your antenna to the angels, and communicate with them. All of life's miracles happen with angelic presence. When you begin to do this, you will see that you have an ever-present friend at your shoulder.

$16.95 • Softcover • 176 PP.
ISBN 978-1-62233-048-5

All Our Books Are Also Available as eBooks on Amazon, Apple iTunes, Google Play, and Barnes & Noble.

Light Technology PUBLISHING Presents

TO ORDER PRINT BOOKS
Visit LightTechnology.com, Call 928-526-1345 or 1-800-450-0985,
or Check Amazon.com or Your Favorite Bookstore

BOOKS THROUGH JAAP VAN ETTEN

Birth of a New Consciousness: Dialogues with the Sidhe

This book contains the wisdom of the Sidhe, a race of human-like beings who are our direct relatives. They are invisible to our five senses and occupy one of the subtle worlds that are part of Gaia.

Embark on a journey, the journey of every soul who comes to Earth. This book stimulates you to raise your vibration and expand your view of reality by giving many suggestions on how to do so. It truly can be called the start of a new consciousness.

$16.95 • Softcover • 6 x 9 • 192 PP. • ISBN 978-1-62233-033-1

CRYSTAL SKULLS: Expand Your Consciousness

Includes 1 Meditation CD

Crystal skulls invoke a sense of mystery. What was their role in ancient times? Are they important for us now? Can they assist us on our spiritual journeys? How? Although much has been written about them, many questions linger. This book addresses these questions on practical, subtle-energy, and spiritual levels.

$25.00 • 256 PP. • Softcover • ISBN 978-1-62233-000-3

CRYSTAL SKULLS: Interacting with a Phenomenon

Discover your energetic connection with crystal skulls. Learn how to utilize these energies for your personal growth and how these special energies affect your awareness and expand your consciousness.

$19.95 • 240 PP. • Softcover • ISBN 978-1-891824-64-7

Gifts of Mother Earth

We live in a sea of energies that are part of the Earth we live on. Most people are not aware of these energies and consequently are not aware that they hold many gifts. These gifts help us to heal, balance, expand consciousness (awareness), and support spiritual evolution. Our ancestors knew the gifts of Mother Earth and used these energies to support their lives and spirituality in many ways. We, modern humans, have mostly forgotten that they exist.

$16.95 • 256 PP. • Softcover • ISBN 978-1-891824-86-9

All Our Books Are Also Available as eBooks on Amazon, Apple iTunes, Google Play, and Barnes & Noble.

Light Technology PUBLISHING Presents

TO ORDER PRINT BOOKS

Visit LightTechnology.com, Call 928-526-1345 or 1-800-450-0985,
or Check Amazon.com or Your Favorite Bookstore

PRODUCTS BY LYSSA ROYAL HOLT

GALACTIC HERITAGE CARDS

The First and Only of Their Kind: This 108-card divination system, based on material from Lyssa Royal Holt's groundbreaking book *The Prism of Lyra,* is **designed to help you tap into your star lineage and karmic patterns** while revealing lessons brought to Earth from the stars and how those lessons can be used in your life on Earth now. Includes a 156-page book of instruction and additional information.

Illustrations by David Cow
$29.95 • 108 cards (3 x 5 inches)
156-page • ßoftcover book (5 x 7 inches)
978-1-891824-88-3

Preparing for Contact

Extraterrestrial contact is happening now. We may ignore the signs of contact because we do not understand them. The contact experience is intricately tied to the nature of human consciousness. When we as a species evolve, so will the nature of our contact experiences.
$16.95 • Softcover • 300 PP.
978-1-891824-90-6

The Prism of Lyra

The Prism of Lyra traces various off-planet races through their own evolution and ties them into the developing Earth. Highlighted is the realization of our galactic interconnectedness and our shared desire to return home.
$16.95 • Softcover • 176 PP.
978-1-891824-87-6

All Our Books Are Also Available as eBooks on Amazon, Apple iTunes, Google Play, and Barnes & Noble.

Light Technology PUBLISHING Presents

TO ORDER PRINT BOOKS

Visit LightTechnology.com, Call 928-526-1345 or 1-800-450-0985,
or Check Amazon.com or Your Favorite Bookstore

DR. JOSHUA DAVID STONE'S

EASY-TO-READ ENCYCLOPEDIA OF THE SPIRITUAL PATH

1

The Complete Ascension Manual: How to Achieve Ascension in This Lifetime

Stone weaves research and intuitive information together in this exploration of self-realization.

$14.95 • Softcover • 320 PP.

ISBN 978-0-929385-55-6

2

Soul Psychology: Keys to Ascension

There are thousands of self-help books on psychology and relationships, but few integrate the soul and spirit like this one.

$14.95 • Softcover • 272 PP.

ISBN 978-0-929385-56-3

3

Beyond Ascension: How to Complete the Seven Levels of Initiation

Incredible new channeled material completely demystifies the seven levels of initiation.

$14.95 • Softcover • 320 PP.

ISBN 978-0-929385-73-0

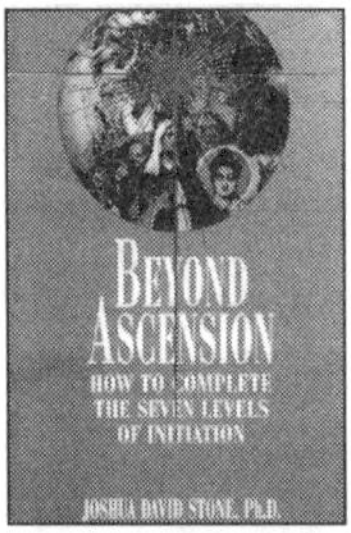

4

Hidden Mysteries: ETs, Ancient Mystery Schools & Ascension This book contains a wealth of information on esoteric teachings of recently founded religions.

$14.95 • Softcover • 384 PP.

ISBN 978-0-929385-57-0

5

The Ascended Masters Light the Way: Beacons of Ascension

This book contains guidance from the saints and spiritual masters of all the religions that have graced this planet.

$14.95 • Softcover • 288 PP.

ISBN 978-0-929385-58-7

6

Cosmic Ascension: Your Cosmic Map Home

In our extraordinary time, there is a new opening and potential to begin our cosmic ascension process.

$14.95 • Softcover • 288 PP.

ISBN 978-0-929385-99-0

7

A Beginner's Guide to the Path of Ascension

This volume covers the basics of ascension clearly and completely.

$14.95 • Softcover 192 PP.

ISBN 978-1-891824-02-9

8

Golden Keys to Ascension and Healing

This volume represents the wisdom of the ascended masters condensed into concise keys that serve as a spiritual guide.

$14.95 • Softcover • 256 PP.

ISBN 978-1-891824-03-6

All Our Books Are Also Available as eBooks on Amazon, Apple iTunes, Google Play, and Barnes & Noble.

Light Technology PUBLISHING Presents

TO ORDER PRINT BOOKS

Visit LightTechnology.com, Call 928-526-1345 or 1-800-450-0985, or Check Amazon.com or Your Favorite Bookstore

DR. JOSHUA DAVID STONE'S

EASY-TO-READ ENCYCLOPEDIA OF THE SPIRITUAL PATH

9

Manual for Planetary Leadership

This book lays out, in an orderly and clear fashion, the guidelines for leadership in the world and in your own life.

$14.95 • Softcover • 320 PP.

ISBN 978-1-891824-05-0

10

Your Ascension Mission

In this book, Dr. Stone shows how each person's puzzle piece is just as vital and necessary as any other.

$14.95 • Softcover • 288 PP.

ISBN 978-1-891824-09-8

11

Revelations of a Melchizedek Initiate

This book traces the author's journey of ascension through the seven levels of initiation.

$14.95 • Softcover • 336 PP.

ISBN 978-1-891824-10-4

12

How to Teach Ascension Classes

This book serves as an ideal foundation for teaching ascension classes and leading workshops.

$14.95 • Softcover • 160 PP.

ISBN 978-1-891824-15-9

13

Ascension and Romantic Relationships

Dr. Stone explores relationships from the perspective of the soul and monad — not just the personality.

$14.95 • Softcover • 224 PP.

ISBN 978-1-891824-16-6

14

Complete Ascension Index

This companion volume to the Encyclopedia of the Spiritual Path series will allow you easier access to the techniques and wisdom of Dr. Stone.

$14.95 • Softcover • 288 PP.

ISBN 978-1-891824-30-2

15

How to Be Financially Successful

This book is like no other in the financial field because it is a holistic approach for life study rather than just another book about money.

$14.95 • Softcover • 256 PP.

ISBN 978-1-891824-55-5

SPECIAL
All 15 Books for $149.95
plus shipping

All Our Books Are Also Available as eBooks on Amazon, Apple iTunes, Google Play, and Barnes & Noble.

Light Technology PUBLISHING **Presents**

TO ORDER PRINT BOOKS

Visit LightTechnology.com, Call 928-526-1345 or 1-800-450-0985,
or Check Amazon.com or Your Favorite Bookstore

MEDITATIONS BY SARAH GODDARD NEVES

12 Steps to a Lightness of Being

$19.95 • Softcover • 160 PP.
6 X 9 • Perfect Bound
ISBN 978-1-891824-99-9

This unique book has been designed as if you were taking a very special spiritual development course in the comfort of your own home. Through its wisdom and guided meditations — **included on the enclosed CDs to boost empowerment** — *12 Steps to a Lightness of Being* will gradually but surely lift your vibration and awaken you. To get the most out of it, take as long as you need on each step before moving on to the next. Commit to doing each meditation or visualization, giving yourself some quiet, undisturbed time to do this, and recall your meditation experiences and insights afterward.

3 GUIDED MEDITATION CDs INCLUDED!

The Twelve Steps:

1. Meditation on the Light
2. Opening to Your Intuition
3. Master Connection
4. Being Happy
5. The Healing Power of Forgiveness
6. Evolving with Love and Light
7. Realizing Your Life's Purpose
8. Awakening to Love
9. You: a Creation and a Creator
10. Soul Reflection
11. Hope from the Stars
12. Becoming a Lightness of Being

All Our Books Are Also Available as eBooks on Amazon, Apple iTunes, Google Play, and Barnes & Noble.

Light Technology PUBLISHING Presents

TO ORDER PRINT BOOKS

Visit LightTechnology.com, Call 928-526-1345 or 1-800-450-0985,
or Check Amazon.com or Your Favorite Bookstore

Shifting Frequencies

Sounds for Vibratory Activation

by Jonathan Goldman

For the first time, Healing Sounds pioneer Jonathan Goldman tells us about shifting frequencies — how to use sound and other modalities to change vibrational patterns for both personal and planetary healing and transformation. Through his consciousness connection to Shamael, angel of sound, Jonathan shares his extraordinary scientific and spiritual knowledge and insights, providing information, instructions, and techniques on using sound, light, color, visualization, and sacred geometry to experience shifting frequencies. The material in this book is both timely and vital for health and spiritual evolution.

$17.95 Plus Shipping

ISBN 978-1-891824-70-8
Softcover • 226 PP.
6 X 9 Perfect Bound

CHAPTERS INCLUDE:

- Sound Currents: Frequency and Intent
- Vibratory Resonance
- Vocalization, Visualization, and a Tonal Language
- The Harmonics of Sound
- Vocal Harmonics and Listening
- Energy Fields
- Creating Sacred Space

Hearing the Angels Sing:

A True Story of Angelic Assistance

by Peter Sterling

Hearing the Angel's Sing chronicles my extraordinary journeys into the higher dimensions of light where I met the angels who ultimately brought me to the realization that my mission was to be a channel for God's heavenly music. The book includes never-before-shared details of my journey of awakening. From the snowcapped peaks of the Rocky Mountains to the tropical jungles of the Mayan temple lands, the red rock towers of Sedona, and ultimately to the Incan highlands of Peru, this is a captivating story that will take you on an amazing journey of discovery!

— Peter Sterling

$16.95 Plus Shipping

ISBN 13: 978-1-891824-96-8
Softcover • 256 PP.
6 X 9 Perfect Bound

CHAPTERS INCLUDE:

- Descension and Birth
- Down the Rabbit Hole
- Windows to Heaven
- Rocky Mountain High
- Angels and Devils
- Harmonic Converging
- Red Rocks Calling
- To Hear the Angels Sing
- Fires of Purification

All Our Books Are Also Available as eBooks on Amazon, Apple iTunes, Google Play, and Barnes & Noble.

Light Technology PUBLISHING Presents

TO ORDER PRINT BOOKS

Visit LightTechnology.com, Call 928-526-1345 or 1-800-450-0985, or Check Amazon.com or Your Favorite Bookstore

BOOKS THROUGH TOM T. MOORE

THE GENTLE WAY

A SELF-HELP GUIDE FOR THOSE WHO BELIEVE IN ANGELS

This book will put you back in touch with your guardian angel or strengthen and expand the connection that you already have. How can I promise these benefits? Because I have been using these concepts for years and I can report these successes from direct knowledge and experience.

$14.95 • 160 PP., SOFTCOVER • ISBN 978-1-891824-60-9

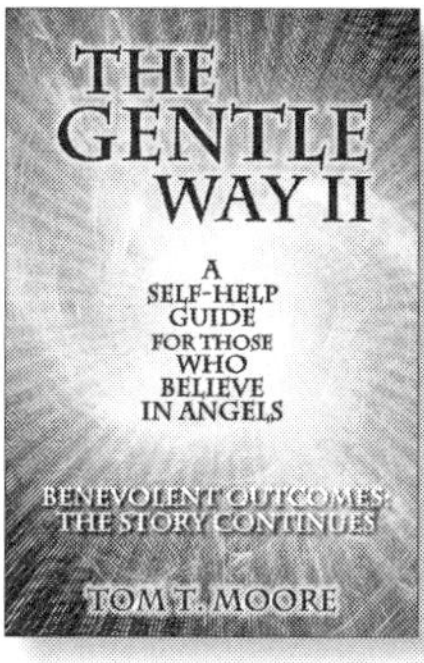

THE GENTLE WAY II

BENEVOLENT OUTCOMES: THE STORY CONTINUES

You'll be amazed at how easy it is to be in touch with guardian angels and how much assistance you can receive simply by asking. This inspirational self-help book, written for all faiths and beliefs, will explain how there is a more benevolent world that we can access and how we can achieve this.

$16.95 • 320 PP., SOFTCOVER • ISBN 978-1-891824-80-7

THE GENTLE WAY III

MASTER YOUR LIFE

I continue to receive truly unique stories from people all over the world requesting most benevolent outcomes and asking for benevolent prayers for their families, friends, and other beings. It just proves that there are no limits to this modality, which is becoming a gentle movement as people discover how much better their lives are with these simple yet powerful requests.

$16.95 • 352 PP., SOFTCOVER • ISBN 978-1-62233-005-8

FIRST CONTACT

CONVERSATIONS WITH AN ET

This book contains vital information about our past, present, and future contact with ETs. Tom relays this information through conversations with "his brother from another planet," Antura.

$15.95 • 224 PP., SOFTCOVER • ISBN 978-1-62233-004-1

ATLANTIS & LEMURIA

THE LOST CONTINENTS REVEALED!

Sixty thousand years ago, Earth had two more continents than it does today, each larger than what we now know as Australia. Why are they no longer there?

$16.95 • 256 PP., SOFTCOVER • ISBN 978-1-62233-037-9

All Our Books Are Also Available as eBooks on Amazon, Apple iTunes, Google Play, and Barnes & Noble.